D1604307

Betrayed by Choices

A Family Story of Murder, Forgiveness, and Redemption

JIM BUFFINGTON, JR.

with Kirk Blackard

Betrayed by Choices

A Family Story of Murder, Forgiveness, and Redemption

"Let the redeemed of the LORD tell their story—
those he redeemed from the hand of the foe."
Psalms 107:2

Book cover and interior design by Jess LaGreca, Mayfly Design

Hardback ISBN: 979-8-9890313-1-3
Paperback ISBN: 979-8-9890313-0-6
eBook ISBN: 979-8-9890313-2-0
Audiobook ISBN: 979-8-9890313-3-7

Library of Congress Catalog Number: 2023916095

Family pictures are from the Buffington family private collection.

News headlines are a collage of hard copies Jim collected
from 1976 to 1996.

A portion of the book sales proceeds will be donated to Bridges To Life.
www.bridgestolife.org

To my grandson,
Palmer James Buffington,
and all the Buffington grandchildren:
this is the family story of your great-grandparents,
James Buffington Sr. and Chere Stieferman Buffington.

—Jim Buffington Jr. (aka Jimmy)

Susan & Dick
Thanks for your long &
great friendship.
All our love—

Marcia & Kirk

Contents

Note to the Reader

Betrayed By Choices is the story of several generations of a family and many of the people they intersected with over a half-century. Some have similar names, some came, some went, and several are easily confused with one another. A family tree and list of significant others noted can be found in the Appendix.

The story is told from various points of view. Short portions written in italics contain important background information presented by the authors. Unless otherwise indicated, the narrative is in Jim's voice. However, several others contributed, and their contributions are in their own words. The authors are especially thankful to these individuals for telling portions of the story: Aaron Buffington, Bryce Buffington, Emily Buffington, Erica Buffington, Gina Buffington, Judson Buffington, Louis Buffington, Marilyn Buffington, Oscar Buffington, Chaplain Richard Lopez, and Ken Rawlins.

CHAPTER ONE

Heartbreak

"She watches over the affairs of her household and does
not eat the bread of idleness. Her children arise and call her
blessed; her husband also, and he praises her. 'Many women do
noble things, but you surpass them all.'" (Proverbs 31: 27–28)

My name is Jim Buffington, Jr. I was eleven years old in 1974. As far as I was concerned, my two brothers and I had a perfect family and a perfect life. We did not have any trauma that I was aware of. Our dad, James Buffington, and mom, Chere Stieferman Buffington, both had regular jobs that provided us a comfortable living. On weekends, Dad was the music minister, and Mom was the pianist at the Allena Baptist Church in San Antonio, where we lived amid a loving church congregation. Our family had recently moved from the cramped and somewhat decrepit church parsonage to a modest, four-bedroom, one-bath, ranch-style house on Lazy Oaks Drive, where each of us had our own bedroom. My brothers, Oscar, nine, and Louis, eight, were my buddies. My mom's parents lived near us, and we enjoyed spending time with them.

Then my life came crashing down like a collapsing house hit by a spring tornado. The day is indelibly etched in my memory.

Our family was driving home on Sunday after a Thanksgiving visit to Dad's parents in Malvern, Arkansas, the small industrial town where Dad was born, about twenty miles from Hot Springs. Around eleven in the morning, a couple of hours into the nine-hour drive, we passed the "Welcome to Texas" sign as we crossed the border from Arkansas. Oscar, Louis, and I were sitting in birth order in the back seat of Mom's Lincoln Continental with suicide doors. I was behind Dad, who was in the driver's seat. Oscar sat in the middle, and Louis was behind Mom. The sky was gray, and the temperature was just above freezing in the rolling hills and piney woods of northeast Texas. Mom and Dad were mostly quiet. We boys were also, except when we were picking at one another or begging for a pit stop.

Dad suddenly called for our attention. With his eyes fixed firmly on the road ahead, he made an announcement of sorts that would forever change our lives. "Jimmy, Oscar, Louis . . . , I've got some news for you. Your mom and I have decided we cannot live together any more. We'll be getting a divorce. I'll move out of the house tomorrow, and we'll work out the details later. It will be tough for a while, but I'm sure you'll be able to handle it."

Louis, Oscar, Jimmy

Dad remained rather stoic, very matter of fact, and didn't really explain why they were divorcing. Mom cried softly, her lips trembling and tears trickling gently down her cheeks. She didn't disagree that a divorce was in our future.

Before that moment, we boys had not a clue that anything was wrong with our parents' relationship, which seemed to have held up well in the fishbowl of the church community. We learned later that problems in their marriage had led to our move from the parsonage. When they saw that they were headed in the direction of a divorce, they gave up the church family, resigned their paid church jobs, and we moved out of the church parsonage. Divorce was not acceptable for leaders in the Baptist Church. We boys had no idea why we were leaving the church. We just thought we were moving to a better neighborhood.

News of the coming divorce was a major shock to Oscar, Louis, and me. We became physically sick to our stomachs and emotionally broken all over, as if kicked in the stomach and hit between the eyes with a baseball bat. We broke down and cried buckets of huge, salty tears—wailed actually. Each cry of anguish bred another one, and we just couldn't stop the gut-wrenching sobs that started in our stomachs and tore through our chests.

Then like a Gulf Coast hurricane seems to blow itself out, we stopped wailing, and a grim silence settled over us as the sad reality of what was happening consumed the car. Mom and Dad did not speak, and we boys whimpered remnants of our cries. That car ride home was the longest, most depressing trip I can ever remember, as we wrestled with the disbelief, despair, and fear exploding inside our bodies and tried to contemplate our uncertain future.

Dad moved out of our home on Monday morning following the holidays. He and Mom hugged awkwardly, and he walked out the door. We didn't understand what was going on. We stood silently, taking in the scene but not understanding it, a puzzle with the borders still incomplete. Six or seven months later, in mid-1975, their divorce was finalized.

After our parents' divorce, we boys lived for a time with Mom in the house on Lazy Oaks. We had a good life in a single-parent family, with a present, loving mother, regular home-cooked meals eaten around the kitchen table, help with our homework, and other stuff that seemed more or less normal.

Dad moved first into an apartment, and later lived for a time with his high school buddy and long-time friend, Ed Currie, Uncle Ed to us. They resided in Ed's house—a small, three-bedroom, one-bath bungalow not far from where we were living. We saw Dad most weekends.

Jimmy, Chere, Louis, Oscar

Each parent wanted custody of us kids. Mom wanted us to live with her, but she especially wanted her three sons to stay together. Dad also wanted us. He told us that Mom had to work so much that we would see

4

her more if he had custody. In retrospect, I believe that was a ruse. He wanted custody mainly because he wanted to be in control and not "lose" to her. I also suspect he didn't want to pay child support.

After considerable back and forth, we boys were told to decide who we would live with—a tough, no-win situation for Oscar, Louis, and me, requiring us to display a level of wisdom well beyond our years. We eventually decided to live with Dad, somehow accepting his position that living with him would enable us to see Mom more. We each had mixed feelings at best. I remember Louis crying in his bed, telling Mom that he wanted to live with her.

Dad moved back into the Lazy Oaks house, and Mom moved to an apartment. We stayed in the house with Dad, spent time with Mom on weekends, and were back in our beds in Dad's house at night. She said everything was going to be okay.

Mom was wrong.

Living with Dad was a combination of sugar and vinegar. He was a hard worker who provided for us financially. He often hugged us and told us he loved us. He was very active in the church. The four of us attended services routinely on Sundays, Wednesday nights, and any other times the doors were open at the large Castle Hills Baptist Church in north San Antonio. Dad joined the choir, and my brothers and I participated in youth activities. He cooked us big breakfasts featuring his special biscuits and gravy on many weekend mornings, which became our best time with him.

However, Dad was often controlling, manipulative, narcissistic, verbally abusive, and probably physically abusive by current standards. Living with him was not the comforting experience of living with Mom. At Dad's, we often were left at home alone and had to arrange our own meals. Other times, he was home, and we lived on fast food. He yelled at us often and whipped us with a belt for really minor things.

Dad seemed to feel he was above the law. An example occurred that Christmas. We boys badly wanted a Christmas tree—a real one that you could smell and decorate and put lots of presents under, as we always had when we lived with Mom. But Dad didn't want a tree. Maybe he was stressed by his financial problems and concerns related to their divorce and just didn't want to deal with the hassle. Whatever the case, we boys persisted in begging for a tree.

One night, for reasons I can only surmise, we were in a grocery store parking lot after the store closed. Dad suddenly said, "You guys have been wanting a Christmas tree. Well, let's get one. We'll grab one from that pile over there."

"But the store is closed. Where do we pay?"

"We'll just take it"

So we did. We stole our Christmas tree. We stuffed it into the trunk of Dad's 1976 Ford LTD, took it home, put it on a stand, and decorated it with ornaments from Mom's stash. As far as I can remember, that year the Grinch saved Christmas.

Oscar, James, Louis, Jimmy

We brothers no doubt suffered the predictable results of the divorce and Dad's approach to parenting, struggling with anger, fear about the future, some level of depression, and other such emotions. Upon reflection, it seems that people getting married is a little like gluing two, two-by-fours together. When boards are bound together, the single entity is neat, orderly, and strong, and it performs its function. But if the boards are separated, they splinter, disintegrate, and fail to perform their function. That's how divorce seemed to work in our family.

Mom and Dad each did some dating, and Dad apparently was having an affair with Charlotte Jacobs. Charlotte had worked as a secretary for Cliff's Fence Company where Dad worked. She went with Dad when he started his own business, Jim's Fence Company. She lived with her husband, an attorney, in a comfortable, two-story brick home in a nice area of San Antonio. Charlotte was a very pleasant, attractive blonde who was Dad's administrative assistant/general gofer and drove a baby-blue Ford Pinto owned by the company. I remember their relationship as being generally discreet. I was not sure at the time, but later confirmed that they were having an affair.

Charlotte and her husband attended the same Methodist church as Linda Morrey, a very pretty, sophisticated, San Antonio socialite and eligible bachelorette about the same age as Dad. She had been divorced since shortly after her daughter Tammy was born, about nine years previously. She and Tammy, who was the same age as Louis, lived in a nice house in a nice part of town.

For reasons known only to her, one day Charlotte told Dad, "We know this great lady, Linda Morrey, in our church. You need to date her and get married, so your boys will have a mother. But we can still continue our relationship."

That is exactly what happened. Dad and Linda started dating in late 1975. We spent time with Linda and Tammy, and came to know one another quite well. Having them in our lives helped make living in a split family easier on my brothers and me.

I'm not sure exactly what eventually happened between Charlotte and Dad. I do know that he apparently kept a relationship with her for a couple of years; her name continued to surface at interesting times in the drama of his life.

Dad occasionally took us with him as he ran errands or visited job sites. On one occasion, I was being nosy and fiddling around in the baby-blue Ford club cab pickup that was normally used by Charles County, a laborer who worked for him. I opened the glove compartment and saw a black, highly polished pistol with a big handle and a small, metallic barrel. Seeing the gun, so unusual and seemingly so out of place, really scared me. I quickly slammed the compartment shut, stifled my curiosity, and fastened my mouth. Although we never had a gun in the family and I wasn't into guns, I later came to understand that it was a .38-caliber revolver. Oscar had also found it and was confident it was a .38. I didn't mention the gun to anyone, and assumed that was the end of it. Was I wrong.

Dad and Linda planned to fly to Little Rock, Arkansas, for the weekend of March 19–21, 1976, although Dad never did such seemingly impromptu travel and never traveled by plane. They planned to introduce Linda to Dad's father, Norris Lee Buffington (Papa Lee to me), and stepmother, Frances Buffington (Granny Fran), and spend the weekend with my great-uncle and aunt, O.B. and Patsy Holiman. They also planned to attend horse races in Hot Springs on Saturday, although neither of them had any particular interest in horses. My brothers and I were to spend a rather routine weekend hanging out with our mom.

However, according to Dad, at the last minute, Linda asked him, "Hey, why don't we see if Chere will change her plans and allow the boys to stay at home for the weekend. I'd really like Tammy to spend some time with them, so they can get to know one another better." Mom agreed to the switch of weekends, so we brothers and Tammy spent the weekend at our house with a housekeeper.

James and Linda

I tried to call Mom at her apartment several times during the day on Saturday, but could not get her. On Sunday morning, Mom's dad, my Grandpa Herman, called. After a brief conversation, he said, "Jimmy, I'm looking for your dad. Do you know where I can find him?"

I responded, "Well, Grandpa, he's out of town this weekend. He's staying at my aunt and uncle's house in Arkansas." I gave him their phone number.

What Grandpa didn't tell me was that police detectives had come to his and Grandma's house a few hours earlier, around three or four o'clock on Sunday morning. The news was as heartbreaking as a knock on the door at that hour would suggest.

Mom had been murdered.

When the police told them what had happened, Grandma Mignon, Mom's mother, fainted. She fell flat on the floor, stunned, out cold. Grandpa managed his shock enough to help pick her up and try to calm her down. He then drove with the police to the morgue to identify his daughter's body—an awful, awful experience in any case, made even worse by what he saw when they showed him Mom's corpse. The attendant's best efforts to make the viewing feel humane failed miserably.

Grandpa Herman never got over what happened to my mom, and the trauma of seeing his daughter with three gunshot wounds to the face, while trying to figure out who on earth would have done that to her, or why. Grandpa's health began a rapid decline, and he died within a year, on January 19, 1977 (my brother Louis's eleventh birthday), of no apparent cause other than a broken heart.

Later that morning, Grandpa called Uncle O.B.'s number and got Dad on the phone. He told him that his ex-wife, Chere, had been murdered.

Dad immediately called "Uncle Ed," told him what had happened, and said, "You need to go pick up my boys and Tammy. Spend the day with them. Do not let them watch TV or see or hear any other media." He briefly shared the heart-stopping news with the Arkansas family members. He and Linda then headed to the Little Rock airport and flew back to San Antonio.

———

"Uncle Ed" called out of the blue as far as I could tell. He said, "Hey, your dad called and said he would like for me to spend the day with you. I'm calling to arrange to come and pick you up. Get ready as soon as you can. I'll be there in a few minutes."

I didn't much like Ed, but he was my dad's best friend. He went to high school with Mom and Dad and knew several of our relatives. Ed was sort of a playboy, around five feet ten inches tall, athletically built on the thin side, dark hair, good physical condition. He had never been married, had no kids, and was a real free spirit who maintained a stable of girlfriends and a gallery of pictures of girls. He drove a 1970's conversion van, often referred to as a "shaggin' wagon" or a "bedroom on wheels." I thought of him as a playboy creep. Spending the day escorting a group of kids did not seem to be the way he would choose to spend his time, and a day with him was not high on my agenda either.

This all seemed odd, so I called Mom's number again. She didn't answer, again. I vaguely wondered why I couldn't get her on the phone for almost two days, why Grandpa was calling, and why Ed Currie wanted to spend the day with us. Somehow, the three things happening at about the same time seemed as weird as snow in San Antonio. Being quite young and outside the circle of adult communication however, I didn't worry too much about it at the time.

Ed picked up Tammy, my brothers, and me, and we spent the day with him. We all piled into his shaggin' wagon and went to a local fast-food restaurant for an early lunch. Then he took us to a movie, *Escape to Witch Mountain*, about two orphan children with extraordinary psychic powers. After that, we spent the remainder of the day just hanging out at his house.

Sunday evening, Dad and Linda returned from Arkansas and came to Uncle Ed's house to pick us up. When they arrived, Dad hugged us as he normally did, then almost immediately sat Oscar, Louis, and me down on the aging, overstuffed couch in Ed's small living room. Ed, Linda, and Tammy moved to the adjacent dining room, where they could see us through the open double doors. An eerie quiet pervaded the room, as though we all knew something bad was coming, but didn't know what it was. Dad looked past us, took a deep breath, and said, with amazing calm, "I've got some bad news. Your mother has been killed. They found her in her car in a parking lot at a school not far from Woodlawn Lake. We don't know anything else now, but we should know more tomorrow."

My brothers and I lost it. We were hysterical. We immediately started crying, wailing. "Mom has been murdered?"

Linda and Tammy heard our outburst, ran in, and we hugged one another desperately. Along with the shock and sadness, I couldn't help thinking, *Who would kill my mom?* I remembered that we were scheduled to have been with her that weekend, and wondered, *Are they trying to kill us?*

The sadness and fear that shattered our hearts seemed worse than death itself. We were stunned, bewildered, not sure what to do next.

Dad didn't have much else to say. However, I do remember him telling us, "Y'all need to quit crying. You're upsetting Linda."

When he said, "stop crying," we swallowed our tears, choked back our wails, and put on our game faces as best we could. Dad was very controlling, and we were afraid of the consequences if we disobeyed him.

Dad took us home. Reeling, exhausted, and in shock, we went to bed on pallets spread haphazardly across the available space on the floor of Dad's bedroom. It was a long, difficult night of tossing, turning, bad dreams, and fear. Our fear of the unknown, and of what might happen next, continued day after day. We spent many nights running from it while lying on pallets on Dad's bedroom floor. And always, Mom's absence was palpable in the profound sadness that filled our hearts.

When I woke up on Monday morning, Dad was not in the house. An unknown, middle-aged Black lady was there to be with us for the day. She was Idell, wife of Charles County, the laborer who worked for my dad and drove the truck where I had seen the pistol in the glove compartment. In my confusion, fear, and sadness, I could only think, *Why is this woman here? Where's Dad?*

That day's newspaper, the March 22, 1976, edition of the *San Antonio Express-News*, flashed, "Slain woman found in car is identified—The nude body of a woman found in the back seat of a car parked at Longfellow Junior High School was identified Sunday. Mrs. Chere Buffington, 29, of 8051 Broadway. She was dead on arrival at the Green Hospital late Saturday. She had been shot three times in the head, police said."

The article continued, "The woman was crouched in the back floorboard of the car with her head partially under the front seat," and "articles of the woman's clothing including a bloody dress were found scattered around the car."

When Dad returned home later that day, he took us boys, along with his brother, Norris, to the Roy Akers Funeral Home to make arrangements for Mom's service and burial. Mom's family was not included, and to the best of my knowledge did not object to Mom's ex-husband controlling the arrangements. He made us three boys go with him through the grim tasks of selecting a casket, deciding on a burial place, and making other such arrangements. Incredibly for a twenty-nine-year-old woman, Mom had left a will giving custody of us to Dad, and if he could not take care of us, to her brother, Herman. She conveyed all her estate to us boys. She also left written instructions for her funeral service. Dad finalized the arrangements, generally following Mom's plan, especially the music.

Dad cried the next day when he saw Mom in the casket at the funeral home—not wailing like we boys had, but more of a controlled weeping, with tears sliding slowly down his cheeks. It floored me nevertheless, as I had never seen him cry before, and he had seemed so matter-of-fact when he told us about Mom's death.

It's common, I believe, that when a loved one dies, you want to see the body, perhaps to say your last goodbye. That is when you are sure their death is real. I wanted to see my mom, to convince myself that this all really was happening. However, as I walked slowly, hesitantly up to Mom's casket, Dad said, "Jimmy, you need to stay way back, because it doesn't look like your mom. Move further back, and it will look more like her."

We moved back, but nevertheless were dismayed at how she still didn't look like herself. Mom was very pretty. But the execution, with three shots in the face, had changed her appearance. We didn't want anyone to see her as she was, so we decided on a closed casket for the funeral.

We then went to the San Jose Mission Burial Park to pick out a grave site. We wanted her buried next to a tree. When we couldn't find a site with a tree in a suitable location, Dad said he would purchase a big Texas live oak with Spanish moss and have it planted near her gravesite. This surprised me, as I would not have thought he could afford to buy a tree. Time would tell if he'd deliver on his promise. We selected a granite headstone. Dad had both his and Mom's names engraved on it, which seems incongruous for a thirty-one-year-old divorced man who was seriously dating another woman, but perhaps not for James Buffington and his need to maintain control.

Afterward, we headed to Mom's apartment to select a dress for her burial. We were met by two San Antonio police detectives who would not let us into the apartment. They told us that Herman, Mom's brother and my uncle, had already been there and taken a dress, which we later learned was in the dry cleaning my mom had picked up the day of her murder. The officers asked Dad to come to the police station to answer some questions. He agreed to do so after the funeral.

———

The service was on Wednesday in the funeral home chapel, with a packed house of church members, Eastern Star and Masonic friends, work colleagues, school friends, various other friends and acquaintances, and a few curious hangers-on. The entire extended family, including grandparents, uncles, aunts, and cousins from both sides, filed into the chapel and sat together on the front pews. A recent eight-by-ten picture of Mom sat on the closed casket. Reverend James McKee and Reverend Bill Fortson, a close family friend, officiated at the service Mom had planned. A lady from church sang *I'll Tell the World that I Am a Christian*, the song that Mom specifically requested in her will. The lady sang in a high soprano voice that sounded like Mom's.

I'll tell the world, that I'm a Christian,
I'm not ashamed, His name to bear;
I'll tell the world, that I'm a Christian,
I'll take Him with me anywhere.

After the funeral service, a seemingly never-ending line of cars caravanned from the funeral chapel about eight miles south to the burial at San Jose Mission Park. Pastor Fortson spoke at a brief burial service. Seeing Mom placed in her final resting place was almost more than I could handle. Pondering the circumstances of her death—being found nude, robbed, apparently raped, and murdered—added insult to injury.

During all the sadness and turmoil of the day, some of Mom's and Dad's best friends from church, Jorgen and Sandy Hoberg, came over to me, took me aside, hugged me, and said some encouraging words. Their gesture seemed very appropriate and well meaning, but somehow oddly

Chere Buffington, 1976

confusing. I didn't understand all that was going on at the time, but their demeanor seemed to suggest that they knew, or suspected, something that I didn't. But I did know that I had a huge hole in my heart, and that my entire life had changed.

———

Relatives from both sides of the family gathered for a late-afternoon lunch at Mom's parents' house after the funeral. My grandfathers, in particular, were good friends, having been brought together by a love of family and the fact that each was a World War II veteran. After lunch, they sat together, just the two of them in a sitting room that had been converted from a back porch. They were listening to a cassette tape of my mom singing, and both were crying softly. Each was in his own world, and also in Mom's world, and the world of the other. They said not a word. The sweetness of Mom's high soprano voice and the heartbreaking sobs of two grandfathers were the only sounds that broke the mournful silence of this time that seemed so sacred.

In the kitchen, Mrs. County was serving food to the family and cleaning up after us. She received a phone call, immediately became visibly upset, and started screaming and wailing. When she finally calmed down enough to talk, we learned that she had been told the police suspected her husband Charles of killing my mom, and he was at the police station answering questions. We could not imagine that one of Dad's employees was being charged with killing Mom.

Dad gathered us boys, and we abruptly left the luncheon—shell shocked—and went home. Scientists say humans often quash thoughts they don't want to think about. That seems to be the case with me, as I have no memory of that night, a missing scene in the movie of my life. I only remember the fear of what would be next.

Nude body identified

MAR 2 2 1976 News

...e recently divorced
mother.

The woman lived alone in
an apartment in the 8800
block of Broadway. She
moved into the apartment
March 1 and had not com-
pletely settled because of a
death in the family.

Her children are in the
custody of the father, an
acquaintance told The
News.

The grisly find was made
by San Antonio School District Security Officer C. W.
Williamson while pa-
trolling various schools.

Neighbors told police
they first noticed the car
parked at the school about 6
or 6:30 p.m. Saturday, some
5 or 6 hours before checked
by Williamson.

The car was unlocked and

the key was in the ignition.
Both backseat windows and
the front right window were
open.

The woman was shot in
the right eye, right eyebrow
and in the forehead.

Hunt on for killer

MAR 2 2 1976

**Police are hunting a
killer who left his
bloody dead victim on
a school parking lot
over the weekend.**

Medical Examiner Dr.
Ruben Santos said the
29-year-old North Side secretary was not raped be-
fore being shot three times
in the head.

The nude, bloody body of
Mrs. Chere Buffington was
found crouched on the
floorboard of a car on the
Longfellow Junior High
School parking lot late Saturday.

Bloodsoaked clothing was
scattered around the interior of the car registered to

See NUDE BODY, Pg. 4-A

Police push killer hunt

MAR 2 2 1976 News

Police today pushed
their search for the
killer who left the
nude, bloody body of a
mother of three on a
school parking lot last
weekend.

The woman was shot
three times — in the
right eye, right eye-
brow and forehead.

However, Medical Ex-
aminer Dr. Ruben Santos
d the former church
nist had not been raped
he body of Mrs. Cher
ffington was foun
uched in the back floo
rd of her own car on th
king lot of Longfello
ior High School late S
day.

Divorced

Bloody clothing w
ttered inside the car.
he 29-year-old wom
d been divorced
arly nine months
ed alone in an apartm
the 8800 block of Br
y.

She had been marri
imes Buffington.
ople was married in
63, separated in
mber 1974 and div
st June, accordi
urt records.

They had three ch
which she was
stody at the time
vorce, but custod
issed to the fathe
greed order last A

Security

Mrs. Buffington,
nded Jefferso
chool before he
iage, was found
ntonio School Di
urity guard
rounds of campus

Slain woman found in car is identified

MAR 2 2 1976 Express

The nude body of a
woman found in the
back seat of a car
parked at Longfellow
Junior High School
was identified Sunday.

Mrs. Chere S. Buffington,
29, of 8051 Broadway, was
dead on arrival at the
Green Hospital late Saturday. She had been shot
three times in the head,
police said.

The manager of an
apartment complex where
he woman lived until a
onth ago identified the
ody, according to
omicide Det.-Inv. Bob
leming.

Articles of the woman
clothing, including a blood
dress, were found scattere
around the car.

Bnarsndrn said the car,
four-door sedan, belonge
to Mrs. Buffington. Th
keys were in the ignitio
and the back windows wer
open when the body wa
discovered, he said.

At least three person
reported noticing the car so
the lot about 6 p.m. Satur
day, police said.

San Antonio Express
23 Mar 1976, Tue · Page 26

Divorced

Mrs. Buffington was a
vorced secretary who
ed alone, Fleming said.
er body was found at
1 p.m. Saturday by Wil-
g H. Williamson, a San
onio School District
rity guard.
illiamson was on
lar patrol when he
d the body in the car

191—DEATHS

BUFFINGTON

Mrs. Chere Sheterman Buffington,
29, of 8051 Broadway, died March
20th. Member Grace Baptist
Church. Charter member of
University Park Baptist Church.
Mrs. Buffington had been a church
pianist and vocalist for a number of
years, member San Antonio
Chapter No. 10 E.S. lifetime re-
sident of San Antonio. Survivors:
Parents, Mr. and Mrs. Herman A.
(Gene) Sheterman, sons, Jimmy,
Oscar, and Louis Buffington, an

Nude Woman Found Dead In School Lot

4977

3/21/76

The nude body of a woman about 30
years old was found Saturday night in
a car parked in the Longfellow Junior
High School parking lot in Northeast
San Antonio.

Homicide detectives said the
woman appeared to have been
severely beaten about the face and
head, but did not know if she had been
raped.

Police were called to the scene
about 9 p.m. by school security
officers.

The car was in the parking lot, 1130
E. Sunshine, and the victim was in the
back seat which was splattered with
blood.

The woman's clothes were strewn
about the front of the auto. There were
no personal effects which could lead to
immediate identification of the
victim.

Officers said the car key was in the
ignition.

EMS technicians reported that the

CHAPTER TWO

Roots

"A man leaves his father and mother and is united to his wife,
and they become one flesh." (Genesis 2:24)

Our story did not end during that terrible week in March 1976. Nor
was that when it began.

Mom's dad, Herman Stieferman, was born in 1910, grew up in Okla-
homa, moved to San Antonio when he entered the military, and served
in World War II. He later worked as a body shop foreman and then an
insurance adjuster, providing his family with a stable income. He was a
Catholic, and attended church regularly. Grandpa Herman was straightforward, gentle, and independent.

Herman and Mignon

Mom's mother, Mignon Stieferman, was born in San Antonio in 1914. Grandma Mignon was a classic southern belle: very put together, attractive, blonde, beautifully dressed, often with a cigarette dangling from her very bright-red lips. She graduated from Mary Hardin-Baylor University, a Christian university in Belton, Texas. Grandma Mignon maintained a lively home for her husband and their children Herman and Chere; her brother, Jay; her parents, Elmer and Imogene Edwards; and a caretaker named Rose. She cooked meals that were homespun masterpieces. She was quite gregarious, made friends easily, was a member of the Baptist church, and maintained an active social life. Grandma Mignon was one my best friends when I became an adult.

Mom, Chere Stieferman Buffington, entered the story on August 16, 1946. She was born in San Antonio, roughly two years after brother, Herman, her only sibling, was born. She grew up in San Antonio, attended the University Baptist Church and public schools, and blossomed into a very attractive woman. She was around five feet, eight inches tall, with piercing blue eyes, fair skin, and radiant facial features. Her brown, slightly curly hair was nearly always coiffed in a traditional beehive. She dressed stylishly and was a classy lady, much like her mother.

Music was one of Mom's big loves. She sang in her school choir at Thomas Jefferson High School and enjoyed singing and playing the piano in church. She loved the church and the Eastern Star organization, a fraternal society associated with the Masons.

Oscar, Louis, and I remember Mom as a beauty, both inside and out. We have good memories of time spent with her. She was a devoted wife and mother who enjoyed being with her kids. She was open and verbal, and often told us she loved us. All three of us

Chere

had a great love for her, and often argued about who would get to sit next to her in church. Like all human beings, she was not perfect, but as kids we viewed her as a saint, totally without fault.

Dad's father, Norris Lee Buffington, traced his roots to Malvern, Arkansas, a town of roughly 5,000 people at the time, near Little Rock and Hot Springs, home to prior generations of Buffingtons. He served in World War II and fought in the Battle of the Bulge, among other engagements. He contracted war induced schizophrenia, now called PTSD, which became a long-term problem. Papa Lee married Glendal Rae Holiman, my Grandmother Glendal, and they had two sons: Norris Jr., and my dad, James, his younger brother.

Glendal, Norris Lee, Oscar

Dad, James Buffington, Sr., was born on April 16, 1944, in Malvern. When he was a youngster, the family moved to San Antonio for his father to obtain medical assistance from one of the military hospitals located there. They lived in San Antonio until about the time Dad graduated from high school. The family then moved to Houston, where they lived until Papa Lee retired, and he and Grandmother Glendal returned to Malvern to spend their retirement with family and friends.

Dad had a pretty conventional youth, doing what boys do in a town of half a million people. Church was a big part of his family's culture and life, and they attended regularly. At one point, Dad considered going to seminary. He ultimately decided it was not in the books for him and chose the music route instead. He attended Thomas Jefferson High School, where he played the violin in the school orchestra and sang in the choir.

James

Mom and Dad attended Thomas Jefferson High School along with Dad's older brother, Norris Jr., and Mom's older brother, Herman, who were best friends. Mom and Dad started dating when he was a senior, and Mom was a sophomore. He was seventeen, and she was fifteen. They got very serious, very quickly.

Chere and James in high school

After Dad graduated and his parents moved to Houston, Dad lived at home with them and started college at the University of Houston. He and Mom maintained a long-distance romance, spending most weekends together. On August 16, 1962, Mom's sixteenth birthday, they had a date—and what a date it was. They eloped across the border to Mexico and got married. They didn't tell anyone. Mom continued to live with her parents in San Antonio and Dad with his parents in Houston.

In January Mom learned she was pregnant, and they told her parents they were married and expecting. To Mom's great surprise, her mother reacted quite calmly and was supportive about the whole matter. She did, however, insist that a secret Mexican wedding did not count, and they had to get married in a Baptist Church. So they had a formal wedding at her church, the University Baptist Church in San Antonio. Pastor Dr. Jimmy Draper, who later became president of the Southern Baptist Convention, officiated at a small wedding in the chapel.

Once the secret was out, and they were officially married, the couple moved briefly into Dad's parents' home in Houston, along with Dad's brother and their grandmother, Willie Wheat Holiman. They were in a ridiculously small house, and Dad's mother, my Grandmother Glendal, was a very controlling lady, frequently complaining, criticizing others (particularly her husband), and otherwise verbally abusing people and creating drama in the family. Dad seemed to be her favorite however, and always managed to get his way. She and Mom fought like cats and dogs. At one point the relationship was so bad that they agreed to not talk directly to one another, and have all communication between mother-in-law and daughter-in-law go through Dad. However, as difficult as she was with others, she was nice to her grandchildren.

Dad worked at his father's Tenneco service station while he was in college. Mom went to court reporter school, got a job as a court reporter for a time, and then—no doubt influenced by her dad and her grandfather, Elmer Edwards, a prominent retired insurance salesman—started working as an adjuster in an insurance company. Mom and Dad were both members of The Order of Eastern Star, and Dad was a Mason and a Shriner.

When I was born in June of 1963, my parents, struggling financially, moved into an apartment not far from Dad's parents' house. Soon after that move, our family joined the Townwood Baptist Church. Dad, charismatic and an extrovert who liked being the center of attention, joined the church choir. I suspect he did so, at least in part, to allow him to perform on stage.

Oscar was born a couple of years after I was, and then Louis came along ten months later. Mom was only nineteen years old and had three kids. Dad quit college and began working for a finance company, but apparently our family continued to have money problems. Their marriage seemed to be going downhill. Mom saw Dad as controlling and demanding, drinking too much, and working and socializing pretty much as he pleased. She became unhappy and depressed. I later learned that during this time they discussed the possibility of divorce.

In the summer of 1969, after I finished kindergarten, the finance company transferred Dad to San Antonio, where he was promoted within the company and also obtained a weekend job as music minister in the small Allena Baptist Church. Mom worked as an insurance adjuster and got a weekend job as a pianist in the same church. We moved into the parsonage, a small, nondescript, but comfortable bungalow with three bedrooms and one bath. Located just behind the church, it had a small front porch with a room on each side. The rooms each had different looking facades and architecture, giving the house a somewhat discombobulated, add-on look from the street. But it was better than the apartments we had lived in, and we soon became comfortable there.

Mom loved her mother. They got along well, and continued to have a close relationship after Mom was married and had her own family. They loved meeting frequently for lunch, always at a Mexican restaurant, where they sometimes visited for hours.

The family developed an awesome Friday night routine that everyone greatly enjoyed. Grandma Mignon prepared a very formal, sit-down family banquet and served it in their formal dining room, on her best China plates, with crystal drinking glasses and silver tableware. Grandpa Herman would get things started with the traditional Catholic blessing:

Bless us, Oh Lord, and these thy gifts,
which we are about to receive,
from thy bounty,
through Christ, Our Lord. Amen.

These meals were sumptuous examples of Southern cuisine. My favorite was baked chicken with Grandma Mignon's special sauce, that we called "chicken on the bone." Delicacies such as this, paired with congenial conversation about work, school, church, and other subjects, made for dinners that the family repeated time and again.

After each meal was finished, Maude, the housekeeper, did the dishes and the family adjourned to the well-appointed living room. We all gathered around the old upright piano that had belonged to Mom's Grandmother Edwards and that I have in my house today. Mom played the piano, and she and Dad sang a duet. Both were talented musicians, and on one occasion even sang the national anthem at an event in the Houston Astrodome. They used their Friday night sessions to practice for singing and playing in church on Sunday. I will never forget the power and grace of their performances, especially their rendition of old church hymns. Dad's favorite song was "How Great Thou Art," an old Baptist hymn he often sang as a solo. Everyone loved Mom's piano solo of "The Entertainer," by Scott Joplin, popularized by the movie, *The Sting*.

When the music stopped, the adults would gather around the kitchen table and play canasta until late at night. My brothers and I stayed in the living room, aggravated one another, watched television, played

Herman, Jimmy, Chere, Oscar, Mignon, Louis

board games, or slept. One of us usually spent the night with our grand-parents and had breakfast with them on Saturday morning. We rotated, and considered the sleepover as a great part of our family experience.

Faith and religion were important parts of our family life. I've heard it said that "faith" is our belief in a higher power, while "religion" involves ritual and a philosophy of life. Using these definitions in our family, Mom was the person of faith, and Dad seemed to focus more on religion.

Mom had a strong personal faith that seemed genuine to all who knew her, and she came across to others as caring and sincere. She and I had natural, comfortable conversations about God, but Mom never made it pushy or preachy. She would come into my room at night, share Bible stories, and pray with me before I went to sleep. She didn't try to

27

force me to believe, but just naturally discussed God, shared her beliefs, and encouraged me. She taught in the kids' ministry at church and played the piano at church services. Mom loved singing Christian songs, not to show off her talented voice, but to express her faith. When she sang, you could hear the strength of her faith in God and knew that she had a personal relationship with Him. She loved singing the song, "He's Got the Whole World in His Hands." Mom made it easy to believe, and she was my leader/teacher of religion and faith.

Dad was a different person. During the week, he prepared songs he was going to sing at church on Sunday and led choir practice on Wednesday night. On Sundays, as the minister of music, Dad sat in a chair on the left side of the stage, with the pastor sitting on the right. Dad stood at the pulpit and led the church in singing, with the choir behind him. However, during my life at home, I don't remember having any faith conversations with Dad, or hearing him pray, or praying with him, or doing other things from which I could discern a faith. Dad was charismatic and tried to maintain a Christian persona, but he often came across as loud, bossy, and controlling.

Looking back, I think Mom was the true Christian believer, and Dad was only a church leader. Something was missing in my dad's life when I was a child. I think it was true faith in God.

We attended services regularly as a family. On Sunday mornings, we all attended Sunday school, and then my brothers and I sat side by side in a pew near the front of the sanctuary as Mom played the piano and Dad led the congregational singing. They joined us during the pastor's sermon, and we sat together as a "perfect" Christian family, all appearing to listen in to the message of the day.

In 1973, when I was ten years old, I talked to Mom about becoming a Christian and being baptized. In our church tradition, baptism is a step of obedience after you decide to become a Christian. It represents the death, burial, and resurrection of Jesus Christ. You are baptized and immersed under water to represent the death of your old life and, when you come out of the water, it represents your *new* life in Christ as a Christian and follower of Christ. It is a public statement of your faith.

Mom was very encouraging, and one Sunday not long after our talk I walked "down the aisle" at the Allena Baptist Church and told the pastor I had put my faith in Jesus Christ as Lord and Savior and wanted to be baptized. The next week, both my brothers walked down the aisle too and told the pastor they had accepted Christ and wanted to be baptized. So the following Sunday, all of us were immersed, one by one, in age order, by our pastor, in the baptistry at the front of the church, behind the choir.

The pastor asked each of us if we were professing our faith as Christians, and we each said yes. Then he dunked us under the water, "in the name of the Father, the Son, and the Holy Spirit," to walk in a new life.

After I walked down the aisle, made my public profession of faith, and was baptized, I felt I was independent. I had made the decision, and I thought I was grown up. My brothers doing the same thing made me realize the impact I had on them. I better understood that my choices impact others.

After a couple of years in San Antonio, Dad found a better job as the general manager of Cliff's Fence Company, one of the larger residential and commercial fencing companies in the area. It had an office and warehousing facility located in an industrial complex not far from the center of the city. The company employed approximately fifty people, including Charlotte Jacobs and Charles County—each of whom became a continuing character in Dad's life.

Mom and Dad's marital difficulties, which spanned several years, seem to have come to a head in 1974 when Mom sought help from the church minister, and Dad became jealous of their relationship. Mom and Dad argued frequently, and on one occasion, just before Thanksgiving, he hit her and gave her a black eye. This led to their split, as Dad moved out shortly after what no doubt was a difficult holiday. We boys started our new life living with Mom.

After Mom and Dad separated, Dad started his own business, Jim's Fence Company. His was a smaller version of Cliff's, with one office, two administrative employees, and two baby-blue vehicles. The company purchased material on the open market when needed and used contract labor. Mom worked nights and weekends as a cocktail waitress at the Sugar Shack, in addition to continuing her work as an insurance adjuster, and looking after us boys.

In May of 1974, Dad's father came home in the early morning from a graveyard shift at Acme Brick Company and found his wife, our Grandma Glendal, dead in their bed. She had been a heavy smoker who suffered from Crohn's disease and had died from a brain aneurysm at the age of fifty-one. Her death was a shock to the entire family, and it delivered quite a jolt to Dad. As her favorite child and mama's boy, they had a close relationship. Whatever Dad wanted, Dad got. It was his first loss of a person close to him, a double whammy of sorts, since it occurred in the midst of his continuing marital problems.

At Grandma's funeral at the Atkinson Funeral Home in Malvern, Mom said to Dad, "James, I sure wish it had been me in that coffin instead of your mother."

One can only wonder what that comment triggered in Dad's mind.

CHAPTER THREE

The Crime

"For everything in the world—the lust of the flesh,
the lust of the eyes, and the pride of life—comes not
from the Father but from the world." (1 John 2:16)

Detectives Robert Flemming and Abel Juarez began investigating
Mom's murder on Sunday, March 21. They soon learned that on Friday
night, Mom was out with Ken McDaniel, a man she had been dating. She
ended their date early, telling him, "I've got to get up early Saturday, because I'm doing a job for James. I have to pick up two of his employees
and take them to their job site."

Dad had promised her fifty dollars for delivering Charles County and
Charlie Moore to their workplace, and she planned to use the money to
buy clothes for us boys.

Around 7:00 a.m. Saturday, Mom went to County's house, rang the
doorbell, and got no answer. Not knowing what to do, she called Dad
at the home of OB and Patsy Holiman in Arkansas, where he and Linda were vacationing, and explained the situation to him. He responded,
"Don't worry about it. They probably got drunk last night and passed out,
so they didn't answer the door. We'll reschedule it."

Mom picked up some dry-cleaning and groceries, and then went to
her parent's house for most of the day before returning to her apartment late that afternoon. When she arrived home, she found two large
white envelopes at the front door with "Jim's Fence Company" on the
return portion. One envelope had been torn open and "Charles house
key inside" scribbled on the outside and "Call Charles 732–5049" on the
inside. "Charles County" was written on the address location of the other envelope.

Concerned that County obviously knew where she lived, Mom called the Holiman's number in Arkansas again, looking for Dad. Patsy Holiman answered, and told Mom that James was out of touch, at the horse races. The two women had a brief conversation, including a discussion about Mom's concern that County obviously knew where she lived. Deep down, Patsy knew something was wrong.

Notwithstanding her concern, Mom called the number on the note, talked to County, and arranged to meet him to deliver weekly payroll checks that were due for digging post holes on one of Dad's projects. She placed the envelope that was addressed to him on the small table where the phone was located, got in her car, and went to their meeting place.

County was one of Dad's few employees. He was twenty-seven years old, medium height and build, with a somewhat modest Afro hairstyle. Charles could not read or write. He stayed in a small shotgun style, wood-framed house with two bedrooms, one bath, and a simple add-on carport, in a ghetto in central San Antonio. He had faced a trial five years previously for double murder with malice in the shooting of a man and woman in their mid-fifties. He was convicted on reduced charges of aggravated assault and assessed a six-month jail term.

County had begun drinking with friends Mary Rodgers and Charlie Moore at a westside lounge around 4:30 on Saturday afternoon. After about an hour, he and Moore left the lounge, telling Rodgers they were going to pick up a check.

A little after 5:30, a witness observed a car and a baby-blue Ford club cab pickup, identical to vehicles used by Jim's Fence Company personnel, parked side by side in the parking lot of Longfellow Junior High School. The witness reported that two Black men were standing between the car and the truck. Shortly thereafter, the men left in the truck, and the car remained in the parking lot.

County and Moore returned to the west-side lounge between 6:30 and 7:00 p.m., drank more gin and beer, and continued their socializing with Rodgers and others. Later that evening, they went to a local grocery store and cashed two payroll checks drawn on Jim's Fence Company.

Around 9:30 that evening, San Antonio school district security officer, C. W. Williamson, was making routine patrols and discovered a 1972 green-and-white Chevy Impala, later determined to be the car Mom had obtained in a trade for her older Lincoln Continental a couple of weeks previously, in the Longfellow Junior High School parking lot. Mom's nude, bloodied body was slumped on the back floorboard. She had been shot three times in the head. Her purse was missing. Williamson called the San Antonio police.

Detectives Fleming and Juarez visited the Robert B. Green Morgue and found a doctor in the process of conducting an autopsy. The detectives then began digging into a long list of possible sources of evidence. They checked out the school parking lot where Mom's body was located, but found nothing of significant evidentiary value; and went to the police vehicle pound where they inspected Mom's car and found the door handles on the Impala had been wiped clean, but Charlie Moore's palm print was on its roof. They interviewed Mom's parents in some detail in the midst of their overwhelming grief and spoke with several witnesses who had seen Mom's car and a truck with two Black males in the school parking lot on the day of the crime.

That afternoon, the officers received calls stating that a fisherman had discovered Mom's checkbook on the banks of Woodlawn Lake, and that another had found her purse in the lake.

The following day, March 22, the detectives proceeded to the apartment building where Mom had lived and interviewed the apartment manager and assistant manager. While they were talking to the managers, Mom's dad and her brother Herman arrived to get some clothes to bury her in. They all entered her apartment together, where they found everything in order and saw the groceries and clothes she had picked up on the day she was murdered. They also found the two large envelopes with scribbled notes that Mom had left on the coffee table.

Later in the day, Detective Juarez drove by Jim's Fence Company and observed a 1975 baby-blue Ford club cab pickup—the same type of truck that the two witnesses reported seeing at the school parking lot. The detectives concluded that someone apparently had used one of the Company trucks in committing the crime.

Around 4:45 in the afternoon, Dad and his attorney, Cecil Bain, showed up at the homicide office. Bain asked if Dad was a suspect. He was advised that Dad was not under suspicion at that time. Dad exhibited considerable nervousness as he was being asked questions concerning his life with Mom and the operation of Jim's Fence Company.

When asked about the letters Mom had left on the table, Dad said that, except for the scribbling, they were in his handwriting and he remembered writing them, but couldn't explain how they got on the table in Mom's apartment. Dad related that Charles County did most of the company's residential installations on a contract basis and often used a 1975 super cab pickup. He sometimes was assisted by Charlie Moore, a man County had introduced as his cousin.

The deputies interviewed County on the day of Mom's funeral, March 24. He apparently figured he was a prime suspect in the murder and would for sure be arrested, so he agreed to go to the police station and answer questions. Around 5:00 p.m. he arrived at the homicide office with his father, Verdo County, and his attorney, Charles Butts, a prominent criminal defense attorney in San Antonio. County was advised of his rights to have an attorney and to remain silent. Statements were taken from him and his father. Charles was released, but the probe of him as a prime suspect in Mom's murder continued.

Detective Juarez contacted Mayola Taylor, County's girlfriend. She told him she owned a .22-caliber pistol that Charles County had been using. She gave Juarez permission to take the gun and test fire it. On March 30, the crime lab confirmed that the bullets removed from Mom's body had been fired from the revolver Taylor had loaned to County.

At 2:00 p.m. on March 31, warrants were issued for the arrests of Charles County and Charlie Moore on capital murder charges in the armed robbery, rape, and shooting of Chere Buffington. Detectives Juarez and Fleming arrested County at Taylor's house on San Antonio's west side later that afternoon. He had a .22-caliber pistol in his possession. He was arraigned before a justice of the peace and locked in jail, with bail set at $100,000.

County implicated Charlie Moore, who had fled the state and was on the run. He also opened Pandora's box when he told Detective Fleming that James Buffington had hired him to kill his wife for $3,000, later increased to $5,000, to be paid from life insurance proceeds. County's attorney, Charles Butts, made a deal with the DA, Charles Conaway, that County would testify that Dad had hired him to kill his ex-wife, if he, Conaway, would not seek the death penalty for County. County was returned to the Bexar County Jail, assuming he had saved his own skin by ratting out the other two.

In addition to the alleged murder pistol, Police recovered Mom's purse and checkbook that local fishermen reported discovering at Woodlawn Lake. Later that afternoon of March 31, County and Moore were charged with capital murder in the Court of Justice of the Peace J. P. Gutierrez. In July, a grand jury indicted each of them for capital murder.

San Antonio Express-News and San Antonio Light, April–July, 1976

A nationwide alert was issued for Moore's arrest. Thirty years old, a contract employee of Jim's Fence Company who claimed to be owed ninety dollars for three days' work, Moore was five feet eight inches tall, stoutly built but not overweight, sporting a short buzz haircut framed by a slightly receding hairline. His piercing-gray eyes and a large, jagged scar on the right side of his face put one in mind of a killer from a Hollywood movie, or a man who raped and killed my mother. He had been charged in 1973 with assault after attempting to murder a nineteen-year-old woman who survived a single shot to the chest.

Moore was located about a year after Mom's murder in the Hobbs, New Mexico, jail, charged with auto theft. New Mexico officials discovered he was wanted in Texas on a murder charge and notified Texas officials. They arrested him on April 20, 1977, extradited him to San Antonio, and locked him in the Bexar County Jail. Bail was set at $50,000.

36

Suspect
APR 23 1977
Back
In S.A.

A 31-year-old man,
rrested earlier this week
Clovis, N.M., was
turned to San Antonio
iday on a capital
irder warrant for the
6 slaying of a divorcee.
harles B. Moore, 31, is
ng held in Bexar
nty Jail in lieu of
)00 bond, set by 186th
rict Court Judge
's Barlow.
ore is charged with
March 20, 1976,
er of Mrs. Chere
gton, whose nude
vas found huddled
floorboard of her
ft on a parking lot
'fellow Junior High
She had been shot
ad three times.

Second suspect in S.A. woman's death captured

Express
APR 21 1977

A second man charged with murder
in connection with the March 20, 1976,
slaying of a San Antonio secretary is
expected to be returned to San Antonio
Friday.

Authorities said Charles B. Moore,
31, is being held in a Clovis, N.M., jail
pending extradition to San Antonio.

Police said the man is wanted in
connection with the slaying of Mrs.
Chere Buffington, 29.

Another man, Charles County, 28, is
in Bexar County Jail in lieu of a $50,000
bond on a captial murder charge in
connection with the Mrs. Buffington's
death.

Officers said the woman's nude body
was found crouched on the back of her
car parked on the Longfellow Junior

High School campus.

The woman had been shot in the
right eye, right eyebrow and forehead,
police said.

The bloody clothing was scattered in
the car, but Medical Examiner Dr.
Ruben Santos said the woman had not
been raped.

Officers later recovered a pistol
believed used in the slaying, the woman's purse and checkbook at two
residences, officers reported.

County was arrested March 31, 1976,
and Moore has been sought by officers
ever since, police said.

Moore was arrested Tuesday in Clovis, N.M., and jailed after Clovis police
discovered the man was wanted on a
murder charge.

Murder
Express
suspect
jailed
APR 22 1977

A second man charg
with capital murder
connection with the sl
Antonio secretary
lodged in Bexar Cou
Jail Friday after b
returned from Clovi
M.
Charged with c
murder in conn
with the shooting d
Mrs. Chere Buffi
29, is Charles B.
31. He was jailed
of $50,000 bond
District Judge J
Barlow.
Moore is al
held on a Curr
N. M. warrant
him with auto
officials said.
Moore wa
earlier in th
Clovis and
authorities
vered he wa
murder cha

San Antonio Express-News, April 21, 1977

Following up on a tip, the detectives contacted Connecticut General Insurance Company and learned that Mom had applied for a $125,000 life
insurance policy (more than $500,000 in 2023 dollars), with double in-
demnity in case of accidental death. Her sons were beneficiaries of the
policy, which had been paid but not yet issued.

A young mother purchasing life insurance on herself for the benefit of three young sons seems highly unusual, and the contemporary record is silent as to why she did. However, years later a letter from Mom's
friend, Carol Gibson, shed some light on what was going on at the time.

> Chere was an easygoing type of person whom I admired for her
> work as well as being a good mother to her boys . . . I can recall
> on several occasions when we were out after work she always
> seemed bothered and nervous. She would never sit with her back

37

to the door of any place we were at. She commented to me one night that James was watching her and she knew it.

. . . On one occasion at the "Sugar Shack" we were shooting pool, joking, and laughing and it was her turn. She all of a sudden froze and told me, "Don't look now, but there's one of James's employees sitting at the bar." Chere had a look of horror on her face as she told me, "we have got to get out of here. It's not safe."

. . . She was shaking and crying and she told me that James had been calling her at work again. He had previously been calling her and threatening her, like he was jealous. He asked her to check into insurance for the boys, something with double indemnity in case of an accident. She seemed concerned and really worried at this point.

She explained to me that she was really afraid of James and what he might do to her and to the boys and that his capabilities were way beyond control. She said she knew that James's employees had been watching her but she didn't know how long, and that they were divorced and James didn't want her, but he didn't want anyone else to have her either. She said she was really scared.

. . . I drove over to her apartment to find that it had really been trashed and torn all to heck and that her clothes were even shredded. She told me that she was scared and didn't feel safe anymore.

. . . She told me she might ask for leave from work and leave town for a while without telling anyone.

Well, I never heard from her again.

The detectives also contacted John Hancock Insurance Company and learned that Mom had three life insurance policies with them, on her life: one for $2,000, triple indemnity for accidental death; one for $10,000, triple indemnity for accidental death; and a third for $98,000. The beneficiary on all three policies was James Buffington.

"Closure" is probably an overworked concept—one favored by the media and people who have never been seriously victimized. Having two prime suspects in Mom's murder locked behind bars should have given the family some sense of a path toward that elusive feeling of finality. But there was a problem.

At the April examining trial to determine if the charges against County and Moore should go to a grand jury, Mayola Taylor testified that County had taken a .22-caliber pistol from under a mattress in her home the day Mom was murdered, and returned it a day or two later. Other testimony had shown that it was the weapon used in the murder. The medical examiner's report confirmed this conclusion.

An autopsy done on Mom's body before County was arrested had reported that all bullets had been removed, and they appeared to be from a .38-caliber weapon. But a .38-caliber weapon was never found. When County was arrested, the coroner, apparently at the urging of the district attorney, changed his report to say that the bullets removed from Mom's body had been in bad shape and couldn't be identified—and he had left one bullet in her that he couldn't retrieve. The district attorney then obtained a court order to exhume her body to retrieve the remaining bullet.

The plans to exhume Mom's body got wide publicity and were detailed in the local papers. The whole matter was like digging up pain and sorrow that had not been really buried in the first place, and adding a level of uncertainty that caused our entire family's grief to become even more profound. In an effort to shield us boys from the additional trauma, Dad had Charlotte take us to Arkansas for a couple of days to hang out with his dad and stepmother. Her doing such a thing was highly unusual, and seemed to stoke as many questions as it covered up.

Mom's body was exhumed on March 31, about a week after her funeral, with the DA participating. When the casket was opened, he allegedly said, "Here it is," and pulled a bullet out of her hairline. The coroner had originally said all three bullets were removed during the first autopsy, apparently also saying they were too damaged to conclude what type, or that they were from a .38 caliber. The story changed to, "He left one bullet inside her head, so an exhumation was needed."

After the exhumation, the coroner changed his statement to, "I found the one bullet" in Mom's hairline during exhumation and it was a .22 caliber. The bullet the DA claimed he pulled from Mom's hairline during the second autopsy was the only one that was a .22-caliber. It matched the .22-caliber pistol County had in his possession when he was arrested. A .38-caliber bullet, the type matching the gun that I had found in the work truck that County drove, was never found. Thus, the only gun that could be tied to the murder was the .22 that allegedly was County's gun, and it connected him. However, questions remained whether the .22 was actually the murder weapon—and about many other issues as well.

CHAPTER FOUR

Life with Dad

"Whoever brings ruin on their family will inherit only wind, and
the fool will be servant to the wise." (Proverbs 11:29)

Our decision to live with Dad after he and Mom divorced worked
reasonably well. We first lived with him in the small, four-bedroom, one-
bath ranch-style house on Lazy Oaks Drive that they had purchased before they separated—where we went with Dad when he abruptly took us
away from the family luncheon following Mom's funeral.

Several months after Mom's death, Dad used the life insurance proceeds to purchase a bigger house. We called it the "big house." Located at
1111 Country Court, it had a brick façade, a two-car garage, two stories,
five bedrooms, and four bathrooms. It was located at the end of a large
cul-de-sac in a really nice neighborhood in north San Antonio. A community club with a swimming pool and tennis court was at the end of the
street. It seemed like a mansion compared to the parsonage or the house
on Lazy Oaks where we previously lived.

1111 Country Court

The three of us boys moved to new schools when our parents left the church parsonage and moved to Lazy Oaks Drive. Each of us had a history of being good students, but the trauma in our lives after Mom was murdered really affected our school performance.

I attended junior high at Garner Junior High School, and I remained obsessed by what happened to Mom. I couldn't think or focus. I had horrible pictures in my head of what she suffered, and these images would not go away. I felt different from my classmates, who seemed to treat me as if I had some terrible communicable disease. I believed I didn't belong.

All three of us boys received failing grades the spring semester of 1976—the semester Mom was murdered. We missed more classes than usual, and continued to be unable to concentrate, complete our homework, or otherwise stay on task. Articles relating to Mom's murder were in the news so much that everyone knew about our situation. Thankfully, our teachers were tolerant, and we each managed to do well enough to pass and be promoted to the next grades.

We switched schools again after our move to the big house. I changed to Eisenhower Junior High School, a bigger school in a great district in a plush area of town. I did well in academics, was on the tennis team, and had an overall good school experience. Almost no one associated me with my mom's murder, as media coverage declined, and we were in a new area of town where few people knew what happened unless we told them. Most of those who did know about Mom reacted positively, with respect, consideration, and love.

Dad's financial situation during this time was a mess at best. He tried to continue his fencing business but, not surprisingly, it didn't work. He was severely distracted by more important issues, and potential customers were understandably wary about signing on with a rumored murderer to build a fence on their property. Dad closed the office and sold what few assets the company owned.

We lived mainly on insurance money resulting from Mom's death. Dad had purchased several term policies on her life, apparently without her knowledge, with himself as the beneficiary. The combined payout from these policies was $350,000. He had also purchased three additional term policies of $75,000 each on Mom's life, with each of us kids designated as a beneficiary. The insurance companies paid, but very reluctantly and after considerable haggling, as they suspected Dad was involved in Mom's death. The money that was payable to us boys was placed in a trust. Dad was guardian of our estate, so he received or controlled a total of $575,000, probably worth slightly in excess of $2 million in 2023 dollars.

Dad blew through that money like a drunken sailor. A few months after Mom's death, he had purchased the "big house" for $82,000, and spent $10,000 on furniture. He also bought Linda a mink coat and a 2-to-3-karat engagement ring. In less than a year, Dad drained all the $350,000 he received and half of the $225,000 in our trust. Exactly how he spent all that money was a mystery.

Dad engaged in some pretty questionable schemes to keep us afloat amidst the extravagant and mysterious spending. One ruse involved kiting checks. He would write a check, say for twenty dollars, and send me into a convenience or drugstore to buy something small and cheap like a candy bar, pay for it with the check, and get the extra cash for him. We repeated the process at several stores and accumulated a bundle of cash. The checks bounced like a ping-pong ball. I didn't really understand what was going on, but I sure did enjoy my cut of the candy.

The real issue seems to have been Dad's acting as though he was above the law. For instance, he had me drive him around town with my brothers in the car. Although I was only thirteen years old, Dad acted as though I was old enough to drive and all would be okay. I enjoyed the feeling of power and control, and didn't see any problem either. Upon reflection, I'm pretty sure my driving allowed him to drink all the booze he wanted without risking a DUI charge.

At another level, our life somewhat stabilized. Our fear about what would happen next was greatly diminished when Charles County was arrested. Although we still had some concern because we knew that another man had been involved, this worry caused underlying jitters, but not a crippling fear.

Life with Dad had its pros and cons. The best part probably involved church. After their divorce and before Mom's death, we went to church with either or both my mom and my dad. Church and faith continued to be a big part of our lives. After Mom's death, we attended church with Dad, sang and heard him sing, were a part of the church community, and saw him at his charismatic best. I then started going to a Methodist church with Dad and Linda, and actually went through the confirmation process in the Methodist Church. Rumors concerning his involvement in Mom's death didn't seem to affect him or his relationship with the church, and our involvement seemed to provide an anchor that brought a semblance of balance to our lives.

On the other hand, Dad's narcissistic, controlling, and overbearing side frequently raised its hideous head. He wanted nothing of Mom's to be seen in the house, and he threw away most things he saw that had belonged to her, or that would remind him of her. He wanted Mom removed from our lives. We were not even allowed to talk about her, particularly in the presence of Linda.

Anything relating to Mom that I wanted to keep, like pictures, keepsakes, or other mementos, had to be behind closed doors in a cabinet in my bedroom. One day I accidently left the cabinet door open, with stuff that had been Mom's there for Dad to see. He came in when I got home from school and said, with more than a touch of anger in his voice, "You left the cabinet door open in your bedroom."

"Yeah."

Dad continued, "I could see the pictures of your mom. That will really bother Linda."

I liked to keep the cabinet door open so I could see the pictures of Mom on the inside walls. But after that day, I made sure to double check anytime I walked out of my bedroom, to be sure that I had closed the door to the cabinet so nobody could see my pictures of her. If Dad told me to do something, I complied. I didn't want to make him mad.

Linda was not living with us and only visited from time to time, but he made us call her "Mom," even though they were not yet married, and we didn't want to recognize her that way. Chere was still our mom. We liked Linda, gravitated towards her because of the genuinely nice person she was, and became very affectionate toward her. Dad, however, couldn't force us to replace our mom.

James and Linda

45

We had little connection with extended family during this time. Mom's parents, and her brother Herman, and his wife, Dana, tried to see us often, but Dad put a damper on their efforts. They knew Dad was a suspect in Mom's murder and apparently had some concerns that he was guilty. Those suspicions were particularly fueled by Charles County's arrest. Dad was pretty sure Herman and Dana suspected him, and his predictable efforts to avoid them precluded much contact with Mom's side of the family. When he and the in-laws were together, we felt like we were walking on thin ice that was quickly melting.

We didn't see much of Dad's parents during this time, either. Papa Lee had lost his wife, my Grandmother Glendal, shortly before Mom was murdered. He soon met Frances Monroe, who owned the Polly Ann Bakery, where he hung out with friends on many mornings, drinking coffee and visiting. They married about a year later. He was living with his new wife, my Granny Fran, in Malvern, Arkansas.

Papa Lee came to San Antonio alone—while his new wife stayed home to run the bakery—in January of 1977 for Grandpa Herman's funeral. We didn't see him again until several months later.

Special occasions often are the most difficult times following the loss of a loved one. That was my experience. On my thirteenth birthday, June 17, roughly three months after Mom was killed, her parents insisted that Dad let us come to their house for a birthday celebration. Dad dropped us off, visited a few minutes, and then left. We boys, our grandparents, and Herman and Dana, had dinner and a cake, they sang "Happy Birthday," and I opened gifts. We boys enjoyed spending time with our grandparents. Dad returned later to have cake and pick us up. There was very little conversation between him and his in-laws. Mom's absence was the "elephant in the room" that stomped much of the life out of the occasion.

Christmas wasn't much better. Linda and her daughter, Tammy, were there with Dad and us three boys. Santa Claus showed up. We shared gifts. We all dressed up, went to church for the Christmas service, and then out to eat. But much of the joy of the season didn't show up. We could not fill the huge, deep void that was left by Mom's absence. We missed Mom, her gingerbread houses, how she decorated our house, her hugs, and the warm feeling that Christmas was with her. Fortunately for us, we didn't know the extent to which Dad was under major suspicion, stressed out, bleeding money, and trying to put on a false face that everything was fine. Having such information would have only made matters worse.

In recent years, I have seen a picture of us that was taken on that day. I am struck by the smiles, given the pain we were dealing with.

Linda, Tammy, and boys, Christmas 1976

During Christmas break of 1976, Dad surprised us when he said, "Hey, we're taking a trip to Carlsbad caverns in New Mexico. We will be leaving in the morning."

Travel to Carlsbad Caverns

My brothers and I reacted among ourselves, "But we've already been to Carlsbad caverns. We've been there a couple of times on family vacations. Why do we want to return? And why now?" It just seemed so odd. But we, with Linda and Tammy, drove west, spent a couple of days revisiting the rocky canyons, flowering cactus, desert wildlife, and two of the deep underground caves, and returned home.

Why did we go on that sudden and unusual vacation? Charlie Moore was in Hobbs, NM, just sixty miles from Carlsbad. Did Dad talk to him while we were there? Did he make the trip to pay off Moore, as some later suspected? I didn't know, and still don't. But it seemed so bizarre, like so many other events that were to occur.

CHAPTER FIVE

An Arrest

"Religion that God our Father accepts as pure and faultless is this: to look after orphans and widows in their distress and to keep oneself from being polluted by the world." (James 1: 27)

In Texas, a grand jury is used to determine whether or not there is probable cause to believe that a felony has occurred. A prosecutor recites alleged facts or provides witness testimony to twelve jurors in a secret hearing. The defendant generally is not present in the hearing involving him or her, and the defense attorney is not in the room. If fewer than nine jurors believe the defendant is likely to be guilty, he or she is "no-billed," not indicted, and released. If at least nine grand jurors believe there is probable cause that an offense occurred, it indicts the alleged perpetrator and the process continues. The indicted person usually is sentenced to jail pending a trial.

Shortly after our visit to Carlsbad, Dad and Linda visited Puerto Vallarta, Mexico, for a short getaway. Upon their return, they told us they were engaged to be married and their wedding was scheduled for May. They called us four kids together, sat us down in the den of the big house, and explained that publicity surrounding the ceremony would be somewhat unusual.

"You're gonna see something in the newspaper in the next few days about Linda and me being required to appear before a grand jury that's looking into your mom's death. We just want you to know it's no big deal. We'll just have to answer some questions and tell them what we know about the situation. You'll probably see articles that say they think Linda and I had something to do with her death. We did not, so there is no problem. It will all be cleared up. But we do have to go to the courthouse and appear before the jury."

Dad's words were a punch in the gut. I knew he had gone to the police to answer questions, but I had just assumed this had to do with the allegations against one of his employees. I never had considered that he was suspected of being caught up in the situation, or that Linda could be involved. Now it seemed like a dark storm cloud of suspicion was floating on top of us.

The investigation of Mom's murder had been going on for roughly a year: the normal police probe, plus an inquiry by the insurance companies that were reluctant to pay out money under the questionable circumstances. County was in jail. Charlie Moore was on the lam. As far as I knew, the probe was focused on them. We had heard little from the police. After the initial media flood, there had been almost nothing about the investigation in the news. In any case, I wasn't really watching television or reading the paper, partially because Dad did a pretty good job shielding us from them, and I was thirteen and interested in tennis and other things.

I learned later that the investigation of Dad had been active since Mom's murder, almost thirteen months previously. Police had assembled what they considered a case for his participation in the crime, although the evidence was largely circumstantial and questionable.

Charles County had told them Dad hired him to do the job—but County was a rather slippery ex-con with an incentive to lie to save his own skin. David Savere, a local college student, claimed he had heard a conversation in which Dad hired County, but Savere also seemed to be of questionable character and was not particularly convincing. Insurance policies provided a motive, but they were not conclusive of guilt. Unusual travel seemed like an effort to construct an alibi, but was not proof of anything. In summary, the police had a strong belief, but a weak case.

The "straw that broke the camel's back" occurred when Charlie Moore was located and arrested and told officers he was hired by Charles County to "kill a White lady." When he disclosed the full story, officials decided they had a case. Dad and Linda were charged and referred to a grand jury, with a hearing scheduled for May 11, 1977. Since both of them were suspected of being involved in Mom's murder, each of them was required to attend the grand jury hearing and testify as a witness in the other's case.

On May 18, as Oscar and I were preparing to board the bus after school, some kids told us there had been an announcement on the school's public address system telling us to go to the principal's office. We went directly there, somewhat reluctant but pretty sure that even Oscar, who seemed to court trouble that led to minor teacher interventions, had done nothing bad enough to warrant the call. When we walked in, we were surprised to see Mrs. Sorber, a family friend who lived down the street from our house. She greeted us warmly and said, "You will not be riding the bus home today. You need to come with me instead. Your dad said that's what you should do."

The principal confirmed the plan, and we headed out without further explanation. Mrs. Sorber had already picked up Louis, whom she had found riding his bicycle home from elementary school. She had him leave his bike in a ditch by the side of the road, get in the car with her, and lay down on the floorboard. Louis was scared, whimpering, trying to catch the butterflies in his stomach. He had no idea why she told him to abandon his bike, go with her, and hide.

Dread hung heavy in the air. We knew something was up, but didn't know what. When Oscar and I got into the car, Mrs. Sorber had Louis get off the floorboard and then told us, "I have some bad news for you boys. Your dad is being indicted by the grand jury—the one he and Linda testified before last week. That means he has been charged with committing a crime, and probably will be arrested and taken to jail later today. Tammy's mom was not indicted. This means she can remain free. What will happen next or in the near future is uncertain. So, your dad and Linda are going to get married before he turns himself in. We are on our way to the church for their wedding."

Linda and Dad had scheduled their wedding for Saturday, May 28, 1977. She had sold her house, quit her job, and moved her belongings into the big house. Both families had focused on planning for the ceremony, which was to be held at Coker United Methodist Church, where we were members and attended regularly. Invitations had been sent to a large group of family and friends for a big church wedding, with reception to follow. I was to play the piano and Dad was to sing to Linda—"One Hand, One Heart" from *Westside Story*. I had practiced with Dad in preparation for their big day.

When we arrived at the church, Dad explained, "So, my attorney has advised me that I'm going to be arrested in connection with your mom's murder. I'm going to turn myself in. I was not involved, so there is nothing to worry about. But I will have to go to jail for a short time. Linda and I are getting married today. She will have custody, and you boys can stay with her. Your uncle and aunt would like to have you with them, but I know you want to stay with Linda."

Whether Dad was anticipating a claim of spousal immunity to prevent Linda from being called to testify against him in a later trial, as the police alleged, was never discussed.

They tied the knot in the church sanctuary, with the pastor officiating a very short ceremony. My brothers and I, Tammy, Mrs. Sorber, and the pastor were the only ones in attendance. We were dressed in street, school, or work clothes. Dad wore a nice shirt, tie, and blazer—perhaps preparing to turn himself in and be photographed as much as to be married. I played the piano and Dad sang "One Hand, One Heart" as planned. We all acted happy, but in reality, the wedding seemed like a glaze of fictional cheer covering a cake of sadness.

An old joke goes that when you are a member of the Baptist Church and get divorced, you become a Methodist. That's what happened to Dad. Dad had been a Baptist, but he and Linda were married in the Methodist church before the police arrested him, perhaps a new definition of "shotgun wedding."

Once the last "I do" was pronounced, and the last hug hugged, and (hopefully) the last tear shed, Mrs. Sorber, an attorney, went with Dad to the police station to turn himself in. In a press interview, he stated, "I am innocent of this charge. My sons and I have been under this type of harassment for a year—something of a personal vendetta in the district attorney's handling of my case." Dad asked for a speedy trial and reiterated, "I didn't do this. I will be found innocent."

Dad was locked in jail that day, May 18, 1977, about a week after the grand jury hearing. The DA recommended that no bond be set.

Linda, who had not been indicted, was now our step-mom. She drove us to her family's home in Poteet, a small Texas town of roughly 2,000 people, the Strawberry Capital of Texas, about forty miles south of San Antonio. The drive to Poteet was surreal, as we pretended to be going to the country for a fun outing, while we were in fact fleeing from the police and press, like criminals on the run or celebrities pretending to avoid publicity. The visit wasn't too bad though, and being with Linda made our situation better. We trusted her, had developed a great affection for her, and were excited that she and Dad were married. More important, Dad assured us that after he turned himself in, he would be released on bail and allowed to return home.

Linda's widowed mother, Mrs. Wheeler, was a strawberry farmer who lived in a nice ranch-style house shaded by big trees and surrounded by a manicured lawn of Bermuda grass interspersed with a few extraneous weeds. Just beyond the lawn were large strawberry fields with seemingly endless raised rows of dark-green strawberry plants with a few red berries, an early hint of the explosion anticipated for June.

Mrs. Wheeler was the matriarch of the small clan of siblings who lived on or near the farm and ran the strawberry operation. She took great care of us. We were at her house for almost a week, exploring the area, including the strawberry patches and processing facilities, gorging on early ripening strawberries, and becoming friends with Linda's siblings, extended family, and friends in the area. But in fact we could not escape reality. Wednesday's evening paper said, in large bold headlines:

Jury alleges: Husband hired wife killers.

A San Antonio man was indicted today for hiring killers who murdered his wife. The indictment came on the eve of his remarriage, scheduled for Saturday. James Glen Buffington, 33, was indicted by the Bexar County Grand Jury for capital murder—for hire.

The lead story on the 10:00 p.m. television news of May 18 was Dad doing a live interview. The newscaster explained that Dad had been indicted by a Bexar County grand jury for capital murder and solicitation of capital murder of his wife, and had surrendered in the sheriff's office around 5:00 p.m. A $15,000 bond was set on the solicitation charge, and no bond was allowed on the murder charge. Dad officially pled not guilty to all charges. He maintained his innocence, and claimed again that a prosecutor in the DA's office was engaged in a personal vendetta against him, and had been harassing him and his three sons.

It was the weirdest feeling, being with Linda, her family, and my siblings in that comfortable home on that almost idyllic strawberry farm, and seeing my dad on the news, accused of murdering my mom. I already lost a mother. Now somehow, deep within my being, I could not escape the nagging fear that I was also losing a father. The life-changing magnitude and uncertainty of it all caused tears to drip from the corners of my thirteen-year-old eyes. My brothers and I could only guess whether this day, May 18, 1977, was the last day we'd ever see our dad in the free world again.

San Antonio Express-News and San Antonio Light, May 18–19, 1977

About a week later, we returned to the big house, happy to get some clean clothes, as we were still wearing what we wore the day Dad got arrested and we fled San Antonio. When we arrived home, Janet Daniel, our neighbor from two doors down, intercepted us and explained that, during our absence, a SWAT team had broken into our house, looking for whatever evidence they could find about the murder.

The SWAT team thought Janet was Linda and confronted her. Both were attractive brunettes, and she had several kids in her car, so they were easily mistaken for us. She told them she was Janet Daniel, not Linda Morrey. In the process, she learned some details about what had been going down in the house. Among other things, the SWAT team had searched the entire premises and removed some files from Dad's office, which was located in a walled-off portion of a converted garage.

Janet also told us that Dad's father, Papa Lee, had flown in from Arkansas to get us kids and take us home with him. With no one in the house, and not knowing where we were, my grandfather sat on the front porch until Janet introduced herself and invited him to stay with their family for several days until we returned. She drove him to the jail to visit Dad, and later to the courthouse to attend the bail hearing.

Linda assured Papa Lee that she would take care of us, and they decided we would live with her in the big house in San Antonio rather than move to Malvern.

Papa Lee returned home without us, but things didn't turn out as planned.

CHAPTER SIX

Bail

"Do not be deceived: God cannot be mocked.
A man reaps what he sows." (Galatians 6:7)

A person indicted for an alleged crime and awaiting trial often can get out of jail by posting bail. A judge typically conducts a hearing to gather evidence and then sets the amount of the bail, or may deny it altogether if he or she considers the defendant a flight risk or a risk to the public. Courts generally require bail amounts that are greater than the financial strength of most defendants. When this happens, the defendant may purchase a bond for 10 to 20 percent of the bail amount to secure the bail and be released.

When Dad surrendered, he was locked in the Bexar County Jail. A bail hearing was conducted on June 6, 1977, before 187th District Judge John G. Benavides. Linda, Oscar, Louis, Tammy, Papa Lee, Herman, Dana, and I attended the hearing in the Bexar County Courthouse. We sat on a bench behind Dad and the officers who were holding him in custody, with almost no opportunity for contact or communication. District Attorney Charles Conaway read the charge from the indictment, and several people testified.

One witness, a Connecticut General Insurance Company agent, testified that he sold a $125,000 life insurance policy with a double indemnity provision to Mrs. Chere Buffington. Proceeds in case of her death were payable to her sons as primary beneficiaries, with James Buffington as the secondary beneficiary. After her death, the company presented an insurance check for $229,600 to Dad and two attorneys as guardians of the sons.

Homicide detective Robert Fleming testified that Charles County told him Buffington hired him to kill his ex-wife.

County's friend, Mary Rodgers, testified to several drinking parties she attended with County and Charlie Moore. County's father-in-law testified that on the afternoon of the murder, he, County, Moore, and some friends were drinking gin and beer at a westside lounge. County and Moore left the bar for a short time and then returned and continued drinking.

County, who was being held in the Bexar County Jail on capital murder charges in Mom's death, was called to testify, but refused on the basis that his responses might incriminate him.

Charlie Moore testified that County had offered him $1,500 to help kill a woman that James Buffington paid him (County) $3,000 to assassinate; and he accepted the offer because he feared for his own life if he refused to go along with the scheme. Moore claimed that he and County took Chere Buffington on a pre-slaying ride around the city on their way to cash a payroll check. Shortly after entering the car, County told Mom to go straight at an intersection and pointed a pistol at her. "Charles. Charles, why are you doing this?" she responded.

"You just might as well be cool because I'm going to kill you anyway, because your husband is paying me to kill you," County told her, according to Moore.

Moore said that at an isolated spot along St. Hedwig's Road, County pointed the pistol at her, forced her to disrobe, and raped her. County laughed like somebody crazy as she begged for her life and offered to buy her release with more money than her husband had offered him for killing her. As she was crying and begging him not to kill her, County held his gun about six inches from her face and shot Mom three times in the head. Moore also testified that he later helped County wash the car inside and out with beer to remove all fingerprints.

David Savere, the twenty-six-year-old St. Phillips College student who had met Dad three or four years previously when he was working as a helper at Cliff's Fence Company, testified that he heard Dad plotting his wife's assassination with County in a conversation while sitting in a pickup about a week before the murder. He claimed Dad said he didn't care how she was killed—by pistol, knife, strangulation, or whatever—

but he specifically asked to have his wife's dead body left nude and her purse removed from the scene to make it look like attempted rape and robbery. Savere also claimed that Dad told them he was leaving town the day before the slaying to go to a horse race out of state. He said the two of them would be "well taken care of" if they killed his wife. Dad was in debt at the time but expected to collect about $40,000 in life insurance money for her death, and would pay them after he collected the money. Savere asserted he had nothing to do with the killing, and said he didn't go to the police because he thought the conversation was not important.

Dad did not testify at the bail hearing, although his attorney made a brief statement attempting to justify a reasonable bail.

Judge Benavides denied bail, holding that based on evidence presented during the hearing, he believed Buffington was a threat to society. Dad was returned to jail to await trial on the capital murder charge.

San Antonio Express-News and San Antonio Light, June 17–18, 1977

Being in jail charged with capital murder wasn't Dad's only problem. The June 22, 1977, edition of the local paper summarized his situation as follows: "Five civil suits and a Sept. 6 trial date for capital murder await James G. Buffington Sr. today after he lost his latest legal battle Tuesday."

The fifth suit had been filed just minutes before Dad's bail was denied. He and another man were named as defendants in an $82,000 lawsuit by two women who alleged they were injured in an auto collision in which the two men were involved. This action was added to a list that included a suit for $51,000 by Coastal Plains Sales and Service Inc. against Jim's Fence Company; judgments against Dad for payment of money owed to BankAmericard and Frost National Bank; and a ruling that he was required to pay over $17,000 for the balance on an overdue promissory note.

The issues listed in the paper weren't the end of Dad's legal problems. A sixth suit was filed against him and his company by a Minnesota firm seeking a judgment of $1,750 on a claim that Jim's Fence Company failed to repair and replace fencing at its local apartment complex as agreed. After that, another Bexar County grand jury indicted Dad on charges of theft of service and theft of property because of two hot checks he allegedly signed and passed to two of his employees.

His trial for capital murder was set for September 6. Oscar, Louis, and I could only guess what was going on and what was next in our lives.

Buffington faces suits, murder trial

By ED KINGSHOTT

Murdered Woman's Finances Studied

By TILI GIRON

A hearing into alleged improprieties in the handling of the financial affairs of the sons of the late Chere Buffington will be held July 25 at the request of the children's court-appointed attorney.

County Court-at-Law No. 6 Judge T. Armour Ball set the hearing Monday after James Aderholt, the attorney appointed to represent the children, questioned the validity of some of the children's court-appointed attorney.

Aderholt has filed at a claim for $2,200 in legal fees and James Bass, Buffington's present attorney, has filed a claim against the estate for $5,000.

According to the court documents, Buffington has already paid attorney Cecil Bain ...

6th suit hits Buffington

Another lawsuit has been filed against a San Antonio businessman facing a Sept. 6 trial date for capital murder.

McNeely-Whitney Associates, a Minnesota-based firm, filed suit in 150th District Court Wednesday against Jim's

Fence Co., Inc. and James G. Buffington Sr.

It's the sixth civil suit filed against the 33-year-old man.

The suit seeks a judgment against Buffington for $1,250.

Buffington, meanwhile, is due in 187th District Court Friday where he is expected to argue he does not have enough money to hire a

lawyer to defend him on the capital murder charges.

District Atty. Bill While contends Buffington has sufficient funds to hire his own lawyer and is not entitled to a court-appointed attorney.

Buffington is charged with capital murder for the death of his divorced wife, Chere, now

Buffington, 29, in March last year.

Her nude bloody body was found in her car on the grounds of Longfellow Junior School. She had been shot three times in the head.

Buffington last week requested Judge John Benavides to appoint a lawyer to defend him. While is fighting that.

Buffington is sued on fence job

JUL 21 1977 Express

Troubles mounted Wednesday for accused killer James G. Buffington who was hit with a suit for damages because of a fence repair job left undone by his company.

Buffington, 33, is in Bexar County Jail without bond on capital murder for hire and criminal

Damage suit adds to woes

Capital murder trial defendant James G. Buffington Tuesday was hit Friby a damage suit filed by two women allegedly injured as a result of a February vehicle collision.

The petition filed by Mary Gonzales and Maria Garcia alleges Buffington was driving one of the vehicles involved

Buffington hit with two new charges

The Bexar County Grand Jury Wednesday indicted a San Antonio businessman facing a Sept. 6 trial on a capital murder charge and two counts of theft of service and theft of property.

The indictments were returned against James G. Buffington Sr., 33, because of two hot checks allegedly signed by Buffington and passed to his employes at a fence company he owned, an assistant district attorney said.

Buffington: Express MAY 27 1977 Not guilty in wife's murder

San Antonio businessman James G. Buffington pleaded not guilty Thursday to hiring killers for the 1976 slaying of his ex-wife.

Appearing before 187th District Judge John G. Benavides, Buffington announced his plea and was returned to jail where he is being held without bond.

The San Antonio man is charged in connection with the March 1976 slaying of Chere Buffington, ... nine months at

Buffington murder trial date set

JUN 4 1977 Express

Hassles Mount For Buffington

James Buffington, charged with hiring a killer to murder his ex-wife, faced a growing number of legal problems Wednesday while confined to a jail ordered by a judge's order.

Buffington was ordered confined without bond Tuesday by Dist. Judge John Benavides after the judge ruled that Buffington could possibly be a threat to society and should remain in jail.

Meanwhile, Buffington also faces several civil court proceedings.

• A trial is scheduled to begin June 28 in County Court-at-Law No. 6 on whether Buffington should keep legal custody of his three children.

He was named guardian after the children's mother, Chere Buffington, was found shot three times in the head, on the floorboard of her car in the parking lot of a school in northwest San Antonio March 20, 1976.

• An $80,000 lawsuit was filed Tuesday against Buffington and another man by two women who claim they were injured when a car driven by Buffington and a pickup truck collided at a downtown street intersection earlier this year. The two women, who were pedestrians, claim the drivers did not exercise ordinary prudence in driving.

• Buffington also ...

company for work to be performed.

• Dist. Judge James Onion has also entered a judgment against Buffington for payment of a $3,184 account from BankAmericard and for payment of a $2,048 note from the Frost National Bank.

• Dist. Judge Peter Michael Curry earlier this week ruled that Jim's Fence Co., of which Buffington is president, has to pay $17,083 for the balance of a promissory note payable to Ray C. Council on March 1.

During the bond hearing Tuesday, a witness testified she had been told by another man that two men, Charles County, 27, and Charles Moore 31, had participated in the killing of Mrs. Buffington.

The woman, Mary Rogers, said she was told by Will Wilburn, County's father-in-law: "You know, those damn fools killed that white woman."

school parking lot.

Two other men — Charles County and Charles Moore — are also in jail in connection with the Buffington murder case.

Buffington, meanwhile, is to appear Monday in probate court on matters related to his divorced wife's will and the custody of their three sons.

Buffington also faces an annulment action filed last month by his second wife. The new Mrs. Buffington, the former Linda Kay Morrey, also wants her own name restored. She filed for annulment barely a week after their wedding on the day he turned himself in to sheriff's deputies following his indictment last month.

Buffington also faces an annulment action filed last month by his second wife ... Kay Morrey. Buffington was being held in county parking lot ... 20, 1976.

His former wife left her sons more than $200,000 life insurance proceeds, according to documents filed with the probate court.

Buffington Charged Again

JUN 28 1977

James Buffington, who is awaiting trial for capital murder for hire in the death of his wife, has been charged with theft over $200 allegedly for passing worthless checks.

Peace Justice Jimmie Gutierrez Monday set bond at $6,000.

Buffington is accused of writing two checks totaling $211 to a local grocery store and to an employe of his fence company. He was returned to Bexar County Jail where he was being held without bond on the capital murder charge.

San Antonio Express-News and San Antonio Light, June–July, 1977

CHAPTER SEVEN

On the Move

"But if anyone does not provide for his relatives,
and especially for members of his household, he has denied
the faith and is worse than an unbeliever." (1 Timothy 5:8)

The bail hearing was the first time I had heard what Charlie Moore or David Savere had to say about Dad being involved in Mom's murder. I was blindsided, stunned beyond words. I believed Dad's claim of innocence, rather than their accusations of his guilt, and was absolutely convinced their testimony was a pack of lies as big as Texas. I was completely supportive of my dad and couldn't believe they could have said what they said about him.

Our family believed Dad would be granted bail, would leave the courtroom with us, and return home. Instead, after Judge Benavides rendered his decision, we could only say brief goodbyes, whisper "I love you" and promise to stick with him until he was released from jail. Dad's immediate future was certain, and bleak, but we felt that all would be fine in the longer term.

The immediate future for Louis, Oscar, and me was much less clear. I could never have imagined how the judge's decision would affect us. Before the hearing, we were seen as victims: kids whose mother had been murdered, whose father had been unfairly taken from them, and who deserved sympathy, support, and love. After the judge's decision to deny bail and keep Dad locked up, many people seemed to see us as in league with the devil, accomplices to murder who were threats to society, to be gossiped about, avoided, and scorned.

Our challenge was to be neither victims nor criminals, and instead to be ourselves and live our lives as normal human beings. The question was whether we could do that—and more immediately, where and with whom we would reside to have a normal life.

Mom had been awarded custody of us at the time of the divorce, but we were later passed to Dad in an agreed order. Now he was in jail for the foreseeable future, with no opportunity to bail out, and Linda had convinced Papa we should be with her, as she was now married to our father and living in our big house in San Antonio. We were off to a rocky start, but the arrangement was okay with us. We began to settle in.

A couple weeks later, in late June, just after my fourteenth birthday, Linda sat us down around the kitchen table and told us she was filing for an annulment of her marriage to Dad; and that our uncle and aunt, Herman (mom's brother) and his wife Dana, were at that moment driving from Austin to pick us up and take us to live with them. This devastating and emotional discussion seemed to forecast a life as uncertain as the weather in a Texas spring, most likely filled with dark days and deluges of tears.

That conversation was when it finally hit my brothers and me that our lives, as far as we could see, had changed forever. We became hysterical, alternating between subdued weeping and uncontrolled bawling. We had lost our mom to cold-blooded murder and our dad to a judicial system we considered incompetent. Now we were losing Linda and Tammy and our big, comfortable house and moving away from family and friends to live in Austin with an uncle and aunt we barely knew—an hour away by car, but an eternity away in our minds. I was fourteen years old. Oscar was twelve. Louis was eleven.

Our tears were still flowing like rain in a Texas drencher when Herman and Dana arrived. They greeted us warmly, hugged us, and made every effort to wear happy faces. We acted like kids who had been abandoned—by our mom, our dad, the system, and now Linda and Tammy. We were being forced to do what we didn't want to do, and to go live with a family we didn't want to live with. The result was predictably awkward.

Jimmy, Louis, Dana, Herman, Oscar

No one knew quite what to say or how to say it. There was more crying than talking. A tenseness fell upon us that almost took our breath away.

We somehow managed to round up our necessary belongings, pile them into Herman's overstuffed car, and head north on Highway 35 to Austin, a carload of desperate souls driving to an uncertain future. In just a little over an hour, we went from life in our big house to abandonment, from stability to throwing stuff in suitcases and leaving for a new town and family. No goodbyes to our grandmother, neighbors, church, or friends.

The trauma was almost too much. My brothers and I continued our weeping and bawling all the way from San Antonio to Austin. We were moving to another city to live with relatives who we knew mainly from brief times together in family gatherings. Herman and Dana were mostly quiet during the drive, perhaps demonstrating their own feelings of shock and discomfort at having three traumatized boys suddenly dropped into their comfortable lives.

Herman (Mom's brother) and Dana appeared to be the original odd couple. They were in their early thirties. He was six-feet-eleven-inches tall, and she was approximately five feet. Herman was very affectionate; Dana was sometimes a little strict. They had one son, Scott, who was a couple of years old. They lived in a modest three-bedroom house in the south part of Austin. My brothers and I were assigned bunk beds in the one available bedroom, where we packed all our belongings into the single closet and the lone dresser.

Prior to her marriage to Dad, Linda quit her job and sold her house in the belief that he was innocent of all charges. After their marriage, Linda could realistically anticipate a situation she had not considered before. Dad was going to jail for who-knew-how-long, and possibly to prison after that. His fencing business had failed. He had purchased the big house with money from his insurance and then sold it to us three kids, to be controlled by the bank appointed guardian of our estate. He spent all his life insurance money and half of ours. He had no money and was facing additional legal actions. In summary, Linda had no husband, no house, no money, no source of income, and no reasonable hope of improvement in the near future. She said she believed that the annulment was justified because she was induced to marry by fraud, and had not voluntarily lived with Dad since learning of his deception.

Dad did not fight the dissolution of the marriage. A hearing was held, and a formal annulment was granted about a month later. Linda vacated the big house and moved in with her mother in Poteet for a time—basically hiding out once again to avoid all the publicity associated with the case.

My brothers and I still wanted to maintain a relationship with Linda and Tammy, and we continued to see them periodically for short visits. However, the visits became less frequent over time as our lives changed and each of us moved in different directions.

In the will she signed in 1970, Mom requested that her brother, Herman, be our guardian if Dad was not able to serve. After we moved in with Herman and Dana, he filed to become guardian for us three kids and the estate of $225,000 from life insurance benefits. He contended that Dad was incapable of being our guardian, because there was no reasonable expectation he would be freed from jail in the future; and that we should live with him and his wife in Austin, rather than with Dad's father in Arkansas. Herman was granted temporary, 120-day guardianship in a negotiated settlement with Dad. Herman was to receive $200 per week to pay for our expenses. He was subsequently awarded permanent custody, and a court-appointed bank became guardian of the estate.

Dad was broke. He filed a petition to be declared a pauper so the state would provide him with an attorney. The DA responded that he felt Buffington had funds sufficient to hire his own attorney. A hearing was held on his "pauper oath," in which he claimed he did not have the money to defend himself against the criminal charges he faced. According to testimony at the hearing, the $225,000 insurance proceeds were held separately for his three sons and the $139,000 he received from his deceased wife's estate had all been spent. He declined to say how.

After the hearing, Judge Benavides ordered two attorneys Dad had previously employed, Cecil Bain and his partner, Tom Thurmond, to continue representing him, as they had already been paid $44,000 to represent him in other matters. The judge also granted motions that required the State to pay for a ballistics expert, an accountant, a fingerprint expert, two investigators, and a psychologist to help pick a jury.

The two attorneys initially refused to follow the judge's order. He found them in contempt and sent them to jail. They shortly purged themselves by agreeing to represent Dad, and were released. Approximately a year later, they were removed from the case, and Marvin Zimmerman and John Hrncir were appointed to replace them.

We didn't want to live with Herman and Dana, a feeling fostered by my dad, who apparently believed they thought he was guilty and would turn us against him. We liked living in the big house, the nice two-story with a tennis club at the end of the cul-de-sac, where each of us had our own bedroom with bath and closet. Moving to a small house, bunking in one small room, living with an aunt and uncle we didn't want to be with, in a city where we didn't want to be, greatly heightened our trauma. The change, along with the tension between my aunt and uncle and Dad, was almost too much to handle.

Our moving in with them was no doubt as difficult for them as it was for us. They seemed to make the best of it, and they made an effort to have their home be our home.

San Antonio Express-News and San Antonio Light, May–June 1977

I started high school in the ninth grade in the fall of 1977 at Crockett High School in South Austin. It was a positive experience, relatively normal except for dealing with periodic news reports about Dad. We attended the Catholic Church with Herman and Dana for a while but preferred the beliefs and practices of the Methodist church. After a time, Dana took us to Faith United Methodist church. The youth choir pastor, Judy Hansen, and her son Chris, who lived down the street from Herman and Dana, took us under their wings and got us actively involved in their youth group. Members of the church and the kids in that group knew what our situation was, but nevertheless made us feel welcome and helped us greatly. They became the core of a gang of close friends, and my refuge during a time of trauma as well as spiritual growth.

The Briscoe family, with three sons near our ages, was special to us, and we spent a great deal of time in their home. What happened to them put our difficulties in perspective. One evening, the two oldest boys, Kevin and Scott, were driving home after a youth group meeting and their car was hit by a drunk driver. Both were murdered. This tragedy was a horrifying loss, especially after the death of our mother and the pending loss of our dad to prison. Kevin and Scott's tragic deaths demonstrated how so many people suffer so much. It created a common bond that brought our church group closer together and made it stronger, and helped us see that suffering can foster faith and be a source of strength.

Being so close to families like the Bennetts, Burnetts, Briscoes, Davises, Fitzgeralds, Hansens, Johnsons, Merrills, and Statons, in addition to Herman and Dana, also helped us see, really for the first time, what a normal family was supposed to be. They gave us people to model our lives after—moms and dads who loved and respected each other, family lives that were stable, dads who were not on television for murdering your mother. They gave us goals to aspire to, and hope that we could move through our current situation to lives of peace and love.

Herman and Dana took us to San Antonio to visit Dad in the county jail, virtually every week at first and then about every other week. I tried to avoid telling my friends what I did on weekends, as the shame and embarrassment of my dad being in jail so appalled me.

The Bexar County Jail was an old, five-story building with a white facade, located in downtown San Antonio. Dad was housed separate from the general population because he was charged with capital murder. He was locked in a one-person cell—a small stall, roughly eight by six feet, with a metal bed, a sink, and a toilet bolted to the wall. It provided isolation, but not privacy. Dad seemed to stay relatively busy for someone imprisoned in county jail, where most residents are short timers, few or no work or educational programs generally are available, and life is as boring as dry toast. He exercised during recreation time, studied in the jail's law library, and spent a great deal of time writing letters to family, friends, and lawyers—often several in a day—and reading and rereading the many he received. He watched church and football on television, and read voraciously, including *Newsweek, Time, Sports Illustrated, U.S. News & World Report, Harpers,* and *Texas Monthly*, which were mailed to him by various friends and relatives. He read books, several written by Oral Roberts, and spent time in Bible study. He actually seemed to relish a breakfast of a "bread, butter, jelly, banana, toasted sandwich."

We were allowed to visit Dad once a week for two hours. Visiting someone in jail is typically traumatic and stressful. The general population area is usually a madhouse, packed with people of all ages, sizes, shapes, colors, and dispositions, including screaming babies, crying spouses, and rambunctious teens, visiting people who are never alone but terminally lonely; longing for confidentiality, with no privacy. It is as noisy as a roomful of drunk politicians, simultaneously too controlled and out of control, a challenge to one's sanity.

Fortunately, we did not have to see Dad in the general population visiting area. Somehow he was able to arrange for us to meet in the attorney visiting area, which was marginally less public, less loud, and less bad. My dad's attorney met us out front and escorted us to a small cell, kind of like a phone booth, adjacent to a cubicle where Dad would be. A glass shield with a window separated the two boxes. Sometimes the window would be closed, we had no contact with Dad, and had to communicate through a shared phone. Other times the window was open, allowing us to have an actual conversation, touch, and awkwardly engage in almost hugs. We considered ourselves as special, and I was thankful we didn't have to suffer the indignity of hanging out with the general population of visitors.

When we visited Dad, it was great to talk, sort of hug when the window was open, and reconnect. It was great to receive his frequent letters. My relationship with him was basically through letters. I was a pen pal with a jail inmate. His letters almost always expressed his love for us and told us how proud he was of us. They predictably encouraged, even hounded us to attend church, stay active in church activities, study hard, and do what was right.

But this proxy for real connection with a present father didn't change the fact that every time I left a visit or read a letter, I relived the anguish of the bail hearing, the annulment, and the move to Austin. I was angry with all the things that were causing me stress. I faced the reality that my dad was in jail, and he was going to be tried for capital murder with a possible death penalty, even though I felt certain of his innocence. I also faced living with an aunt and uncle I didn't want to be with, listening to a dad who didn't trust Herman, and waiting for Dad's trial.

Our situation affected my brothers and me in similar but different ways. My face broke out with a rash. Oscar had stomach pains. Louis was withdrawn and quiet. Dealing with school was difficult for all of us. A letter written by Herman to our guardian ad litem in the spring of 1978 captures the pushes and pulls, the good and the bad, of our situation and its effect on us:

We knew upon getting into this mess it would not be easy, but nine months of hell is just about enough. I am weary of James

Buffington Sr. I don't know as to his guilt or innocence of the murder charge, but he certainly falls short as a human being.

... (Dana's) love for those three boys is unbelievable. We have come back from visits w/ James when the children have vomited their guts up. Dana was right in the bathroom cleaning them up, cheering them up, and trying to calm them down as though each one was her own.

I suppose sons have a natural desire to love their fathers and believe the best about them. In my case, I now know that many of Dad's actions were beyond the pale; but at the time, they did not destroy my belief in him or my love for him. As I heard the heavy steel doors in the Bexar County Jail clank shut behind him, I had a rather simple feeling about the complex situation: the testimony against Dad was a pack of lies, he was innocent, he would be found not guilty in his trial which had been set for September 6, and I loved him.

In a letter to him dated May 12, 1978, I wrote:

Well tomorrow is the last day I'll be able to go to the house & call it ours. I wish none of this would of ever happened. Then I could come home to you. We sure do miss you lots dad & love you so much. But soon, I know, we will be together as a family again. I can't wait for that day. I know you can't either.

... P.S. I love you Dad !!!!

Later in the year I wrote a letter to Judge Benevides, opposing the sale of the furniture in our house.

For one, selling our house isn't the best interest of the children. Right now we do not have our father—we do not have our home. The only thing us 3 boys have is our furniture. ... If and when my father is acquitted, we will need every piece of that furniture. ...

Because of all this criminal mess, when my father gets out of jail, which I know he will because he is innocent. I won't get into that right now. We will have to start a brand new life. We will need the furniture.

I perhaps saw what I believed, rather than believed what I saw—but I saw Dad as good rather than bad. The police and others who said bad things about my dad were his enemies, so they were my enemies as well.

Then the trial was upon us.

CHAPTER EIGHT

Letters from County Jail
1977-1978

"Therefore judge nothing before the appointed time; wait until the Lord comes. He will bring to light what is hidden in darkness and will expose the motives of the heart." (1 Corinthians 4:5)

After Judge Benavides denied bail in the June hearing, James remained in jail, awaiting trial until January, 1979. His letters from the Bexar County Jail were mostly to his sons. Following are some excerpts.

June 7, 1977. Great to see you. Things will get better. Don't get involved in defending your father. Everyone is entitled to their own opinion on any subject. You can't expect everyone to believe in me. Keep the faith.

June 22, 1977. As you know by now, I was refused bond. All we can do is be grateful the trial is less than 80 days. There is only one relationship that is forever & that is your relationship with Jesus Christ. Death alone separates any relationship on earth. I know you have been hurt by divorce between Chere & I, then her death, then Mom's [*Linda*] and I pending annulment, but God promises that your relationship with Jesus is forever, & he promises that he will not put more on you than you can handle, just keep your faith in him. A lot of times, the more you love Jesus, the more your faith in the Lord is challenged. The reaction I expect from Mom [*Linda*], Tam, and you boys, first, not to be bitter, & 2nd , that this whole situation teaches us to let Jesus be the motivation in our lives & not the things of the world. To be grateful each day for the blessings God has given us . . . I started to lie to mom. Made bad business decisions, lost self-control, got into trouble, things that are hurting me now.

July 4, 1977. I realize it's not easy with Dad in jail for Father's Day, 4th of July, and Labor Day, but it's going to be nice to be together for Thanksgiving, Christmas, and New Year's.

July 23, 1977. Read John 15:7. Also, pray daily about problems and situations that are on your mind.

August 5, 1977. I'm sitting here enjoying a big red & a cigar & waiting to go to the law library this afternoon.

September 8, 1977. I have had a busy day today. I went to recreation this morning. Came back for lunch. Went to library this afternoon & prepared for tomorrow. Just had supper & now waiting my turn for shower. Will read papers & by then Dallas Cowboys game will be on.

October 26, 1977. Received four letters from you yesterday and will try to answer them all in this letter. Pray, keep the faith, stay in church, study hard, and stand up for your convictions.

October 31, 1977. I know you completely believe I'm innocent; I'm afraid that is not a belief or wish shared by everyone involved.

November 18, 1977. I have lost all sense of time here. Every day is the same but Sundays still come out strong because of church services I watch. . . . I do realize that the love we have is not determined by what a jury in a trial decides, but it was good to hear you say it in your letter.

November 23, 1977. I believe all parties involved realize the psychological impact on the boys with having their father in jail. My opinion as the Natural Father is that the monthly visit I have each month with the boys is helpful to them.

November 25, 1977. I have not seen attorneys but in last night's newspaper they had a big write up about trial. Said that judge had set trial for February . . . Received several items in mail yesterday from Judge Benavides. First, he denied my motion to remove Cecil & Tom as attorneys. He granted my motion for a speedy trial & set trial date for February.

San Antonio Express-News and San Antonio Light, November 1977

December 15, 1977. I know how you feel; I would like to be able to sit up & look at the Christmas tree & and talk to my dad. I just know that in time we will be together as a family again. I hope eventually Linda will recover & start to write again & let me know about Tam.

December 24, 1977. Christmas Eve has arrived. I love you very much & we look forward to all doing together again next Christmas.

January 6, 1978. Jimmy, I hope this month goes fast for you & that you do not worry too much. I do enough for all of us.

January 15, 1978. Good ol' Channel 5 had me on news Friday. Only station that gets a thrill out of taking pictures of me walking on sidewalk with leg irons.

January 22, 1978. You will always have adversity to face at different times in your life, and you will never achieve having everyone agree with your opinions. The making of a man is being able to determine in your own mind as to what is true and false, right or wrong, fair and unfair. Then you are a man when you can realize that situation is false, wrong and unfair, and can respond with truth, right, and fairness; with a little forgiveness and love thrown in for good measure.

February 27, 1978. Times like this, you fall back on scripture, "all things work for good for them that love the Lord."

March 26, 1978. God has been good to me even though we are in the midst of a great crisis in our lives, but because of our belief in Jesus, we have a great source to turn to in this hour of need.

April 9, 1978. Sundays just are not a good day for me. Monday through Saturday goes by so fast, on Sunday I miss my three sons very much.

June 20, 1978. I hope you are receiving my letters. A letter goes to Austin usually every day.

July 18, 1978. Obviously the change of the trial to Judge Curry's court, was the first good thing to happen to us since I have been in jail. . . . One major change, & it is a biggie, is that money is now approved for a proper defense that judge Benevides denied.

July 27, 1978. Went to court and Judge removed Bain & Thurmond as my attorneys. New attorneys are Marvin Zimmerman and John Hrncir.

August 7, 1978. New attorneys feel all this will be over by Christmas so our motto of "Home for Christmas" & "Victory in 78" can still be a reality.

August 10, 1978. Charlie Moore wrote a letter to the federal judge here that Charles Conaway and a DA investigator checked him out of the jail last month & drove him around town threatening him with the death penalty if he did not say what they wanted him to at my trial.

September 2, 1978. Started my diet & boy am I hungry, but I will stick to it. . . I should be able to drop 40 pounds the next two months.

October 22, 1978. The waiting time is almost over. It has just been a long wait. Will be a year and ½ the 18th of next month.

November 28, 1978. The trial has finally begun after all this time we have had to wait. Yesterday the first fifty jurors received a talk . . . I wrote you previous that Judge Curry ruled that I was not to have chains put on me. Yesterday, I was taken immediately to the courthouse. Right behind was the normal chain gang of inmates. Just as they arrived at the front door to the Courthouse, a "fool" came up and shot one of the inmates six times and killed him. Judge Curry has stepped up security for me as a result. I will be leaving now for the Courthouse each morning at different times with no set schedule. I can now have anyone I want removed from the Courthouse & I am brought in the back way to the courthouse.

December 2, 1978. Tuesday, Mr. Carpenter, bailiff, had to shove a cameraman to one side as bailiffs were escorting me down hallway in Courthouse. Press made a big deal out of it. Finally, Judge Curry had a meeting in his office with all three TV stations & told them any further interference with bailiffs by news media people, he would ban news media from the courthouse entirely. Trial should begin on Monday December 11th. Do you realize that all of this can be over with possibly by Christmas or New Year's?

CHAPTER NINE

Trial

"You shall not murder." (Exodus 20:1)

In 1964, a moratorium was placed on executions in the United States, and in 1972, the United States Supreme Court ruled that death penalty laws in all fifty states were unconstitutional. However, Texas law was revised in 1973, and the death penalty became legal in the State again in 1974. The first execution in Texas after the new law was implemented was on December 7, 1982, and since that time the State has executed over 560 people, more than any other state. A finding of guilt of capital murder adds a name to the list.

A capital murder trial is blood sport: a take no-captives, winner-take-all, cutthroat brawl between a prosecution team aiming to end a life and a defense team aiming to save one. Each team is comprised of hired guns: investigators, forensic experts, jury selection consultants, financial wizards, psychologists, psychiatrists, legal secretaries/assistants, second chair attorneys, a lead "first chair" attorney, and on and on. The lead attorney is the team's "quarterback," responsible for trial strategy and implementation that aims to convince a jury that his client represents truth and justice incarnate.

The Bexar County district attorney fielded a full prosecutorial team in its battle to convict Dad. Charles Conaway was lead attorney. A thirty-eight-year-old with a bald head, wire-rimmed glasses, and perpetual pipe in his mouth, he was a graduate of the University of Texas and the University of Texas School of Law. A veteran of the Army Reserve and twelve years as assistant district attorney, he was leader of the DA's capital crime section, considered the top prosecutor position in Bexar County. Conaway built his reputation by winning convictions in several major capital cases. His professional ethics were questioned in at least one of them.

The Buffington defense patched together a full team as well. As Dad filed a pauper's petition maintaining he couldn't afford to pay for his defense, the State paid the fees, and the court reviewed each selection. Most were approved, including the fee of John Hrncir, the lead attorney for the defense team. Born June 13, 1942, in Taylor, Texas, he was a tall, charismatic man, with a full head of dark hair and a thick mustache. He graduated from St. Mary's University Law School in 1971 and worked as an assistant district attorney in Bexar County before entering private practice as a criminal defense attorney. He and Dad became friends during the course of the trial.

The trial was held in the "old" Bexar County courthouse, completed in 1896 in the heart of downtown San Antonio, not far from the River Walk. This largest historic courthouse in Texas was designed with a Spanish influence and built with Pecos red sandstone on top of a foundation of Burnet pink granite. It was originally four stories tall and later

Old Bexar County Courthouse

expanded to six stories. Each corner was a tower in the range of 130 feet tall. The courtroom was of traditional style, with cream-colored walls and dark-oak trim. A podium for lawyers to speak from and tables with three large chairs for defense and prosecution teams were convenient to the jury box and separate from an area for spectators. A raised bench for the judge sat in front of the symbol of the State of Texas.

Presiding Judge Peter Michael Curry ran the show from a big, high-back chair behind that bench. He was straight from central casting. Sixty-one years old, with a bald head framed by short gray hair and a white mustache, Judge Curry was a child of Lebanese immigrants, and a graduate of Thomas Jefferson High School in San Antonio and the University of Texas. At UT he met and roomed with future Texas governor, John Connally, who he helped become president of the student body. Curry spoke five languages. He joined the U.S. Army Air Corps during World War II and was assigned as an intelligence officer. Governor Connally appointed him to the 166th District Court, where for thirty years he presided with authority, flair, wit, and a devotion to fairness and justice.

Dad's trial started on Monday, November 17, 1978, when a big room full of potential jurors arrived at the courthouse and reported to the 166th District Court to begin several days of overwhelming boredom and waiting, interspersed with a few moments of mental and moral challenge, as they participated in a jury selection process called *voir dire*. One hundred and fifteen prospective jurors were examined by Judge Curry and the prosecution and defense attorneys, in one group questioning session and additional individual interviews.

The prospective jurors were "death qualified," meaning they were questioned about their ability to fairly consider both aggravating and mitigating evidence and render a death sentence in an appropriate case. The objective was to select jurors who were competent and suitable to serve in the case and find a balance where each attorney attempted to select jurors whose biases aligned with his case and reject those whose biases he didn't like.

Some prospective jurors were rejected for cause—when the lawyer making the challenge convinced the judge they were biased or incapable of following the law. Some were dismissed by peremptory challenges, a limited number of challenges where the attorney did not have to explain why he or she objected to a particular juror. Two were dismissed when they expressed general objections to the death penalty, rather than stating unambiguously that they would automatically vote against the imposition of capital punishment no matter what the trial might reveal, a matter to be heard from later.

The process consumed thirteen days. A jury of eight men and four women was selected.

———

December 15 was the first day of trial testimony. The courtroom was packed. A large gaggle of reporters jockeyed for the best position to hear, see, and be seen. Underemployed lawyers crowded together on the back rows of the spectator section, fiddling with their file folders to appear busy while hoping to learn what they could, or keep up with the local legal gossip, or just enjoy the fight. Courthouse employees and hangers-on from the general public drifted in and out and filled the cheap seats. Some members of Dad's family and friends were present to show their support.

Judge Curry swore in the jury and instructed them in their duties and responsibilities. He explained that a person commits the offense of murder if they intentionally or knowingly cause the death of another person. The offense becomes capital murder if the person employs another to commit the murder for remuneration or the promise of remuneration. The burden of proof is on the State, and the defendant is presumed innocent until guilt is established beyond a reasonable doubt by legal evidence. The jury was instructed to consider the evidence and reach a decision as to whether Dad was guilty beyond a reasonable doubt.

Charles Conaway stood and addressed the jury in a strong, confident voice intended to influence the jurors without unreasonably intimidating them. His thoroughly prepared and rehearsed opening statement, a prologue to the story of the case that the prosecution intended to present, appeared friendly and spontaneous, with Conaway seeming to connect directly with each juror.

Conaway claimed that Dad paid a killer to execute Mom, his ex-wife. He maintained that Dad was insolvent and tried to insure her without her knowledge. When this didn't work because he had no insurable interest, he provided her the money to insure her own life, and also had

84

his three children insured. Dad then approached Charles County with the idea of murdering Mom for pay. County agreed to do it, and Dad offered payment amounts that increased over time, to be paid from the life insurance proceeds. He specified that she should appear to have been raped, or robbed, or both; and her body had to be found so that the insurance companies would pay.

Conaway continued, stating that Dad arranged for Mom to deliver some paychecks to County and Charlie Moore. When Mom showed up, the two men got into her car, drove to the east side, raped her at gunpoint, and shot her three times in the face. They took the checks, cashed them, and had a drinking spree. Dad traveled to Arkansas that weekend so that he would be out of town at the time of the murder.

Conaway also claimed that in the interval between the time of the murder and Dad's jailing, $369,000 in insurance proceeds were paid and spent. He said he didn't know where the money went, but that "James Buffington 'lived high and happy' for nearly a year on the 'blood money' he collected as insurance after his ex-wife's slaying." There was speculation that he either spent it, hid it, or gave it to Charlotte Jacobs.

———

Dad pleaded not guilty to the charges filed against him. A few days later, he wrote a letter to my brothers and me that included the following:

> I hope you will be able to come for a visit soon. It was Nov 2nd since I've seen you. Surely we will be able to see each other for Christmas.
>
> Have enjoyed being able to visit with Papa. Friday morning, I was in a conference room getting ready for trial: (Hair, shave, etc.); bailiffs were there, attorneys; Papa; Sheriff Garza came in to wish me luck; Judge Curry came in & wished me luck; & about 10:30 AM the trial began.

Fortunately, I cannot be convicted on the opening remarks of Mr. Conaway & that a jury & not the news media will decide the issues.

Attorneys buy my lunch each day & Judge Curry allows Papa and I to visit a lot.

Sheriff Garza made arrangements for Papa to visit me here in the jail yesterday & today.

Keep the faith. Merry Christmas.

Love, Dad

Thirty-two witnesses paraded to the stand to testify for the prosecution. The testimony had some high points—and low points. Detectives Robert Fleming and Abel Juarez testified that they were the first to investigate the murder. They described a long list of contacts, including visits to B. Green Morgue, where a doctor was in the process of conducting an autopsy; the school parking lot to check the scene of the offense; and the apartment building where Mom lived. Detective Fleming testified to numerous aspects of the probe, including testimony that several days after the murder, Dad visited police headquarters and asked if he was a suspect in the slaying. He "appeared nervous. Very nervous." Fleming also testified that Dad's company "owned a pickup similar to the one seen at the school parking lot several hours before Mrs. Buffington's body was found."

Police Detective Richard Stengle testified that bullets from a gun County's girlfriend loaned to him, which was seized by police, matched the bullet removed from Mrs. Buffington's head.

County and Moore, each charged with murder in Mom's death, shuffled slowly into the crowded courtroom to testify for the prosecution. The crowd at first became quiet as library mice, then a buzz of murmurs rumbled through the almost all-White horde that filled the courtroom to the rafters. The presence of two thirtyish Black men—not overly large but big and stout enough to appear menacing, bright-orange jail jump-suits hanging loosely from their shoulders, shackled hand and foot with handcuffs and chains, charged with raping and killing an attractive White mom with three boys, and guarded by several large bailiffs wearing big white cowboy hats—riveted everyone's attention.

County was called to testify. He claimed protection of the Fifth Amendment to the US Constitution and refused to testify on the basis that his testimony could incriminate him.

Moore, an ex-convict and admitted alcoholic and drug addict, spilled his guts in graphic detail. He testified that County told him he was hired by James Buffington to kill his ex-wife for a payment of $6,000. Moore maintained that County forced her into the back seat of her car, ordered her to take off her clothes at gunpoint, and raped her, as she repeatedly begged for her life. County climbed back into the front seat and, as they were driving down a country road, he reached around and fired his .22 caliber pistol into her face as she scribbled on a check book in her attempt to pay him to spare her life.

County told Mrs. Buffington, "You know, your husband hired me to kill you." He fired two more shots as blood spurted from her face.

Moore continued, "She lived a while because you could hear her sniffling and crying. Then she died, and we took her to the school parking lot where they found her body."

The eight men and four women sitting at full alert in the jury box were motionless, numbed at the overwhelming sadness of what had happened to my beautiful mom. All began to cry in their own way. Most avoided eye contact, while a few sought comfort in a visual connection with others. Some chewed on their lower lip; some held their head in their hands; some tried to disguise their crying, and failed miserably. Some wiped away their tears. Others let their tears slide down their faces. All were consumed by the human capacity to objectify another human being, abdicate all responsibility for her destiny, and kill her so easily.

Conaway had presented evidence to a sympathetic jury. Things got even more intense when the medical examiner, Dr. James Duff, testified that Mom was shot with a .22 caliber pistol at close range, and showed pictures of the result to the jury. The jury grasped in all its gory detail the prosecution's case for what had happened to James Buffington's ex-wife. Crying turned to sobbing. Eyes became bloodshot and puffy. Glasses fogged up. Noses began running. Tears escalated from a trickle to a flow.

Evidence relating to insurance policies, premiums, and payments seemed to come from all directions to establish a motive for Dad to want Mom dead, and to hire someone to kill her. Testimony from insurance agents Gary White and David Chasen suggested that Dad received a total of $369,000 in insurance proceeds upon Mom's death. One witness testified that Buffington asked if he could insure his former wife without her knowledge, and he was told that he could not. Bobby Jacobs, manager of the Prudential Insurance Company office in Austin, testified that Dad sent one of his employees to the company's office the day before his ex-wife's death to pay the lapsed premium on her $40,000 life insurance policy. Herman Stieferman, my uncle, Mom's brother and also an insurance agent, testified that he sold his sister an $11,000 insurance policy several weeks before her death, and that policies of $150,000 were taken out on each of the Buffington's three sons. Testimony indicated that Buffington or his sons, who he had custody of, were beneficiaries of the policies.

Testimony was also presented suggesting that Dad was a control freak who carried a mean streak in his psyche, and was probably capable of hiring an assassin to kill his wife. Gordon Caton, Mom's former employer, told the jury that he received a telephone call from James Buffington in the fall of 1974, saying his wife would not be at work because, "Quite frankly, I hit her a couple of times where it will show." Caton also testified that Dad threatened him because he "had a drink with Mrs. Buffington one day."

San Antonio Express-News and San Antonio Light, December 1978

Evidence was presented that money did in fact change hands, if in a somewhat bizarre way. Idell County, Charles County's wife, testified that three days after Mom's death, her husband telephoned Dad and asked for his money. After the conversation, Charles asked Idell to go to a telephone booth at Jim's Hamburgers, a small café near Bandera Road, to pick up the payment. Shortly after she arrived at the café, Buffington showed up, carrying a diet cola can, appearing skittish and apprehensive. He left the can in the booth after pretending to use the phone. When he was gone, Idell retrieved the can and used straws to fish out three $100 bills that had been stuffed inside.

The prosecution completed its case on Wednesday, January 3, after seven days of testimony. The following day, Dad's court-appointed attorney, John Hrncir, told Judge Curry, "Your honor, at this time, the defense rests."

The defense's decision not to present any evidence was surprising, but not unprecedented. The defense attorneys declined to give reasons for their unexpected move, saying Judge Curry had instructed them not to talk to news outlets. It should be noted however, that in a criminal case, the defendant is presumed innocent until proven guilty. The prosecution has the burden of convincing the members of the jury, beyond a reasonable doubt, that the accused is guilty as charged. The defense may choose not to present evidence, in the belief that the government did not meet its burden of overcoming the defendant's presumption of innocence, and perhaps also because of concern that evidence presented, or the defendant's demeanor, would cause the jury to reconsider a not guilty inclination. We could only hope that the State had not made its case in the eyes of the jury.

Dad wrote my brothers and me on the last day of testimony:

Tomorrow the case goes to the jury. I had several attorney visits this weekend including Mr. Bass.

We should have a verdict by Tuesday night or Wednesday.

We could be together this weekend with an acquittal or a hung jury.

Keep the Faith. I love you & miss you. I am very proud of you guys.

Happy New Year.

Love

Dad

Prosecution and defense attorneys met with Judge Curry on Friday to work on the court's charge to the jury: his directions concerning the law of the case, questions for the jury to answer, and directions as to what alternatives they had in determining Dad's fate. At 10:00 a.m. on January 9, 1979, the jury was charged to consider the evidence and reach one of three possible conclusions: guilty of capital murder as charged in the indictment, guilty of murder, or not guilty.

The attorneys for each side presented closing arguments. Each summarized the evidence supporting his case and any reasonable inference

San Antonio Express-News and San Antonio Light, January 1979

that could be drawn from it, attacked any holes or weaknesses in the other party's case, and presented his most compelling arguments intended to reach the minds and hearts of the jurors. The defense attorneys maintained that Dad was as innocent as a newborn lamb. The prosecutors claimed he was the epitome of evil.

Louis, Oscar, and I were not allowed to attend Dad's trial. Dad didn't want us in the courtroom. He had put us on the potential witness list so we would be sequestered and denied access to the proceeding. We were scheduled to be present for the closing arguments, but at the last minute, Dad, Herman, and Dana nixed that idea. So we boys went to school on the days court was in session, and later watched news of the trial on TV, read about it in the papers, and devoured whatever Dad wrote in his letters.

Not being allowed to attend the trial seemed a little like a cover-up. My two best friends, Chris Hansen and David Burnett, each a couple of years older than I, agreed. The three of us hatched a plan. They skipped school, drove to San Antonio, sat in the row behind Dad and listened to the closing arguments. When they returned, I asked them how they felt about what they heard. David hedged, saying he wasn't really sure. Chris looked me square in the eye and said in a low, confident voice, "Jim, I hate to tell you this. Your dad did it."

Until Chris said, "Your dad did it," I had never thought it was possible that my dad had hired someone to kill my mom. My first reaction was to go deeper into denial. Chris had to be wrong. He didn't understand. However, his comment planted a small seed of doubt in the back of my mind and convinced me I really needed to discern the truth for myself. I needed to be more thoughtful about what my dad did and didn't do, said and didn't say; view what had happened from a broader perspective; even do my own investigation by talking to witnesses and others involved when feasible.

I could only wonder what truth the jury would discern.

CHAPTER TEN

Verdict

"The heart is deceitful above all things and beyond cure.
Who can understand it? 'I the LORD search the heart and examine
the mind, to reward a man according to his conduct, according
to what his deeds deserve.'" (Jeremiah 17: 9–10)

Dad's trial was not a "non-event" for us boys, but it didn't seem to be a really big deal either. I was fifteen, Oscar was thirteen, and Louis was twelve. We were immersed in school and church, active in building a social life, and preparing for Christmas. Not attending the proceedings separated us from the all the drama. More importantly, even after hearing Chris's assessment that Dad "did it," we remained convinced that he was innocent, and we believed without question the judicial system would find the truth and exonerate him. We looked forward to Dad being released, and the four of us returning home as a family.

The jury had a different view. On Monday, January 3, 1979, after nearly ten hours of debate, they found Dad guilty of hiring Charles County to kill my mom, a capital offense for which Dad could suffer the rest of his life in prison or die by lethal injection. Herman and Dana sat us down immediately and told us point-blank what the jury concluded. We were absolutely devastated. Their best efforts at empathizing with us and comforting us failed miserably. We were totally devastated that Dad had been convicted of killing Mom. A cascade of tears that originated with the divorce and grew time and again with Mom's murder, Dad's indictment and incarceration, Linda's annulment, and our move to Austin, now gushed forth like a broken water main. As in the past, the tears were propelled by sadness, disappointment, loss, fear, and uncertainty. But this time, anger was the biggest factor. We were angry at the judicial system that we were sure had convicted an innocent man. We were angry at the lawyers who let it happen. Perhaps we were angry at Dad for letting his life become such a mess. We were even angry at Herman and Dana for telling us about the verdict and being messengers of such bad news. They were handy, so we took our anger out on them with all the passive-aggressive tricks three hurting boys could muster.

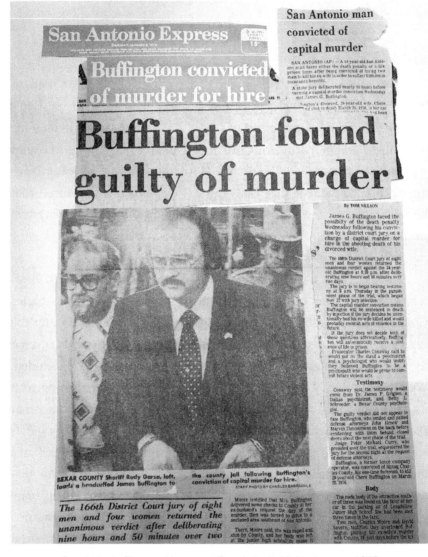

San Antonio Express-News and San Antonio Light, January 1979

The task of deciding Dad's penalty began on Thursday after Monday's verdict. The jury was asked to consider two questions: whether Dad intentionally caused Mom's death, and whether he would be likely to commit future violent acts. A "yes" answer to both meant that Dad would be assessed a penalty of death by lethal injection.

The testimony in the punishment phase largely boiled down to dueling psychiatrists. Bexar County psychiatrist, Dr. Betty Schroeder, testified that Dad had a psychopathic personality and was a sociopath. She said, "Mr. Buffington is smooth with the ladies. He is a crafty and wily man."

Dallas psychiatrist, Dr. James Grigson, was scheduled to testify on Thursday, but heavy snow and bitterly cold temperatures stranded him at his hunting lodge in north Texas. Jurors spent the day playing cards and dominoes and reading books in the locked courtroom. Grigson, nicknamed "Doctor Death" by some press accounts, was a forensic psychiatrist who had testified in 167 capital trials, nearly all of which resulted in death sentences. (He would be expelled by the *American Psychiatric Association* and the *Texas Society of Psychiatric Physicians* in 1995 for unethical conduct.) After the delay, he battled the weather, made it to San Antonio, and testified, among other things, that Dad would be likely to commit violent acts again, even in jail.

Defense attorneys called two local psychiatrists, Dr. Richard Cameron and Dr. Nevil Murray, who testified they believed Schroder and Grigson's examinations were too cursory to produce their diagnosis, and they would have been unable to make a determination that Buffington was a sociopath with no conscience based on the type of examinations that the two State witnesses performed.

After the testimony was completed, prosecutor Conaway asked the jury to assess the death penalty, saying, "If there ever was a case that calls for the death penalty, this is it."

Defense attorney Hrncir said, "It occurs to me that you ladies and gentlemen of the jury may not like James Buffington too much. Don't you forget, he's still a fellow human being."

95

The jury began deliberating at 9:02 p.m. on Friday, and recessed for the night at 10:42.

Once Dad was convicted of capital murder, the worry and uncertainty of waiting roughly three days to learn his fate was almost unbearable. Reading news articles was devastating, particularly reading ones claiming Dad was a psychopath and a sociopath and thinking about the possible implications. Looking friends directly in the eye seemed almost impossible. Decent sleep could not be found.

Saturday morning, after deliberating for a total of about three hours, the jury returned with a verdict. Herman and Dana sat us down again and told us that what started bad got worse. Dad was assessed the death penalty.

Hearing this news was so traumatic, so mind-numbing, that I don't remember much about what was said or what we did. I felt my life was over. I began crying uncontrollably again. Learning my dad was to be intentionally killed by the State put all kinds of things into my mind. I feared for him and worried about him. I would soon be an orphan. My life as I had known it was over. I would be labeled as the son of a murderous death-row inmate.

My identity now also seemed tied to Charles County and Charlie Moore, each of whom was seen as Dad's accomplice. County was convicted of capital murder in June 1979, and given the death penalty. Moore was in jail at the time, and in July 1980, he pled guilty to murder (rather than capital murder, because he cooperated with the DA) and was sentenced to seventeen years behind bars.

I couldn't help wondering, at least a little, about who my dad was. The situation seemed to involve compounded grief: the intense sadness, shock, numbness, denial, and anger resulting from the loss of a loved one, made worse by an assault on the identity that made me who I was.

BUFFINGTON FACES NEEDLE DEATH
Page 3-A

Jury still out on Buffington

Work to Resume Saturday
By DANNY GARCIA and BRUCE BEAL

The jury which must decide if James Buffington will spend the rest of his life in prison or die by lethal injection. But this murder-for-hire death of his ex-wife went to bed late Friday without reaching a decision.

Buffington sentencing delayed

Icy roads on the Texas-Oklahoma border delayed testimony Thursday in the punishment phase of the capital murder-for-hire trial of James G. Buffington Sr. in 166th District Court.

Jurors spent the day playing cards and dominoes and reading books in a locked courtroom while prosecutors awaited the arrival of Dallas psychiatrist Dr. James Grigson.

Grigson, however, was reported stranded at his hunting lodge near Lake Texoma.

District Judge Peter Michael Curry ordered testimony to begin at 9 a.m. today after prosecutors reported Grigson would not be able to arrive in San Antonio until Thursday night.

The jury of eight men and four woman convicted Buffington Wednesday of causing his ex-wife's death by employing Charles County to kill the woman.

The nude body of the 29-year-old woman was found in her car on March 26, 1976. She had been shot three times in the head.

Jurors, after hearing testimony from Grigson and other witnesses, will begin a second round of deliberations to determine whether Buffington, 34, should be given the death penalty or sentenced to life in prison.

The jury has been sequestered since beginning deliberations Tuesday night to determine Buffington's guilt or innocence.

Buffington fate delayed

The punishment phase of the capital murder trial of James G. Buffington was delayed Thursday when a Dallas psychiatrist scheduled to testify was unable to reach San Antonio because of inclement weather.

Dr. James P. Grigson was to testify that he believed Buffington to be a psychopath who constituted a threat to society, according to prosecutor Charles Conaway.

Grigson was stranded at a lodge at Lake Texoma on the Texas-Oklahoma border because of ice-covered roads and could not reach Dallas to catch a flight to San Antonio, Conaway said.

Buffington 'Sociopath'
By BRUCE BEAL

A psychologist testified Friday that James Buffington is a "sociopath" and would be a continuing threat to society.

The testimony from Betty Schroeder, a psychologist for Bexar County, came during the sentencing phase of Buffington's capital murder trial.

She said a psychopath has little or no conscience, although he does understand the difference between right and wrong.

Describing an interview she had with Buffington at the jail, she said: "Mr. Buffington is smooth with the ladies. He is a crafty and wily man."

"He is a personality..." the

SUNRISE
San Antonio Light
LATE MORNING

San Antonio Light

BUFFINGTON AWAITS SENTENCE

Death Jury Recessed

Buffington To Fight For Life

Jury sentences Buffington to death
Story, Column

Buffington

(Continued from Page 1.)

Court jury which Wednesday found Buffington guilty of hiring two men to kill his ex-wife, asked that he be sentenced to life in prison rather than death.

John Streett, another attorney for Buffington, also on Grigson's testimony, that Dallas psychiatrist "spends cent of his time at trials, defendant sociopathic."

"You have the power to this man to death or send t pentitentiary alive," Stre "There Buffington is dead ing you can do can bring h During testimony in th ing phase of Buffington's er Friday, San Antonio p Dr. Betty Schroder said has little or no cons understands the differe right and wrong.

However, the defen Richard Cameron and Murray, two local psyc the stand and they b they would have bee make a determination tion is a sociopath science based on the t nations that were Grigson and Schroder

Buffington given death sentence
By The Associated Press

SAN ANTONIO — James G. Buffington, convicted Wednesday of hiring two men to slay his estranged wife for $369,000 in insurance money, was assessed the death penalty Saturday by a state jury.

Jurors took three hours to return the sentence against the 34-year-old Buffington. The jury earlier had deliberated about 16 hours before delivering the guilty verdict.

Buffington's divorced, 29-year-old wife Chere was found shot to death March 26, 1976, in her car in a junior high parking lot. She had been raped and shot three times in the face.

Two men, Charles County and Charles Moore, are awaiting trial on capital murder charges in the slaying of Mrs. Buffington.

San Antonio Express-News and San Antonio Light, January 1979

Witness Tells of Bid

For 'Assassination'

COUNTY GUILTY

Continued from Page 1A

emotion as the verdict was announced.

Butts asked that the jurors be polled individually and Palmquist began calling off their names and asking them if that was their verdict.

Each juror's response "Yes," came

dignity as possible — stripped down naked in the back seat of a car," Burris said.

Comparison

Burris compared Moore's emotional and sometimes admittedly lying testimony versus County's rather

The state called 32 witnesses in the trial which recorded eight days of testimony. Late Wednesday evening, Butts issued a written statement which claimed County had been double-crossed by the district attorney's office.

Butts contended County had cooperated with the district attorney in

County found guilty

By ALAN BAILEY
Of the Express Staff

BROWNSVILL[E]
woman, nine-m[onth]
Charles County [in the]
murder Wednes[day]
contract execut[ion of]
Buffington.

The jury deliber[ated]
minutes before retu[rning]
verdict at the Came[ron County]
Justice as the m[orning]
came to a quick clin[...]
Thursday mornin[g] jury will hear testimony
will begin hearing

three individuals indicted for the murder of Mrs. Buffington, a 29-year-old

County's sentence

to be decided

SPECIAL TO THE NEWS
BROWNSVILLE — The

backseat of her car.

Mrs. Buffington's nude body was found March 20.

parking lot of Longfellow Junior High School in Northwest San Antonio.
[cour]troom   Wednesday
[readi]ng Judge Preston Dial
[...]an Richard Hinojosa,
[...]tched a unanimous

[...]ve," replied Hinojosa.
[...] verdict to Dial. The
[...]ead the verdict and
[...]im Palmquist, to read

or given a reduced his court-appointed
sentence in exchange for Butts, stood up in the
his testimony.

find the defendant

DEATH FOR COUNTY

Continued from Pa[ge]

last January, by a jury in T[exas]
County.

A third individual, Charles M[oore,]
accused of being an accomplice triggerman, County, is schedul[ed to]
stand trial for capital murder month in Bexar County.

As the jury's decision was read courtroom at the Cameron Count[y]
of Justice, County stood with his appointed attorney Charles Butts.

Both County, with his hands him, and Butts, with his arms stared at the floor as court cler[k]
Palmquist read the decision emotion was visible and County as if he expected to hear the sentence in light of Wednesday's — 13 minutes — deliberatio[n]
reaching the guilty verdict.

Butts had the jurors individually. And each juror resp[onded]
with a firm "Yes," to the v[erdict]
except for one female juror who [was]
fairly audible yes in the courtroom.

The jurors had answered yes t[o]
special issues given by Judge P[reston]
Dial, who had brought the case he[re on]
a change of venue from Bexar Cou[nty]

County

gets death

By ALAN BAILEY
Of the Express Staff

BROWNSVILLE — Charles County must die for the 1976 contract killing of Chere Buffington, a jury of nine men and three women decided Thursday.

Jurors returned their verdict at 5:40 p.m. after deliberating less than 15 minutes in deciding whether County should die by injection or spend the rest of his life in prison.

The same jurors Wednesday had found County, 30, guilty of capital murder in killing Mrs. Buffington, a 29-year-old divorced mother of three, so her ex-husband, James G. Buffington, could collect $379,000 in insurance.

With the decision Thursday, County will join Buffington on Death Row at the state prison in Huntsville.

Buffington, the mastermind behind the brutal murder, was sentenced to die

[...] were that asked him if he was "a killer shrink," [id]entified so in a magazine article.

Grigson said he was the subject of [th]at article, and he had testified in [so]me 50 cases involving almost 100 [pe]ople on Texas' Death Row, but he [sa]id, "I didn't put them on Death Row. [T]hey put themselves there because [th]ey killed one or more people."

Psychiatrist

The psychiatrist, who received his [in]formation about County from the San [A]ntonio Police Department and had not [a]ctually interviewed County, said the [a]ct County was laughing while he fired [th]ree shots into Mrs. Buffington's face, [a]nd the fact he killed her while she was [b]egging for her life, made County an [e]xtremely dangerous sociopath.

Butts did not call any witnesses to [t]estify on County's behalf or on his good [c]haracter.

In his closing plea for the death [p]enalty, Burris asked the jurors, "Have [y]ou ever heard of a more diabolical [k]illing or a more heinous crime than this one?

"He teased her about death. He [a]ctually enjoyed what he was doing and [h]e deliberately planned it in cold [b]lood," Burris said.

Butts filed a series of motions with [t]he court protesting the death penalty [a]spect. One motion noted the law did [n]ot prescribe the type of lethal solution that is to be injected into the person for his execution.

"The injection might be with the saliva of a mad dog or the blood of a rabid bat," contended Butts, claiming the Texas law prescribing death by injection was cruel and unusual punishment.

Testimony in this case showed that Mrs. Buffington's nude body was discovered on the back seat of her auto in a parking lot at Longfellow Junior High School in San Antonio March 20, 1976.

She had been shot three times in the

Murderer given 17 years

Charles H. Moore, one of three men convicted of the March 1976 slaying of Chere Buffington, was assessed 17 years in prison Friday by 175th District Judge Preston Dial.

Moore, 33, pleaded no contest July 30 to a reduced charge of murder in connection with the killing-for-hire slaying.

No date was set by Dial for formal sentencing.

Prosecutors reduced the capital murder charge against Moore after he agreed to testify in the capital murder

Charles County. Both men were sentenced to death.

The attractive Mrs. Buffington, a divorcee and mother of two sons, was found dead March 20, 1976, on the floor of her car.

Buffington, 35, was convicted here last January of plotting to kill his 29-year-old ex-wife so he could collect $369,000 in life insurance he had taken out on her life.

County, 30, was convicted last June in Brownsville of raping and killing Mrs.

San Antonio Express-News and San Antonio Light, June 1979 and July 1980

I was fifteen years old. Several years previously, I had become a Christian and turned my life over to God. Since then, I experienced trauma and suffering from my parents' divorce, Mom's murder, and Dad's arrest, but facing the idea of the State of Texas intentionally taking my innocent dad's life was over the top, just too much for me to handle. It bothered me, it scared me, it hurt me. I don't think I blamed God, but I did not know how God could let this happen to my family and to Dad. I believed that Mom's death and Dad's planned execution were due to County and Moore making some really bad choices. They, not God, caused us to suffer.

However, although I didn't blame God, I sometimes doubted if He was in control, and I became angry that God allowed all the suffering. I dealt with my anger by talking with my friends, attending Bible Study, going to church, and praying. I felt I had to be an example to my brothers, and I could not let them down. Instead I had to protect them and be strong for them.

The death penalty sentence was the most my faith had been tested. I had real doubts about my faith for several years.

CHAPTER ELEVEN

Letters from Death Row
1979–1983

"Then he blinded the eyes of Zedekiah; and the
king of Babylon bound him with bronze fetters and
brought him to Babylon and put him in prison until
the day of his death." (Jeremiah 52:11)

When the jury found James Buffington guilty of capital murder and criminal solicitation, and assessed the death penalty on January 11, 1979, James was in the Bexar County jail. He continued his prolific writing.

January 17, 1979. I am fine & read mostly. Should be going back to court in about a month. Will let you know when.

I miss you guys and love you a lot.
Keep the faith.
Love, dad

Imposition of the death penalty results in an automatic direct appeal to the Texas Court of Criminal Appeals, the State's court of last resort for criminal cases. On February 2, 1979, James Buffington filed an appeal. His court-appointed attorneys argued that the trial court erred in excusing two venire members (potential jurors) who expressed only general objections to the death penalty, rather than stating unambiguously that they would automatically vote against the imposition of capital punishment no matter what the trial might reveal, in violation of a rule established in a then-recent Supreme Court case. His appeal was denied, and he was assigned to the Ellis Unit to await execution.

March 9, 1979. I have just been called out to be transferred; my new mailing address will be:

> James G Buffington—TDC # 630
> Ellis Unit - Death Row
> Huntsville, Texas 77340

Will write you soon.
Love, Dad

March 10, 1979. I was transferred yesterday & sure is a lot better here. The scenery is beautiful. Really enjoyed the trip.

March 15, 1979. My first week here has really gone by fast. The food is great & it will be hard to diet here. I have been working hard to fix up my cell. Fixed me a seat out of newspaper to place on the "John" so I have a chair to sit in to read and write letters.

Diagram of my cell:

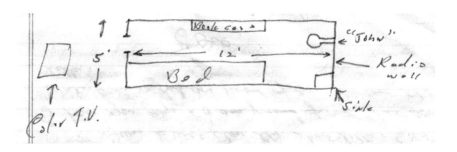

March 15, 1979. I am by myself in a single cell. My meals are brought to my cell. I do get out each morning to take a shower and be issued a clean uniform. Then I get out on Mondays, Tuesdays, and Fridays for a recreation period in a large room with tables. There are 15 men in my recreation group. Also get out on Wednesdays for a haircut when needed. I do talk with guys during the day. Obviously the inmates that live beside me. Duffy, that spent a year with me in the Bexar County Jail is two cells down from me. Also, Rusty that also was with me a long time in the B. C. J. is a level above me but I see him occasionally.

. . . I am also able to buy the things I need here, which is a lot since food & uniforms is all they provide here. But OB and Papa send me a set amount of money each month & the members of Perfect Union have a fund set up for me, so I am receiving the $60 each month that is the maximum you are allowed to spend here. Really makes a difference when you can buy what you need here and receive plenty of mail. In March, even though I arrived here the 9th, received my first letter the 14th, I still received 53 letters here in March.

April 16, 1979—I feel that it is appropriate that I begin this journal on my birthday. The purpose of this journal is to enable me to have a record of events that occur on death row; to leave a record for my sons; to have a source of information to use for books that I intend to write; and to help me better understand myself.

I would like to record the events of March 9, 1979; I had gone to bed late the previous night and had been in bed only an hour when jail guard, Miller, woke me up and told me to prepare myself to be on the "chain," (jailhouse term for inmates being transferred to another jail or prison). I had been waiting to be transferred after my trial judge, Peter M. Curry, had denied my motion for a new trial on February 22, 1979. I had been packed for days so it was a simple matter to dress and stack my packed boxes. At 4:00 a.m. Miller opened my cell door and led me into the main booking area on the first floor of the Bexar County Jail. I watched the other inmates standing in line; some holding Bibles, a few with a file folder, and here I was, with four full boxes looking for a "redcap." Finally, after twenty-two months of incarceration, I would be leaving for death row and a new and different life than what I had experienced in the tank life of an inmate in the county jail. At least on death row I know I would not have to watch rapes, beatings, and drug abuse. Two of Bexar County's finest loaded my books into the transfer van. I had wanted to take my fan, but Lieutenant Alfredo, in his usual state of mind being afraid to make a decision, stated that policy was to take nothing. I assume he thought the transfer guards had loaded four empty boxes for me. After all, what would the community think if a convicted murderer was allowed to take a fan to death row. It was a boring five-hour trip to the Diagnostic Center in Huntsville, Texas. I was there only an hour; just long enough for a haircut, pictures, and a spray job that a sheep herder would not believe. I was then transferred in a van to the Ellis Unit. I was met at the rear gate by a captain. I loaded my boxes in a laundry cart and that is how I entered prison; pushing a laundry cart over the asphalt as the sun slowly set in the West.

April 16, 1979. Your father is getting old and grey. Thirty-five years old today.

Keep the faith.
Love, Dad

In January 1980, James was briefly returned to San Antonio to appear in a hearing that would consider the prosecutorial misconduct charges against District Attorney Charles Conaway. He was attacked and beat up the night before the hearing, the only such incident during his time behind bars. He believed Conaway had arranged it in an effort to affect his testimony.

January 16, 1980. I have to print due to stitches in middle finger of right hand. It took about 30 stitches to close up cuts in my face & 8 to close a cut in back of my head. I am fine but will take a few weeks to feel & look human again. They told me yesterday that DA was filing "aggravated assault with a deadly weapon" against the Mexican that hit me with a metal cup when my head was turned. Now I know how David Crockett felt at the Alamo.

April 29, 1980. Starting this morning, we are having more recreation time. Instead of just one recreation time for ninety minutes, we went out twice today for an hour each time. That was great and will increase our total recreation time from 4½ hours a week to six hours.

James continued his prolific correspondence during the time he was on death row. The essence of most of it can be characterized with five F's:

__Family:__ Nearly all his correspondence during this period was with his sons, his dad, and less frequently with other family members. Most letters started with the reference to, "I love you," referred to how much they were missed or how he was looking forward to a visit, or mentioned past family occasions or hopeful future ones.

__Food:__ Letters contained frequent references to the food being served—rarely complaining and frequently characterizing the food as better than one would have expected, particularly on holidays and special occasions. There were occasional comments about his diet and attempt to lose weight. He lost approximately 100 pounds.

__Football:__ James was a strong supporter of the Dallas Cowboys and the University of Houston Cougars, as well as most Southwest Conference teams. His primary interest was football, but he had an interest in other sports as well. He watched all available games on television and listened to many on the radio. He even conceded that the Houston Oilers and the Texas Longhorns weren't all that bad.

Finances: Having money "on the books" was important to him, as it allowed him to obtain certain "luxuries" not otherwise available. He occasionally asked relatives for money, and frequently thanked them for money they had sent. On one occasion he complained bitterly about the price increases at the commissary, noting that "money makes the big difference as to what your living conditions will be like."

Faith: James's writing frequently mentioned church, asked about the boys' church life, and encouraged their continuing involvement with church. He made frequent references to listening to spiritual music and to church services on the radio or television. Nearly all letters contained a reference to "keep the faith."

January 23, 1983. I regret my situation has caused you so much pain.

January 30, 1983. The atmosphere here on J23 wing is more relaxed now that executions have been stopped by the US Supreme Court until a hearing is held . . . but 1984 could see them dropping like flies. I don't expect to be here then. With the close hand experience I have now I am convinced there must be a death penalty. A few like John Shippy and Randy Wollis (*are exceptions*) . . . , and I don't believe John or Randy should have the death penalty but life sentences instead. These I only associate with. The rest is impossible for you to understand unless seeing them and knowing them firsthand to realize the reprehensible, violent Agents of the devil that exist here. Don't ever worry that an execution in Texas or anywhere else is going to bother me. I'm in support 100%.

On May 11, 1983, the Court of Criminal Appeals reversed Buffington's murder conviction and ordered a new trial on the basis of an error in jury selection.

May 22, 1983. I may still be here but your father is no longer convicted of this terrible crime and I know this takes a great load off your shoulders.

June 5, 1983. I am fine now but have my moments of anger. Prior to my reversal I tried to take my life one day at a time. But since the reversal I look back at the years Conaway took away from me to be with you, Oscar, and Louis. The grief Papa and Fran had to bear with me on death row. Let's just say I'm not pleased at times with the Bexar County judicial system.

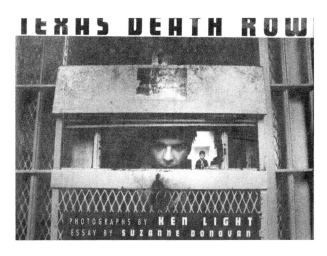

James playing chess on Death Row, from the book, *Texas Death Row*.
James is the arm on the far left.

CHAPTER TWELVE

Texas to Arkansas and Back

"He will cover you with his feathers,
and under his wings you will find refuge; his faithfulness
will be your shield and rampart." (Psalm 91:4)

Dad's death sentence caused a deluge of pain, sadness, and unease, but it also brought a measure of certainty to our lives. We became certain that our living situation had to change.

Our edgy relationship with Herman and Dana deteriorated further when Dad was sentenced to death row. They were even more convinced of his guilt, and were not able to hide what they believed from Louis, Oscar, and me. We often seemed to blame them for our problems and fault them when they couldn't fix them. Our friends knew our dad was on death row, which introduced an unwelcome stigma and caused stress that often made our stomachs feel like we were on a plane in constant turbulence. Each of us continually wondered what would be next, but believed we'd never be going home to San Antonio with Dad. We felt like orphans and, by the fall of 1979, it was pretty clear that we were not where we needed to be. We didn't want to live with our uncle and aunt, and they didn't want us to live with them. We needed long-term stability, and it was time to move and give them some relief. Some consideration was given to our moving into a Methodist boy's home, and a couple from church offered to have us live with them. Neither of those worked out.

Thankfully, our grandparents, Papa Lee and Granny Fran, came to our rescue. They had only been married about three years, since Glendal, Papa Lee's first wife, died of a brain aneurysm. They offered to take us in at their home in Malvern, Arkansas, even though they were empty nesters, were still on an extended honeymoon, and were not prepared to take on three teenage boys who were dealing with some unique issues.

Just before Thanksgiving, Papa Lee drove to Austin and collected us—for one more move. He rented a midsize, orange on white, U-Haul trailer and hooked it behind Granny Fran's two-door Pontiac Grand Prix sports car. We crammed our bunk beds, dresser, and clothes, along with other assorted stuff, into the trailer and headed north, once again like a carload of desperate souls looking for a better life. Once again, we were facing the twin trials of change and uncertainty.

Louis, Jimmy, Oscar, Papa Lee

We didn't want to move, but we needed to get out of Herman and Dana's house and allow them to get back to a more normal life. We hated to be separated from our friends, particularly those at Faith United Methodist Church. But we didn't want to tell our grandparents "no," and we didn't really have any other options.

Our parting was traumatic; sweet and sour at best. A big group of our friends gathered on our uncle and aunt's front lawn, reminisced about our time together, and handed out hugs and handshakes. Herman and Dana expressed their love and concern, but too many pregnant pauses and too few big hugs made our parting difficult and awkward. They all wished us well. The weight of our sadness pushed more than a few big, salty tears from the corners of our eyes.

As heartfelt and appreciated as the goodbyes were, they called attention to the magnitude and apparent permanence of the change that had been dropped on us, making us feel forsaken once again, as though our aunt and uncle had joined a crowd of people who didn't want us in their lives. We were devasted by the feeling of loss again. This time we were not just switching to another house or transferring to another school. We were deserting our Texas home, ditching our friends, and transplanting ourselves in another state. We would be living in a very small, country town with a population of around 10,000 people who didn't talk like us, with our step-grandmother, Granny Fran, who we hardly knew. We'd enter a strange new school mid-semester and never return to live with our dad.

It seems somehow fitting in retrospect that we left town after sunset and drove into the dark to our new home in Malvern on Thanksgiving weekend. I will admit that we had a tough time feeling that we had much to be thankful for.

Papa Lee was tall and skinny, with a thin head of hair, nearly always covered with a Chicago Cubs baseball cap. He usually dressed in a shirt with a collar, and nice slacks. Very friendly and affectionate, but not overly talkative, everyone called him "brother." He rarely talked about himself and never talked about his World War II combat experience at the Battle of the Bulge. He liked hanging out with friends at the Miller Drugstore in downtown Malvern and betting small stakes on horse races run in Hot Springs. Papa loved his grandkids and often told us we were his pride and joy. He operated a brick oven in his job at Acme Brick in Malvern, "the brick capital of the world," and owned the Polly Ann Bakery with his wife Fran.

Although gray-haired, Granny Fran was about ten or twelve years younger than Papa, shorter and thinner, vivacious, attractive, sometimes a little testy, and capable of using an occasional off-color word that seemed out of place from her lips. She was a joy to be with. She was also a competent, independent businesswoman who later taught us about finances, running a business, and avoiding idle time. My brothers and I credit her with instilling us with strong work ethics.

Papa Lee and Granny Fran Buffington

Our grandparents' house was even smaller than Herman and Dana's. It was a 1,500 square foot, nondescript, red-brick bungalow on a big, wooded lot, with a living room that had a big picture window, two bedrooms and one bath, a washing machine in the bathroom, and a clothes dryer in the carport. A modest home, but probably middle class at that place and time. We boys moved into one bedroom, set up our bunk beds and one dresser, and designated a corner for each of our piles. Our grandparents claimed the other bedroom and the five of us shared the bathroom. Fairly soon after our arrival, Papa and Granny Fran expanded the house to include a master bathroom for them, and a den with a fireplace.

Granny Fran sold her Grand Prix and bought a four-door Pontiac Bonneville that accommodated all five of us. Papa drove a well-used, black-and-white Chevy pickup truck, with a three-speed stick shift on the console. It looked a little like a milk truck. In this vehicle, I learned to drive with a stick shift and a clutch.

We started school the Monday after Thanksgiving. I was in the eleventh grade and my brothers were in junior high. Malvern High had three grades (tenth, eleventh, and twelfth) and roughly 700 kids.

We immediately encountered a couple of surprises. Although Austin no doubt had its share of racial discrimination in the late '70s, most of it was pretty subtle and not all that obvious to young White kids like us. We quickly learned that Malvern was different. It had a Black side of town and a White side of town. We lived on the White side, close to the margin between the two. Our bus picked up kids from the Black side first, then came to our house. When we boarded for our first trip to school, the back seats were almost filled with Black kids, and the front was essentially empty. We didn't know the difference, and sat in the back. Later in the day, some White kids advised us of our "mistake," and told us we should sit in the White section.

All involved, including us three kids from Austin, seemed totally oblivious to the fact that in September of 1957, roughly twenty years previously, President Eisenhower federalized the Arkansas National Guard to support integration of the schools in Little Rock, Arkansas, only about forty-five miles away.

This clear segregation surprised and shocked my brothers and me. In our experience, towns were mixed and didn't have a White side and a Black side, and buses didn't have Black and White sections as Malvern did. However, the school seemed to be integrated, except for the predominantly Black basketball team, and everyone seemed to get along. In retrospect, we were living on the leftovers of the South's Jim Crow era.

In recognition of the good reputation of our Texas schools, all three of us were enrolled in advanced classes. In Austin, I studied Latin, was in the Latin club, enjoyed it, and wanted to continue. When I asked about continuing this activity, I was advised that Malvern didn't have Latin classes or a Latin club. So I concentrated on English.

Notwithstanding the differences, we soon assimilated into our new school and adapted to the new, small-town culture that, among other things, included a significant number of family relationships—mainly cousins, including Fran's granddaughters, Cheri and Shannon Monroe. I had several rewarding classes, joined the high school choir, engaged in fun social events, hung out with new friends, and often drove Granny Fran's car down a well-worn path on the town's main drag between the Sonic drive-in and the bowling alley. On one occasion, in a parade before a football game, I drove it with a cage on top holding a big house-cat, because we were the mighty Malvern Leopards. We were all about fun, football, and Friday nights.

Our lives soon settled into a fairly predictable, small-town routine. We attended the Third Baptist Church, where a few hundred "brothers" and "sisters" met in a traditional red-brick building with four large white columns in front and a large white steeple on top. Phil and Sarah Brumley, a young married couple in their twenties who lived just across the street from us, and also attended Third Baptist along with his parents and grandparents, invited us to attend church with them. The Brumleys and their extended family in the area "adopted" us and, along with the church family (such as the Chenaults, Cunninghams, Elliotts, Goldings, Lyons, and Whites), gave us a sense of connection that had a significant, positive influence on our lives, similar to what we had had in Austin. These and others at Third Baptist provided examples of what positive, productive families look like: two parents at home rather than none, family dinners together instead of fast food, family outings rather than visiting a prison on weekends, and not trying to keep a part of your life under cover.

The Polly Ann Bakery, owned by our grandparents, was where Papa met Fran. The bakery and coffee shop, located on Malvern's Main Street, was where people gathered at the tables in front each morning to have donuts and coffee. Fran believed work was good for the soul, so we toiled away in the bakery quite a lot, typically after school, on weekends, and during the summers away from school. Louis worked mainly as a cashier, Oscar operated the donut fryer, and I was responsible for mopping the floors and general cleaning. Our Granny Fran involved us in the financial aspect of the operation as well, which taught us some business skills that came in handy later.

I got a job at a fast-food joint called Andy's, a lot like Wendy's, during my senior year in high school and worked there during the summers while I was in college. I also spent time as a cashier and as a full-service attendant at a gas station, filling gas tanks, washing windshields, checking oil and tire pressure, and often just gossiping with friends who dropped by for a visit.

Our Uncle OB and Aunt Patsy, who had hosted Dad and Linda in Little Rock the weekend Mom was killed, frequently had us in their home on weekends, a couple of times a month at first and then less often as we developed friends and became more involved with weekend activities in Malvern. This gave us a change of scenery and provided our grandparents a small measure of relief and privacy. They would pick us up after school on Friday and return us to Malvern on Sunday afternoon. OB and

Patsy didn't have any kids, and lived in a really, really, nice house on a hill, overlooking the Arkansas River. The house had a walk-out basement with guest rooms and a pool table, and we got the entire downstairs to ourselves. We typically went to the Emmanuel Baptist Church with them on Sunday mornings, followed by a nice brunch. OB and Patsy didn't cook, so we ate brunch, and almost every other meal, at a nice restaurant somewhere in town.

Aunt Patsy was outgoing and bubbly, a lot of fun to be with. Uncle OB was more reserved, a Baptist Deacon and Sunday school teacher who was a wonderful mentor and example for us. A strong man of faith and a graduate of the University of Arkansas, he persuaded Louis and me to attend there as well.

***

Papa Lee took my brothers and me to visit Dad on death row about once a month. We left on Friday after school and drove roughly 300 miles and five and one-half hours to a Holiday Inn in Huntsville, Texas. The difficulty and stress of the trip to see our dad in prison was countered by the joy of anticipating time with him. Because of the distance we had to travel, we were allowed a four-hour visit, which began early Saturday morning.

The Ellis prison unit, that housed death row until 1999, was in the South Texas Piney Woods, about twelve miles down a long, winding, country road north of Huntsville. It was a "real" prison, like in the movies: a huge, forbidding maximum security lockup housing over 2,000 men with a few small windows surrounded by double rows of razor wire coils. Small, white shacks, manned by rifle-wielding officers, guarded each of the corners. The entire complex was in the midst of one of the prison's farming operations, where in times past one would probably have seen white-clad convicts dragging long, heavy white cotton sacks on the ground behind them as they picked row after endless row of cotton.

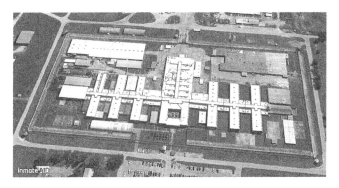

Texas Department of Corrections (TDC) Ellis Unit

Death row was a prison within a prison, a special segregation unit at one end of the huge complex. It confined roughly 300 inmates in cement enclosures the size of a small bathroom, with steel-mesh doors with slits at the bottom through which guards slid meal trays. The area was as loud as a spring thunderstorm, with constant prison ruckus of yelling and taunting and clanging doors. Inmates on the row could work morning and afternoon shifts at various jobs and had several hours a day of group recreation. They were generally alone in their cells only at night. Many of these "freedoms" were eliminated in 1999, following the first escape of a Texas death row prisoner since a member of the Bonnie and Clyde gang busted out in 1934.

Prisoners were provided free room, board, and the barest of essentials. They needed extra spending money, if possible, to make life somewhat less unbearable, but they were not allowed to have actual cash on their person, as cash was considered contraband and not allowed. Each inmate had an account where people on the outside could put money "on the books" to be used to purchase personal items at the prison commissary. Dad was not bashful about asking people to put money on his book. Papa Lee and OB sent him money regularly. I sometimes contributed from my earnings at the fast-food joint or from money I received as beneficiary of the trust from Mom's life insurance. Others helped from time to time. All considered, he was probably one of the "richest" men on death row, although our visits were just about the best presents we could give him.

We arrived in time to pass through the sallyport at the front gate, be subjected to interminable security procedures, and be escorted to a usually empty visitation room, empty because, as compared to county jail, there were fewer inmates, and they typically, sadly, got fewer visits.

We were separate from Dad, who was in a "cage" behind a screen of glass that prevented all physical contact but allowed us to talk directly without using a phone. We always bought him a soda from the commissary, had a guard deliver it, and began our visit. Four-hour visits with nothing to do but talk sometimes dragged. Dad usually picked up the slack by asking about our lives, mainly what was going on in school or church, or talking about his life, his case, or his plans for after his release. He usually expressed his innocence, as well as his confidence that his attorneys would get him off, and we would return to our "normal" life together.

Sometimes a visit seemed to take forever; other times it flew by, but each time our reconnection caused us to relive the loss and trauma of what put our dad on death row. The worst part was when our time together was over. Each time we ended a visit, we felt like we were losing our dad again. Our excitement of seeing him was offset by the sadness of seeing him on death row; our hope of living with him again was offset by the reality of the direction things seemed to be headed; and our pleasure of seeing him was offset by the dread that we would be "found out" in Arkansas.

Our drive back to Malvern was always noticeably different than the drive to Huntsville: quiet, little talk, much reflection, and worry. The good news was that the long drive allowed us to wind down and somewhat accept life without our parents; and when we returned to Malvern, no one knew where we had been. We had left the "where is Mom and Dad" trauma in Texas, and we continued to avoid it in Arkansas.

My high school graduation was held on the school's football field on a pleasant evening in late May 1981. Approximately 222 seniors sat in chairs on the field, facing the home-side bleachers. We sang the school alma mater, listened to unmemorable speeches, and marched across a temporary platform to receive our diplomas. I was awarded a scholarship for my first year at the University of Arkansas. Afterward, a bunch of us loaded into a car and went to a nearby state park, where we hung out and may even have consumed some adult beverages.

My graduation was a fun time, but also one of those heartrending reminders that I didn't have any parents present to be proud of me. I was happy to pass this milestone and thrilled that my brothers, my grandparents, and my aunt and uncle were able to attend, but I felt the sting of melancholy as the absence of my parents sucked some of the energy from the occasion.

Each of us brothers lived in Malvern until we graduated high school and left for college. All considered, our time there was a great, small town, growing-up experience, and probably one of the best times of our lives. There was little tension and stress. Papa Lee didn't think his son had been involved in the killing of our mother, as Herman and Dana had. Even though Malvern was a small town where most people knew my grandparents because of the bakery, no one was aware of our story. No one asked why we three boys from Texas just moved in with our grandparents in the middle of the school year. We didn't talk about Mom and Dad, and my grandparents didn't either. We became just three normal kids, living a small-town, growing-up experience in mid-America. It helped us heal, and it helped save us.

I enrolled at the University of Arkansas that fall—a late change from my earlier plans to attend the University of Texas. I started out studying accounting, but soon discovered, as they say, that I didn't have the personality to be an accountant. I switched my major to marketing, where I could pursue a degree in marketing management and enjoy the sales side of business. A marketing professor, Dub Ashton, who had an incredible knack for immediately learning everyone's name in a large class, helped me see how much I enjoyed working with people, and he was a significant influence on my professional life. He changed my thinking about life and business and was key to my figuring out what I really wanted to do in my professional life.

Several kids from Malvern were there as well, and I roomed at first in a dorm with Mike Barr, a friend from high school. I was active in the Baptist Student Union, where I worshipped and became friends with other students, including Blake Henson, who became the best man at my wedding (and I at his) and a lifelong friend.

In mid-August of my sophomore year, evangelist Bailey Smith presented one of his "Pointing The Way" crusades on campus. At the worship service, he spoke from Revelations 20, which teaches that upon death we stand before the throne and are judged on the basis of what is found in two books: the Book of Works and the Book of Life. He cited verse 15, "Anyone whose name was not found written in the book of life was thrown into the lake of fire," and he made his point with two small stands on stage, each with a book on it.

I had been struggling with my faith, particularly since Dad was convicted and assessed the death penalty, and I had serious doubts whether my name was in the Book of Life. I recalled Jesus's parable of the weeds from Matthew 13, where the good seed stands for the people of the kingdom, and the weeds are the people of the evil one. I understood that many times Christians and non-Christians can appear to look alike, like good seeds and weeds. I wondered if my Dad was really a Christian, even though he looked like a "good seed" before he was arrested and convicted. I wondered if my faith was like his. I kept those doubts to myself, but I knew it came down to a choice to make a heart decision to hold Christ in my life. So during the invitation at the end of the service, I walked forward to resolve any doubts as to whether I was really a Christian. I recommitted my life to Jesus.

A couple of weeks later, the weekend of Sunday, September 4th, I was home in Malvern, Arkansas. I spoke at Third Baptist Church and "told the world," or at least Malvern, that I was a Christian. The church bulletin listed my name with the title: *Let the Redeemed of the Lord say So– Jimmy Buffington*. On the following Wednesday, September 7, 1983, I was baptized, for the second time, at the First Baptist Church in Springdale, Arkansas, along with several of my college friends who made the same decision. I confirmed my faith, and since then I've never had any doubt about whether my name is in the Book of Life.

I have subsequently pondered the question of how all the suffering and trauma from the death of our mom and the arrest, conviction, and incarceration of our dad on death row affected my faith. I concluded that my suffering was caused by other people's bad choices, but it also led to good things such as perseverance, inner strength, endurance, patience, and eventually joy. Suffering taught me to totally depend on God and know that He would get us through the trauma. This has given me great peace, and a stronger faith.

***

During my senior year, I lived in a three-bedroom, two-bath apartment in a complex near the campus. My first apartment was designed for the college scene, with gardens, a couple of swimming pools, and a bus line handy to campus. With graduations and such, roommates came and went like drunks in a county jail.

One day I walked into the apartment, and this well-dressed, attractive, petite, brunette girl was sitting on our sofa. I said, "Well, who are you?"

She answered, "I'm your roommate's girlfriend."

I was struck immediately. My first thought was something to the effect of, *He doesn't deserve you. I'm gonna pursue you even if you are dating my roommate.*

Her name was Marilyn. She had recently finished college and was working in Fayetteville. I fell for her on the spot. We eventually became friends while hanging out with my roommate and other mutual friends. I sometimes told her, "Marilyn, you're going to marry me someday," and

I asked her out. She laughed off my advances, but I was persistent and continued asking. She was equally persistent, and continued saying no. After about a year, the last week of school, I laid it on the line: "Would you just go on one date with me?"

Marilyn, no longer dating my roommate, said, "Fine." It was not the enthusiasm I had hoped for, but better than "No." We went on that one date, and I for sure had a great time. We went across the state line to Missouri, about forty-five minutes away, to the most expensive restaurant I could find. I planned to propose that night, but concluded it was a little too soon, and I chickened out.

I graduated, with plans to move to Austin. Before I left, I asked Marilyn to come see me there. She answered with the noncommittal, "Well, I've never been to Austin."

About a month after I moved from Arkansas back to Austin, Marilyn came to visit. We toured the University of Texas campus and the state capital, and had a great evening at a restaurant on 6th Street. We traveled to Port Aransas to the beach to get out of town, hang out somewhere new, walk its seemingly never-ending shoreline, and do some serious talking. I wanted her to marry me, but I was afraid there was a deal breaker. I didn't want children. I didn't have a good feeling about fatherhood; and as an older brother, I was tired of taking care of two kids. I didn't want any more of that.

However, when the issue came up, I learned that it was not a problem. Marilyn's parents were great, and her mother was a wonderful stay-at-home mom, but Marilyn had decided that was not the life she wanted. She wanted a professional career instead, which at the time meant no children. The potential deal wasn't broken. I breathed a sigh of relief and, as we were walking down the jetties at sunset, I proposed—without a rehearsed speech, a plan, or a ring.

She answered immediately, "I will marry you if you get a job."

Again, not the enthusiasm I had hoped for, but better than "No."

Shortly thereafter, I told Marilyn about Dad. I told her everything—about the divorce, the murder, the arrest, the trial, death row, my belief in his innocence, and the uncertainty of the future. She listened quietly and accepted the story with the understanding, grace, and love she has shown throughout our life together.

Shortly thereafter, we visited him in the Bexar County Jail. Dad was impressed.

Marilyn returned to Fayetteville, and I got a job in Austin with Tracor Aerospace. We married on October 12, 1985, at the Third Baptist Church in Malvern. Its big sanctuary accommodated many local family and friends, plus our friends from Austin and from college. We had a very simple Baptist ceremony, followed by cake and punch in the Fellowship Hall on Arkansas-Texas football weekend. Many of my Texas friends and family were there, along with a cadre of Arkansas Razorbacks. We "called the hogs" in the middle of our reception. The horns won, 15 to 13.

Calling the Hogs, October 12, 1985

We spent our first night at the Capital Hotel in Little Rock, flew to Dallas for one night, then traveled to Colorado Springs for four wonderful days. From there we flew to the coast of Oregon, where my grandparents had relocated, and enjoyed several days at their beach house.

Marilyn moved into the two-story townhouse apartment in South Austin where I was living. She had been working for Dillard's in Fayetteville, and transferred to the store's management team in Austin. We attended Faith United Methodist Church, where my brothers and I had joined when we were living with Herman and Dana. Many of the same families, including my uncle and aunt, were still in Austin. We saw them frequently, as time had dissipated the tensions that developed when we were living with them. We continue to be close today. My grandmother, Mignon, also lived in Austin, and we saw her frequently.

Our life in Austin was typical for newlyweds: getting to know one another better, establishing our respective careers, developing a cadre of friends, training Marilyn to live like a natural-born Texan, except that we visited my dad, her father-in-law, frequently, at the Bexar County Jail in San Antonio as he awaited his second trial. We faced only occasional reminders of his situation.

One of the most memorable occurred sometime in 1987, when there was a knock on our door. It was the police, looking for James Buffington and announcing, "We have a warrant for your arrest." I was not aware of having done anything that would call for my arrest. Turned out, the police were working old cases of various sorts against my dad, and had mistaken me for him. I was able to convince them that I was James Buffington, Jr., that they were looking for my dad. I managed to avoid going to jail.

The Texas Court of Criminal Appeals had reversed Dad's death penalty conviction in May 1983, and ordered a new trial. Although the reversal was ordered on the basis of an error in jury selection, Dad pursued an appeal in federal court that contended the State should not be allowed to try him again, because of, among other things, prosecutorial misconduct in the first trial. A lady who had worked in the Bexar County District Attorney's office had come forward, claiming some men on death row, including Dad, should not be there because of the DA's misconduct. She had the original transcript of the interview when Charlie Moore was first arrested for murdering Mom. The transcript that was submitted to the defense in Dad's trial, where he was assessed the death penalty, was different. Fake language had been inserted, several page numbers had been chopped off, and some pages were removed.

The court agreed the prosecutor had altered the documents and represented from the witness stand that they were true and correct, which was considered a grievous breach of his oath as an attorney in general, and particularly of his oath as a prosecuting attorney. However, the court concluded that although the DA was allegedly guilty of prosecutorial misconduct because of the altered transcript, his actions had not changed the likely result, and even this egregious action did not give Dad a free pass. So the judge ordered a second trial. Dad's appeal of this mandate for a new trial rather than immediate release was denied in October 1984, and he remained behind bars.

We could only wonder if the second trial would produce a different result.

CHAPTER THIRTEEN

Letters from County Jail
1983-1988

"Then the King will say to those on his right, 'Come, you who are
blessed by my Father; take your inheritance, the kingdom prepared
for you since the creation of the world. For I was hungry and you
gave me something to eat, I was thirsty and you gave me something
to drink, I was a stranger and you invited me in, I needed clothes
and you clothed me, I was sick and you looked after me, I was in
prison and you came to visit me." Then the righteous will answer
him, "Lord, when did we see you hungry and feed you, or thirsty and
give you something to drink? When did we see you a stranger and
invite you in, or needing clothes and clothe you? When did we see
you sick or in prison and go to visit you?' The King will reply, Truly
I tell you, whatever you did for one of the least of these brothers
and sisters of mine, you did for me.'" (Mathew 25:34–40)

*Following the Court of Criminal Appeals' reversal of James Buffing-
ton's murder conviction and order of a new trial, he was returned to
the Bexar County Jail to await his second trial. His letters from county
jail continued.*

July 23, 1983. When you see me I will be wearing leg-irons. They are
doing all they can to make me look like a criminal rather than a pre-trial
detainee.

December 4, 1983. I really am a happy fella. I sleep well and sound without any medication. I don't worry and turn large and small problems
over to the Lord. About 3½ years ago I read the scripture Philippians 4:6:

"Be anxious for nothing, but in everything by prayer & supplication with Thanksgiving let your request be made known unto God."

August 10, 1984. Just completed final exams and turned in my term papers. Now it's just a matter of waiting for grades to be posted for College to mail my diploma with your father being a graduate with an associate of arts degree.

August 16, 1984. Today your mother would have been 38 years old. Good qualities of your mother live on in you and your brothers. I still miss her very much.

April 26, 1985. This will be my last contact with you until I can get off restriction. As stated in the grievance, not allowed phone calls or stamps . . . I have never said life is fair. This is a good example. I went to great lengths not even to give an appearance of being involved in the strike. Now I'm locked up because jail decided I was the ring leader.

May 3, 1985. Kangaroo court is defined in Black's Law Dictionary as "Term descriptive of a sham legal proceeding in which a person's rights are totally disregarded and in which the result is a foregone conclusion because of the bars of the court or other tribunal."

June 15, 1985. I must say you know how to pick a wife. Marilyn is super. I'm sure everything was strange to her yesterday, yet, it was as if she had come by the house to visit. She is smart, attractive, Christian, Baptist, republican, voted for Reagan, willing to have children, Bryant girl, enjoys sports, no bias against your father, loves Oscar, Louis, and Gina, employed, and obviously very much in love with you.

August 26, 1985. Not long until it will be James and Marilyn Buffington. Wish I could be there for the wedding.

June 29, 1986. [*Letter to Marilyn*] I want to thank you again for the visit. Of course all my talk about having you live so close didn't help you both to discuss your future plans.

December 9, 1986. This afternoon my attorneys . . . brought me the written recommendation of the Federal Magistrate not to dismiss my case . . . The magistrate ruled, "a more egregious or deplorable example of prosecutorial overreaching than that in the case at hand is hard to imagine . . . this Magistrate finds that petitioner is entitled to the relief requested only if the remainder of the evidence, exclusive of that of Moore, would have been insufficient to support a verdict of guilty. This magistrate concludes that the remainder of the evidence would have been sufficient, although circumstantial, to support a verdict of guilty."

January 23, 1987. I love you. Today two men in my cell were set free. Eventually my time will come.

> I received the money order. Thank you for all your support.
> Marilyn, all I want for Christmas is a grandson.

February 20, 1987. I love you. Instead of the March money, please send the $25.00 as indicated in this letter. It is near spring and there is romance in the air. Genevieve [*A slightly built Catholic chaplain who counseled inmates at Bexar County Adult Detention Center—often visiting cells with a guitar strapped across her shoulder, and playing liturgical songs she had written.*] will have a birthday Sunday March 29th. So will have flowers delivered Saturday the 28th.

February 25, 1987. The timing has a lot to be desired in when I met Genevieve, . . . Obviously, I wish I had met her in a time frame once released from or already out of law school. But she has focused my eyes on the future and my determination to be vindicated and back into a productive place in society.

It is not Genevieve's fault that she is a Christian, intelligent, educated, BEAUTIFUL, and can put up with my TERRIBLE personality. Plus Tom Cruise or some other lucky guy can come along and steal her heart before I can get out of here and court her full time.

March 5, 1987. Celibacy does get old especially when around a 32-year-old attractive woman.

March 6, 1987. Also met with Genevieve. Explained my feelings about her birthday and she was relieved. The truth is it had reached a point that she would blush when we would meet on the elevator, if you can believe. . . .Obviously, I still want her body but we have agreed to stay in a role of good friends until day of my release: that day I throw hat in the ring to court her.

March 12, 1987. I think my woman is MAD with me . . . All I had been writing was about her good qualities and about her!!! . . . My guess is she is paranoid about anyone ever knowing she had received letters and phone calls from me. . . . If I get a call from special management, you know someone has got hold of one of my letters to Genevieve.

March 16, 1987. I'm still being given plenty of opportunities to serve the Lord here. In our morning service, I led the Hymn singing and the prayer. Plus we had a second service in the afternoon. I bought the complete works of Josephus and hope to complete that this year. . . . Still on daily schedule to read the Bible again this year.

April 6, 1987. I love you two. I'm still excited about your move to Arkansas. God has really blessed this family.

July 1, 1987. Today Genevieve and I worked three hours on Rusty's [*an inmate scheduled for execution for murder of a woman during a robbery attempt*] rosary and funeral. An emotional draining time for us.

July 23, 1987. [*Genevieve*] hit me with one bombshell after another . . . Andy with serious doubts about my innocence—from mainly talking with you & she laid other personal problems on me. . . . I made mistakes & continue to make mistakes. But of the crime charged, I am innocent.

November 29, 1987. Glad you could meet Andy [investigator for court appointed lawyer] & Genevieve. I think you agree I did a good job as "cupid" and you could see how easy it was for me to fall in love with her. But your father did the right thing and the 3 of us have a good relationship & they are very supportive of me.

Christmas 1987. I appreciate all that has been done for me by the family. Not your fault that I've been incarcerated for over a decade. Yet we are Blessed as a family and can enjoy this holiday season.

January 29, 1988. Yesterday was Genevieve's last day here as a chaplain. My weekly private counseling session she gave me each week for almost the last two years will be missed.

April 16, 1988. This is a "good" and "sad" birthday for me. Of course, it shows how the Lord has blessed this family even though I now face my 11th birthday incarcerated.

   . . . I especially miss Mom [*Chere*] this week . . .

July 29, 1988, Letter # 1. Andy was here late morning and obviously concerned I was going to trial. He cannot see me getting a fair trial.

   I guess my body had all it could take & last night, I started the "throwing up" action. I got terribly sick.

   There was a meeting in D.A. office yesterday and they are ready to enter negotiations. This has not helped my stomach.

   I want a trial—but not at the price of my death—a plea bargain or plea bargain negotiations before my trial may hurt you & others, but my execution due to an unfair trial will hurt you more.

July 29, 1988, Letter # 2. I authorized John Hrncir to offer 40 years. State is offering 60 years. All I know at this point is John and Sam Ponder started negotiations Friday.

I am eligible now for parole on any of these sentences. I am convinced I made the right decision. (*The plea bargain did not work out.*)

August 25, 1988. I believe God is going to use me in the Catholic Church.

In my Christian life, I believe God is calling me to be used to minister to others then you should rely on the guidance of the Holy Spirit in Christian lives and not a hierarchy of men.

September 19, 1988. In two weeks my 5½ years of waiting will be over & trial should begin unless 5th circuit issues a stay.

San Antonio Express-News and San Antonio Light, 1986–1988

CHAPTER FOURTEEN

Second Trial

"Then you will know the truth, and the truth will set you free."
(John 8:32)

On December 31, 1985, the 4th Court of Appeals affirmed its 1984 ruling mandating a retrial, leading to James Buffington's second test of fate. However, it was further delayed by more legal maneuvering, including fourteen pretrial motions filed by his attorneys in state or federal courts.

Among others, in September 1986, James filed an application for a Writ of Habeas Corpus. (Asks a court to overturn a conviction because of a state or federal constitutional violation, that may include matters not in the existing court record.) He also filed a Special Plea of Double Jeopardy. (Claims a violation of the constitutional protection against being made to stand trial more than once for the same criminal offense.) These filings contended that he should be released from prison and a retrial barred because in the first trial (December 1978–January 1979) "the record revealed utterly unacceptable prosecutorial misconduct to the demonstrable prejudice to appellant, or substantial threat thereof . . ." in violation of the double jeopardy provisions of the United States and Texas constitutions. Evidence was again presented showing that the prosecutor, Charles Conaway, had altered an exhibit by deleting four pages, altering one page, and removing the page numbers from the bottom of each page, and this was done during the trial for the purpose of denying James's lawyers the ability to effectively cross examine Charlie Moore, a key witness against James. But again, the writs were denied.

These were followed by a series of state and federal appeals in which James contended he should not be tried again. In a forty-five-page order issued on Mar 13, 1988, US District Judge Prado denied James's claims, allowed the trial to go forward, and set a trial date of August 1, 1988.

I felt good about the retrial, as I continued to believe Dad was innocent of Mom's murder. Credible evidence that the district attorney had altered the record in order to convict him in the first trial strengthened my belief. In addition, evidence demonstrated that Charlie Moore, a key witness against Dad, lied on the stand in the trial when Dad was convicted. These two evidentiary problems for the prosecution seemed to make proof of guilt all but impossible. I hoped the jury would see it the same way.

Dad's lawyers asked the judge to set a $50,000 bond for his release, pending the trial. A hearing on their motion was conducted in late June. Seven character witnesses testified for Dad, including a doctor, two jail chaplains, two attorneys, and me. We all testified to the effect that Dad was a man of character and not a flight risk. I also testified, among other things, that my grandmother, Mignon Stieferman, did not believe her former son-in-law was involved in the murder of her daughter, and wanted him to be released on bond. However, the judge denied bond and sent Dad back to the Bexar County Jail to await his trial.

Dad's attorneys also filed a motion for a change of venue, alleging he couldn't receive a fair trial in San Antonio because of all the publicity; and another motion to suppress testimony from Charles County and Charlie Moore, his alleged Black coconspirators, arguing that their presence before a jury in the trial of James Buffington, a White man, would inflame the jury and all concerned. The judge denied both motions, and the trial began on Monday, October 31, 1988, before a jury of nine women and three men.

I was working for Tracor Aerospace and had recently been promoted and transferred from Austin to their plant in Camden Arkansas, a town of roughly 12,000 people in the south-central part of the state, about 100 miles south of Little Rock. Shortly before the trial began, I got a call from

San Antonio Express-News and San Antonio Light, August 1988

Defense seeks bond for murder suspect

By JOHN McALLEN
Express-News Staff Writer

Defense lawyers are trying to get a bond set for a former businessman accused of hiring two men to murder his ex-wife in 1976...

SATURDAY, JUNE 25, 1988

tered, was found in her safe on the parking lot of Longfellow Junior High School.

The Texas Court of Criminal Appeals reversed the conviction in 1983, but Buffington's retrial was delayed because his lawyer, Mark Stevens and John Hrncir, pursued a separate appeal in federal courts.

The lawyers contended that prosecutorial misconduct in Buffington's 1978 trial was such the...

Prade's ruling will be appealed to the 5th Circuit of Appeals in New Orleans. The attorney asked Curry to delay setting Buffington's murder trial date until the 5th Court ruled.

"My new bond is only $5,000 low, declaring, 'I really don't care what the federal system does anyway'...

Curry has repeatedly expressed reservations against the federal courts by issuing an order reopening the case three months...

Judge denies Buffington bond motion; Aug. 1 capital murder trial scheduled

A San Antonio man accused of hiring two employees to murder his ex-wife 12 years ago had lost a bid for freedom pending his trial set for Aug. 1.

James G. Buffington, 44, was remanded to the Bexar County Jail without bond after a two-hour hearing before 186th District Court Judge Peter Michael Curry.

Buffington is charged with capital murder in the death of Cheré Jean Buffington, a 39-year-old secretary. Her nude body was found stuffed in the blood-soaked back seat of her auto parked behind Longfellow Middle School, 1530 E. Sunshine St., by a security guard on March 30, 1976. Her head had been shattered by a bullet.

Buffington was sentenced to death by a jury in 1978, but a new trial was ordered by the Texas Court of Criminal Appeals in 1983 because of an error in jury selection. However, because of findings of prosecutorial misconduct at the trial, a federal court proceeding prevented Buffington's new trial until this year.

U.S. District Judge Ed Prade denied defense attorneys' pleas to dismiss the capital murder charge against

Buffington because of the prosecutorial misconduct.

The court-appointed lawyers, Mark Stevens and John Hrncir, said they will appeal Prade's decision to the 5th Circuit U.S. Court of Appeals in New Orleans. They said they expect the 5th Circuit to stay the murder trial until the appeal is exhausted in the federal court system.

Assistant District Attorney Julian Lopez asked Curry Friday to take judicial notice of the evidence in Buffington's 1978 trial and to order the defendant held without bond.

Defense attorneys called seven witnesses, including the defendant's son, James G. Buffington Jr., three Bexar County Jail chaplains, a retired physician, a junior college instructor and two lawyers. They testified they believe Buffington would not fail to attend a court setting if he was released on bond.

"In my opinion, there is zero chance that James Buffington will ever miss a court appearance," testified attorney Andy Logan, a childhood friend of the defendant.

Buffington denied bail as kin cry innocence

By HECTOR D. CANTU
Courthouse reporter

The former mother-in-law of twice-convicted capital murderer James Buffington Sr. believes he is innocent of a charge he hired two men to kill her daughter in 1976, Buffington's son testified Friday.

The younger Buffington, who was 12 at the time of his mother's death, was one of seven character witnesses — including a doctor, two jail chaplains and two attorneys — who appeared at a hearing on a motion to have state District Judge Peter Michael Curry set a bail for Buffington.

The judge denied the motion and ordered Buffington back to jail without bond.

All the witnesses testified they believed Buffington was not a threat to the community.

Buffington's son, James Buffington Jr. of Arkansas, testified his grandmother does not believe her former son-in-law committed the crime.

"She feels, first of all, that he didn't do it," the younger Buffington said. "She wants him to get released on bond."

Attorney Andy Logan, who said he went to elementary school with Buffington, testified he would be willing to help raise $5,000 for his former classmate if a bond was set.

After the hearing, Buffington, 44, had no comment on the ruling when questioned by news reporters as he was led back to the jail by courtroom bailiffs.

Defense attorney Mark Stevens said he would appeal the judge's decision to the 4th Court of Appeals.

Buffington was convicted June 2 of paying two men $3,000 to murder of his wife in 1976 so he could claim hundreds of thousands of dollars in insurance money.

The nude body of Cheré Buffington, 39, her head shattered by a bullet, was found in her auto on the parking lot of Longfellow Junior High School.

Buffington was convicted of capital murder in 1978 and 1979, but both convictions were overturned by the Texas Court of Criminal Appeals on technicalities.

In the past 11 years, Buffington has spent time in both the Bexar County Jail and in the Texas Department of Corrections.

His defense attorneys have contended Buffington should not be retried on the capital murder charge because of prosecutorial misconduct in Buffington's 1978 trial.

An appeal of the case is pending before the 5th U.S. Circuit Court of Appeals in New Orleans.

Despite the appeal, Curry last month set an Aug. 1 trial date.

SAN ANTONIO LIGHT   TUESDAY, AUGUST 2, 1988/D5

Buffington, lawyers study evidence as murder trial nears

By HECTOR D. CANTU
Courthouse reporter

Defense attorneys for James Buffington, accused of hiring hit men to murder his wife, spent Monday weighing evidence prosecutors have gathered in the murder case.

Buffington nine years ago was convicted and sentenced to death in the killing of his wife, but the decision was overturned and a new trial ordered.

His new trial is scheduled to be-

> *Buffington nine years ago was convicted and sentenced to death in the killing of his wife, but the decision was overturned and a*

RESS-NEWS, San Antonio, Texas, Thursday, August 4, 1988

Judge to rule on moving Buffington murder trial

■ A district judge will decide Thursday whether James G. Buffington's capital murder trial will be moved outside Bexar County.

Judge Peter Michael Curry, for three hours Wednesday, heard tech-year-old mur...

Judge to query Buffington lawyers

■ A district judge asked prosecutors and lawyers in the James G. Buffington capital murder case to report Wednesday whether they are ready for trial.

Judge Peter Michael Curry, after meeting with the attorneys Tuesday, said lawyers are having difficulty producing some witnesses.

Buffington, 44, a former San Antonio businessman, is accused of hiring two employees to murder his ex-wife 12 years ago.

Lawyers spent Monday and Tuesday reviewing evidence from an earlier trial of Buffington and two others convicted in the murder.

Curry said Buffington will be brought to 186th District Court Wednesday. He said attorneys and motions will be heard for the rest of the week. A possibility exists the trial may be postponed, the judge said.

John Hrncir attend Buffington's fair trial in was convicted a penalty nine year.

Lopez and stung the pro...

with capital his ex-wife a 29-year-old dy was found soaked back behind Long-1130 E. Sun ty guard on bean shot in...

criminal Ap for Buffing-an error in because of misconduct...

Buffington to be tried in San Antonio

■ A former businessman accused of hiring two employees to murder his ex-wife 12 years ago will be tried in San Antonio, probably in October.

District Judge Peter Michael Curry Wednesday denied a plea by James G. Buffington, 44, for a change of venue in the capital murder re-trial.

Defense attorneys John Hrncir and Mark Stevens contended Buffington cannot receive a fair trial in Bexar County because of publicity in the case.

Buffington is charged with hiring two employees to kill his ex-wife, Cheré Buffington, 39. Her nude body was found on the blood-soaked back seat of her auto on the parking lot of Longfellow Junior High School, 1130 E. Sunshine St. A bullet had shattered her head...

Prosecutors contended Buffington paid the two men to kill his ex-wife in 1976 so he could collect insurance money...

Buffington was sentenced to death in 1978 but won a new trial two years later...

Reporters, lawyers talk on Buffington

Move of Buffington trial sought

By HECTOR D. CANTU
Courthouse reporter

Two local news reporters testified Monday they believe accused capital murderer James Buffington Sr., charged with hiring hit men to kill his wife, can get a fair trial in Bexar County.

However, three local attorneys

Hearing is scheduled to resume today.

Media called in Buffington ca...

By HECTOR D. CANTU
Courthouse reporter

Defense attorneys for accused capital murderer James Buffington have subpoenaed television and radio representatives for a change of venue hearing.

Media publicity on the case has created a "climate of contempt" in the community, making it unlikely a fair and impartial jury can be impaneled, defense attorneys are arguing.

The scheduled trial will be Buffington's second for allegedly having his wife killed so he could collect insurance money in 1977. His first conviction was overturned.

The hearing for the change of venue is scheduled Monday before state trial Judge Michael Curry.

Thursday, Curry heard five additional motions, including a move to declare a charge a violation of double jeopardy protection, the double jeopardy protection...

Prosecutors and defense attorneys...

Buffington is charged with hiring his wife, Cheré, to be killed...

my boss, asking me if I'd been arrested for murdering my wife—as he had seen in the local newspaper. More than a little embarrassed, I responded that the person in question was my dad who was charged with murdering my mother; but since he raised the issue, I did need some time off to attend the upcoming trial proceedings. The company granted me a leave of absence without pay for roughly a month and, shortly thereafter, Marilyn and I headed to Texas. We stayed with Ted and Janet Daniel, our old neighbors from the cul-de-sac where the "big house" of our childhood was located.

Dad's second trial was not held in the historic old building with the Spanish influence where the original one was held. Instead it was conducted in the new courthouse adjacent to the old one. It was a big, light-colored box structure that had a more modern look. The courtroom was very conventional, with the obligatory judge's bench, council tables, witness stand, jury box, and seating for spectators. As in the first trial, the room was packed with spectators, including more reporters than seemed necessary.

Potential witnesses scheduled to testify in a trial are typically "sequestered," or prohibited from attending the proceedings when they are not testifying. This prevents them from tailoring their testimony based on what other witnesses have said, which helps the jury find the truth by noting inconsistencies in the testimonies of different witnesses. I was scheduled to testify, so I was sequestered.

Marilyn and I decided that since I couldn't attend the trial proceedings, she would do so, take notes, and brief me at the end of each day. Not surprisingly, Marilyn agreed to the arrangement willingly, but with some trepidation. She later explained, "As I walked along the sidewalk, making my way to the San Antonio courthouse, I had mixed emotions. Part of me was excited, because I always had a curiosity about court proceedings. However, there was also a part of me that was full of apprehension and dread. The fact that my father-in-law was on trial for capital murder and criminal solicitation, and could be sentenced to the death penalty again, gave me these feelings."

Most of my time each day was spent loitering in the hallway outside the courtroom, warming the long wooden bench, fighting off super-aggressive media reporters looking (unsuccessfully) for words from a son of the accused, and waiting for breaks in the proceedings. During recesses, I went into the courtroom and visited Marilyn and Dad. He wore no handcuffs or leg irons, and wore one of the suits his attorney provided him. He sported a new little mustache that frankly made him look like a mafia thug.

Marilyn usually sat a few rows behind the defense table where Dad was sitting with his attorneys. There was little communication between her and Dad, except for some short visits during breaks and an occasional nod, smile, or other nonverbal acknowledgement. A "spiritual advisor" of Dad, Maria, sat next to Marilyn throughout the entire trial. Maria was an attractive Hispanic lady, with long, flowing dark hair, fetching eyes, stylish dress, and a husband. She had formerly counseled prisoners as a volunteer on death row. Marilyn had just met Maria, whose presence was a great support to her, and no doubt to Dad as well, as the two appear to have become close—probably way too close.

On January 12, 1989, he received the following poem she had written for him:

Kindred Spirit

So many laughs
So many tears
So many fears calmed
    With warm embraces
So many hurts soothed
    With gentle hands
So many tender kisses
    To share the love
So many hopeful prayers
    To lighten the load

Sharing love to resurrect
Sharing love to die
So much life to give
So much life to receive

Two lives
Two friends
Two hearts
One traveled road
One soul

Marilyn explained her feelings about her role in the trial this way: "The trial was foreign to me. I knew how desperate Jim was to find out what happened to his mother, so I made every effort to capture every detail during the proceedings. I felt it was my obligation to Jim and his family, and it was my way of honoring his mother, who I never knew. At the same time, I felt it was necessary to be objective, so I tried to just sit back and listen as if I were a reporter or semi-interested bystander. If I let my emotions sneak out, the heaviness of the situation seemed almost too much to bear.. . . I also felt very sorry for Jim, as I watched him bravely walk up the courthouse steps, loiter in the hallway outside the courtroom door, and shoulder the weight of what was happening to his family."

At the end of each day, we visited briefly with Dad and then met for an hour or so in a conference room in John Hrncir's office located in San Antonio's only real high-rise building, a short walk from the courthouse. I typically wanted to know what was said in the testimony.

John, and his partner, Mark Stevens, wanted to know what was *not* said: Marilyn's perception of how the day had gone, holes in the case, questions she had, and such. They used her as a surrogate juror to get a feel for what members of the actual jury might be thinking.

After each debriefing session, we returned to the Daniel's house, talked nonstop with them about the trial, ate dinner, and watched the 10:00 p.m. news to get the media's lurid perspective on the day.

Marilyn summarized her feelings as follows, "The tremendous burdens were heavy for both Jim and me during that time, but God was by our side every step of the way, showing his great faithfulness to us."

Her extensive notes, plus trial records, press accounts, and just being so close to the action combined to give me a good feel for the case and provided information about things I previously was not aware of.

The cast of characters was much the same as in the first trial, but there were some changes. We boys had grown up. A fifteen-year-old high school kid at the time of the first trial, I was now a college graduate and an aspiring business executive with a new wife. Oscar and Louis, eleven and ten respectively at the time of the first trial, had grown similarly. I guess you can say Dad looked like he had gone in the other direction. He had lost more than 100 pounds, down from more than 300 at the time of the first trial.

Judge Michael Curry also presided in this trial, with the same even-handed, fair competence that he had exhibited in the first trial in 1977. He was kind to everyone, particularly Dad's father, took great liberties in allowing us to visit with Dad during breaks, and even allowed our family and a few others to have lunch together in a nearby conference room.

John Hrncir was again the lead attorney and quarterback of the defense team. However, Charles Conaway, chief prosecutor in the first trial, had been removed from the case because of his prosecutorial indiscretions. Julian Lopez replaced him as lead attorney for the prosecution. He graduated from the University of Texas at Austin with a bachelor of arts in Government in 1977, and from the University of Texas School of Law with his JD degree in 1980. Lopez spent four years as a felony prosecutor for Cameron County in Brownsville, Texas. After leaving Cameron County, he became a lead prosecutor at the Bexar County Criminal District Attorney, Special Crimes Division, for three years. He was assisted by Bill Harris, whose brother Phil was a good friend of Dad from their high school days.

Lopez began with an opening statement along the lines of Conaway's in the first trial, presenting the same charges, outlining the same facts, asking for the same result. Then he continued by examining most of the same witnesses, a total of thirty-two representing the State's case.

The supporting cast of characters had changed as well in the decade since the first trial. The school security guard who found Mom's body in her car in the school parking lot had passed away, and another witness who reported seeing two men in a truck near Mom's car was too ill to testify. Charlie Moore had been sentenced in a plea bargain to a seventeen-year sentence, released on parole, and subsequently rearrested and sentenced to life in prison as a habitual criminal after committing armed robberies in Houston. He refused to testify. Charles County, the alleged triggerman in the murder, was on death row, and he too refused to testify.

Mr. Lopez set the wheels in motion by introducing Mom's bloody dress, pictures of my brothers and me, and evidence showing her as the classy lady and young single mother she was. Charles County and Charlie Moore were again paraded into court in the mode of a Hollywood drama, Black men with their hands cuffed behind them and their legs shackled, guarded by several hefty, mean-looking officers with huge white cowboy hats on their heads and long dark pistols on their legs.

Although neither of the convicts testified, they were noticed, and their presence made a statement to the jury. The crowd of spectators seemed impressed by the dramatic demonstration, but did not react with the same emotional fervor seen in the first trial. Our family and County's family sat near one another and occasionally conversed. One could only guess whether this affected the jury.

David Savere, the local college student and former employee of Dad, who claimed in the first trial that he had heard a conversation in which Dad hired County to kill his wife, testified much the same, but had an addition to his story. Savere said again that Dad told County in his presence that he wanted Mom killed, and he wanted the murder to look like a rape and robbery—with her being found nude and her purse missing—as this would help him get the insurance money on her life. However, this time,

Savere claimed that the District Attorney's office rigged his body with a hidden recorder to tape a conversation with Dad. Prosecutors claimed they didn't know what happened to the tape, which had not been mentioned in previous trials of defendants linked to the case. Dad's attorneys argued that in the recording, Dad denied involvement in the murder of his ex-wife, and they filed a motion for a mistrial because the mystery tape was not available. The motion was denied, and the tape was never located.

I believed the members of the prosecution team were lying, that there was no way that Dad was responsible for Mom's murder. I testified that I thought he was innocent, but Lopez really grilled me in particular about the incident on the day of the funeral when Dad allegedly went to the telephone booth at Jim's Hamburgers and left a can in the booth with three $100 bills stuffed inside. I testified that this could not have happened, because I was with my dad the entire day. I later felt betrayed by Dad when his attorneys told me that the incident had in fact actually happened, about a week after the day of Mom's funeral, on a day when

San Antonio Express-News and San Antonio Light, November 9, 1988

I was not with him. My testimony probably supported Dad's argument that he didn't pay the accused killer, when in fact he apparently did.

Dad's attorneys called twelve witnesses to testify for him. They swore, among other things, that Dad became the first jail inmate to receive a San Antonio College associate of arts degree, was very religious, led singing in jail church services, and counseled fellow inmates, helping them cope with their situations. The prosecuting attorney responded, "He hasn't changed. He's still running a scam. It's not a time for mercy; it's time for justice."

There was an inference in the first trial that Dad had intended to murder my brothers and me. The idea received more emphasis in the second trial. During my testimony, Lopez was not nice to me as he focused on how I felt about my dad having life insurance policies on my brothers and me when we were twelve, eleven, and ten: term life insurance, not an investment, that would only pay if we were killed.

Lopez snapped at me, "You're defending your dad when he had a $75,000 policy on your life? You're a smart businessman. Do you think it's normal to have that much term life insurance on a twelve-year-old boy and your two little brothers? Do you understand the difference between term and whole life insurance? This was not an investment. It only paid if you died."

I understood how term life insurance worked, and I didn't understand why Dad had purchased those policies. However, I stood my ground as the DA pushed me hard to admit that Dad had hired killers to murder Mom and us boys. Even under the heated pressure, I continued to maintain Dad was innocent. During a break following one exchange, I looked at my dad. He smiled, pumped his fist in the air, and mouthed words to the effect of "Good job. Keep up the fight."

My reaction was, *What is he saying? I'm just trying to tell the truth. I'm not here as part of a fight. This is not a game.* I felt odd and extremely uneasy defending my dad, while deep down thinking, *You took out term insurance on my life? And now you are treating this as a game?* The exchange had raised questions, fostered uncertainty, sown seeds of doubt.

I later encountered information supporting the idea that Dad did arrange for us to be killed but may have had a change of heart. We were supposed to be with my mom the weekend of her murder, but at the last-minute, plans were changed, and Dad agreed we could spend the weekend at our house with Tammy and a housekeeper. For whatever reason, apparently Dad did not pass this information to County or Moore. This may have saved our lives. I learned more about that later.

There were no witnesses for the defense in the first trial. In the second one, Linda Morrey, Dad's second wife, and Charlotte Jacobs, his former secretary, were called by the State, but both really supported Dad's defense. I testified for Dad. Each side rested its case on Tuesday, November 8. Afterward, Dad asked his attorney to ask the judge if we could take a family portrait. He did, and the judge agreed to what would be our first family picture in over a decade. We gathered in a conference room adjacent to the judge's chambers, visited, had a meal, and took a family photo—but not necessarily a photo of family bliss. It was a tough, awkward situation, as we were facing a decision whether Dad would be scheduled for execution again.

Then the waiting began—in the courtroom, in the hallways, in John Hrncir's office, and on the streets of San Antonio.

Jim, Marilyn, Oscar, James, Gina, Louis

CHAPTER FIFTEEN

Second Verdict

"Do not take revenge, my dear friends, but leave room
for God's wrath, for it is written: 'It is mine to avenge;
I will repay,' says the Lord." (Romans 12:19)

At the beginning of the trial, I wanted to believe Dad was innocent, and I was confident that he was. I even told the Court that if he were paroled, he could live with Marilyn and me. However, during the trial, the DA's questions about the details of the term life insurance policies that had been taken out on us boys created a queasy feeling in the pit of my stomach. In addition, I discovered some new information when reading Marilyn's notes, information that was riddled with questions and ambiguities.

Although she did not tell me, Marilyn had believed before the trial that Dad was guilty. After the trial, she still thought he was guilty and believed the State had presented enough evidence to prove it. She was shocked by several things she heard, the most significant of which was the strong circumstantial evidence indicating that Dad planned to have his sons—her husband and his brothers—killed.

The jury got the case at 3:15 p.m. on Wednesday, November 9, 1988. The first vote was eleven not guilty and one guilty. Presumably, the one guilty vote was a man whose demeanor and behavior from the beginning suggested he didn't like Dad. The other jurors seemed to empathize with us boys and our families.

The jurors recessed an hour for supper and returned for deliberations until 10:20 p.m. They were sequestered for the night. The next day, after twelve and one-half hours of deliberation, they found Dad guilty of the lesser charge of murder. They were scheduled to reconvene on Monday to assess a penalty.

Since the jury found Dad guilty of murder, and not capital murder, the death penalty was off the table. Consequently, the State asked the jury to sentence Dad to life in prison. The defense asked the jury to sentence him to no more than ten years, and place him on probation, rather than return him to prison. Dad's attorneys called eleven supporting witnesses, including my brothers and me, four Bexar County Jail chaplains, and a former cellmate. We all testified to his good character, and the jail staff said that Dad had been a model prisoner during his eleven years of incarceration. They said he taught other prisoners on death row how to read and write, and was a lay minister to other prisoners in the Bexar County Jail. We boys recalled the day of Mom's funeral in 1976, and testified, among other things, that we had maintained a father-son relationship, and the proceeds from insurance policies on Mom's life were used to send us through college and get us started on our respective careers. The prosecution did not call any witnesses.

The jury deliberated in the penalty phase for less than an hour and assessed the maximum sentence of life in prison and a $10,000 fine. In interviews after the trial, several jurors said they were confident Dad had committed capital murder, but there was not enough evidence—beyond a reasonable doubt—that he had promised or paid remuneration for Mom's killing to convict him.

We were relieved when the jury convicted Dad of murder, but not capital murder. There would be no death penalty, no worries about an execution, no execution. He had already served eleven and one-half years in prison and had been a model prisoner. With the life sentence, he could be free on parole immediately. Dad's reaction was as if he had won a lottery, or like Christmas in November. His main objective had been to get off of death row, and this was accomplished. With credit for time served, he could be released in very short order.

In hindsight, I don't believe the jury liked my dad and probably thought he was guilty of capital murder. But I believe they liked us boys, empathized with our situation, and wanted to save us the trauma of having our dad executed. So they gave him a life sentence rather than death. Our testifying for him probably saved his life.

San Antonio Express-News and San Antonio Light, November 1988

Marilyn and I maintained a list of questions when discussing the case and reading her notes each night. The list of concerns was eventually comprised of some fifty-odd queries to ask Dad that would help us make our own judgment as to what had happened. One of the most significant issues in my mind concerned Charlotte Jacobs, whether she was the person who had been seen in Mom's apartment on the day of the murder and, if so, why she was there. The police maintained that Charlotte was not there, and that Mom was seen at her apartment around noon, talking to the apartment manager. Mom's mother said that was impossible, because Mom was at her house all day, from 8:00 a.m. until almost 4:00 p.m.

After Mom was murdered, her parents had gone to gather her things from her apartment to put them in their house. Her mother observed that Mom's wig—the one she occasionally wore when she didn't have time to do her hair—was missing.

Charlotte looked very much like mom, in size, stature, complexion, and even some facial characteristics. But her hair was blonde, rather than brunette like Mom's. We came to believe Charlotte was in the apartment, and when she saw the apartment manager, she put the wig on to disguise herself as Mom. Mom had only lived there a week or two, so the manager would not have recognized the deception.

We then developed a theory as to why Charlotte was in Mom's apartment.

Ken, who Mom had been dating for almost a year, was with her the evening before she was murdered. She told him she had to get up early Saturday morning because James was paying her fifty dollars to pick up two men and take them to a construction site. We suspect this was the first part of the scheme—to have the victim contact the killers.

The following morning, when Mom went to pick up County and Moore, no one answered the door. She went to a pay phone, called Dad in Arkansas, and explained what had happened. When he told her not to worry about it, that they could take care of it another time, Mom left and spent the day with her parents. Thus the murder didn't occur as scheduled.

We theorized that Charlotte decided to make sure Mom was murdered anyway. So she went looking for her and somehow got into her apartment. At the trial, Charlotte testified that she had written the addresses on the envelopes containing the paychecks that were to be delivered on the day of Mom's murder and that were found on Mom's coffee table. Also, there was a note stating, "house key inside," suggesting that possibly Charlotte had a key to Mom's apartment.

We know that County and Moore also went to Mom's apartment looking for her during the day. And finally, we know that around the time of Mom's murder, Charlotte was at the Eastern Star Building, just a block or so from the crime scene.

In addition, there was convincing evidence from which a motive for her participation in the conspiracy could be inferred. She was Dad's secretary at Cliff's Fence Company and went with him when he started his own Jim's Fence Company. I suspected that Charlotte and Dad were having an affair. Speculation at the time was that he either spent the money he received from the insurance policies, hid it, or gave it to Charlotte. All would have provided a reason for her to work with him on the scheme.

Charlotte Jacobs was never charged with a crime. However, I now strongly suspect that she was doing her part in the plot, and perhaps had arranged the murder. Had she? Could she have been involved in the plot without Dad's complicity? This strong suspicion, plus Marilyn's doubt about his innocence, the jury's guilty verdict, Dad's apparent cavalier attitude about my testimony, and the list of open questions combined to shove my belief about his innocence from a developing concern to serious doubt. I needed some answers from Dad.

Marilyn and I visited Dad the night after the verdict was rendered. We entered the jail's attorney visiting room, intent on asking some questions and getting some answers, not just about Dad, but also about some details concerning Mom's death that had surfaced in the trial. The two of us were assigned a small booth separate from Dad, but were able to talk with him directly without using the phone system. He was friendly, welcoming, even excited, at first. He had dodged the execution and was contemplating a bright future, perhaps living with us, after release on parole, which would be soon because of his credit for time served.

Our first few questions were straightforward softballs: a little rehashing of the trial, anticipation of his life in the free world, parole issues, and such. Then I told him I needed to have some tough questions answered. I referenced the paychecks that were delivered to his employees on the day of Mom's murder, and asked him, "Who was the lady coming down the stairs from Mom's apartment at noon on Saturday the twentieth, the day she was killed? Was it your secretary, Charlotte Jacobs? Were you two having an affair?"

Dad was quiet for a little too long, then crossed his arms over his chest, hunched forward, and glanced toward the ground. The tenor of the conversation changed from open to defensive, from cordial to acrimonious. Dad stated that he and Charlotte had been having an affair, confirming our suspicions and what appeared to us to have been a "chemistry," almost a flirtation, between the two of them in the courtroom. Then he made several comments that seemed to be an effort to justify the relationship and defend Charlotte. We were stunned by what we were hearing. I took a long breath, steadied my trembling hands, and continued asking for details, but received few answers.

Dad's face turned red, small beads of sweat began to moisten his goofy looking mustache, and his voice became less subdued. He looked me directly in the eyes and, with great indignation propelled by unrestrained anger, blurted out, "I did it . . . And she deserved it!"

CHAPTER SIXTEEN

Aftermath

"He heals the brokenhearted and binds up their wounds."
(Psalm 147:3)

Marilyn and I had pulled the truth from Dad, and we didn't like its feel. We glanced at one another and then glared in silence at him, saying nothing through mouths that were agape with shock and despair. My mouth was dry, my cheeks were red, and the muscles of my face seemed paralyzed. Emotions of all kinds gushed through my body. The greatest were anger and the deep feeling of betrayal at what Dad did and what he was doing. Not only did he have Mom killed and lied to me all these years, and finally confessed only when he was pretty sure we were on to the truth, but he was not sorry for what he had done. He actually blamed my mom, and seemed to see himself as the victim. Now he was taking me for granted, assuming he was getting out of jail within a week, and that I would support him regardless.

When my voice returned, I told Dad emphatically that I would do everything I could to keep him in jail and prevent him from being granted release on parole.

Marilyn and I stood, grabbed one another's hands, and left the room in silence, walking slowly into a different world, less than thirty minutes from the time we had arrived.

We left the jail and drove directly to the San Jose Mission Burial Park where Mom was buried—for me to make amends. Dad's confession changed my perspective and helped me see something I hadn't seen before. I could now see that for the last decade plus, I had mostly forgotten her. Since the day Dad was arrested, my focus had been on him and meeting his needs. I had treated Mom as an appendix in the drama of Dad's life. My visit to the cemetery would be an apology to Mom for allowing so much to be about him, and so little about her.

We drove deep into the cemetery, parked our car on the side of a small road, and made our way to Mom's grave, located under the shade of the big live-oak tree that Dad had planted at the time of her burial. The tree was big then, and much larger on this day. We cried at the pink, granite, dual headstone we had placed for Mom and Dad to be buried side by side, with Mom's name and "August 16, 1946–March 20, 1976" etched on one side, and Dad's name and "April 16, 1944– " on the other. I reflected on what I had learned since Mom's death, and regretted that we purchased the dual headstone for her grave. I didn't give much thought at the time as to what we would do when Dad's time arrived.

We stood silently, still holding on to one another, comforted only by the pleasant breezes of a clear mid-November day in San Antonio, and the certain notion that Mom was at peace. In my mind's eye, I told her that I loved her, confessed profusely for seeming to take her memory for granted since the time of her death, and asked for her forgiveness. A river of tears flooded our eyes, charged by the thoughts of my love for my mom, her murder, and the aftermath of sadness, anger, pain, grief, disappointment, and frustration. I had never sobbed like that, even with the announcement of the divorce, Mom' death, or Dad's arrest. When the tears finally stopped flowing, we walked back to our car and drove slowly away, silenced by the realization that we were not only the children of a murder victim, but also the son and daughter-in-law of a murderer.

I have never figured out why Dad chose to confess that he was responsible for Mom's death. His motives are not for me to judge, but I saw no evidence of love, remorse, repentance, yearning for forgiveness, or any of the other principles of the religion that he wore on his sleeves. It seems that his anger got the best of him when he figured out that we were on to him, and to Charlotte's likely involvement. Perhaps he was trying to protect her. He also probably felt free to confess finally, because he had already been charged, tried, convicted, and sentenced, and felt there was nothing else we could do about it. Perhaps deep down, he was demonstrating a feeling of remorse and a subtle cry for forgiveness. Who knows? Whatever the case, his confession opened a floodgate of emotions in me and was the beginning of a vastly different relationship with him.

———

The task of telling people—brothers, grandparents, aunts, uncles, and others—about Dad's confession was difficult, requiring us to remember those we needed to talk to, think of just the right words and, most difficult of all, relive the whole, sordid situation, time and again. All were surprised that Dad confessed. Some were not surprised that he had arranged to have Mom killed, and some could hardly believe that he had—particularly Mom's mother, who never thought Dad had her daughter killed.

The family essentially stopped writing or visiting Dad, although he continued to write us from time to time. We turned our focus from staunchly defending him to keeping him in prison by protesting his parole, mostly by sending letters to the parole board, explaining why he should be kept behind bars. Following are excerpts from the letter I wrote on May 29, 1989, protesting Dad's parole:

Dear Board Members:

Please receive this letter as my official protest of the parole of my father, James G. Buffington, Sr.

. . . My mother put up with years of verbal abuse from my father. I also remember one event when he physically abused her. He seemed to have such control over her life. My mother finally divorced my father in June of 1975 at the young age of 28. She was finally on her own without my father.

. . . Please do not release this man who so brutally had my mother murdered. He has yet to take responsibility for his crime and has not shown any remorse for ending this precious life.

. . . Dad is not welcome in our home. He is not welcome in my brothers' homes either.

. . . Please keep this protest letter in my father's file as my continuing protests of his release, for any future parole considerations.

Papa Lee changed his position as well. A local paper featured the following headline: "Killer's father making sure his son never leaves prison," quoting Papa as follows: "He's guilty and I know it. I wrote him a letter, and I told him that I'm going to see that he stays in jail."

Killer's father making sure his son never leaves prison

By BILL HENDRICKS
Express-News Staff Writer

The father of James "Big Jim" Buffington — twice convicted of having his ex-wife murdered to collect $300,000 in life insurance — has vowed to see that his son never leaves prison.

"He's guilty, and I know it," Norris L. Buffington, 71, said of his son last week in a telephone interview from his home in Waldport, Ore.

"I wrote him a letter and I told him that I'm going to see that he stays in jail," he said, adding that he believes his son might harm someone else if he goes free.

The elder Buffington said he plans to visit San Antonio later in the year and meet with 166th District Judge Peter Michael Curry.

Curry presided at the second Buffington capital murder trial 15 months ago, and Buffington's father said he wants the judge to use his influence to prevent the son from being paroled.

Parole bid rejected

The Texas Board of Pardons and Paroles rejected Buffington's parole bid last December, a board spokeswoman said. He has been scheduled for parole consideration again in January 1993.

Buffington, 45, was convicted and received a life sentence in connection with the March 20, 1976, shooting death of Chere Buffington.

He was first convicted in 1978 and received a death sentence, but the conviction was overturned by the Texas Court of Criminal Appeals.

Bexar County prosecutors convinced two juries that Buffington, a fence contractor, hired two of his employees to kill his 29-year-old ex-wife.

Prosecutors not only convinced jurors at the first trial, they per-

James Buffington was twice convicted of having his ex-wife killed to collect life insurance.

suaded the defendant's father as well.

Norris Buffington said he believed his son was innocent until he sat through the first trial.

Soon after his son was arrested, he said, he asked him if he were guilty.

"No, dad, I didn't have anything to do with it,' " he quoted his son as saying.

"That first trial, the defense didn't call anybody," the father recalled last week. "And, shoot, they gave him the death penalty.

"I still can't understand. If he was so innocent, why didn't the defense put something up? They didn't."

Charles County, now 41, a foreman at Jim's Fence Co. in 1976, was convicted of shooting Chere Buffington in the face and leaving

her body wedged between the seats of her car.

He received a death sentence at his 1985 trial but has appealed the verdict.

The other Buffington employee, Charles Moore, was allowed to plead guilty to a murder charge and testified against County and Buffington.

Moore served part of a 17-year sentence, but was later convicted of armed robbery and sentenced to life in prison.

The elder Buffington said the slaying and trial testimony, portraying his oldest son as a liar who coolly planned the murder, have never left his mind.

The father said he was living in Arkansas when Chere Buffington was slain.

He recalled that shortly before the murder, his son called him from San Antonio and plans were made for the two of them and other family members to spend a day at the horserace track in Hot Springs, Ark.

Used dad for alibi

Chere Buffington was murdered on the day that Norris Buffington, his son and the others were at the racetrack, trial testimony showed.

"He used me for an alibi," the father said. "I still don't know how he could sit there at the races — knowing."

Buffington, who weighed almost 300 pounds when he was arrested in 1976, and his ex-wife had three sons, aged 10 to 13 at the time.

Trial testimony showed Buffington had attempted to buy insurance on his sons' lives, too.

Norris Buffington said he believed his son might have been planning to kill the children.

"I got no use for him," the father said. "I'll fight him as long as I live."

San Antonio Express-News, February 1989

154

On June 26, Papa Lee wrote Dad as follows:

I am not going to write you again or talk to you on the phone until you write the boys and apologize for running their mother down. Until you tell them the truth. I will never help you with any money or anything. I still can't believe that you would do your sons that way.

The following day he wrote to Marilyn and me:

I want you all to know how sorry I am about the two letters you got from your dad. He still has revenge in his heart, for your mother divorcing him. I never thought your dad would stoop that low. He has cooked his goose with me. I wrote him a letter last night and told him I would never write him or talk to him on the phone until he apologizes to you and Marilyn, Louis, Gina & Oscar and tell you the truth about the death of your mother and running your mother down. Your mother was a good mother, and all those things he says will come to haunt him. I had believed for a long time your dad was Guilty, for he was the only one who benefited by her death.

    Jimmy I know your mother is in Heaven, and if your Dad don't change his way, He sure won't get to heaven. I'm sorry, but I've lost respect for your dad.

Dad's trial received a lot of media attention, and my brothers and I were exposed to much that was not kind to us. Many members of the media remarked that when I testified for my dad, I betrayed my mom. Marilyn and I had dealt with the media enough that we weren't greatly affected, but they were a real problem to my brothers and other family members, who had not been exposed to them as we had been.

    We eventually reached out to several reporters, and told them my dad had confessed to the crime and did not seem sorry or remorseful at all. We asked them to ask the people of San Antonio to protest his parole. Support for Dad evaporated like sporadic raindrops on a San Antonio summer day. In December 1988, his parole was denied, and was not scheduled for reconsideration until December 1993.

Dad's attorneys appealed the conviction, alleging that six generally technical errors had occurred in the second trial, and that the results should be overturned. The court overruled the first five allegations. It agreed with the sixth point of error, that the trial court erred in assessing a fine of $10,000, on the grounds that the applicable sentencing statute at that time did not allow the imposition of a fine. It reformed the judgment to omit the portion of the punishment assessing the fine but left Dad with a sentence of life in prison.

In January 1989, he was returned to the Ellis Unit of the Texas Department of Corrections, but this time not on death row. On death row, he had been isolated in a single cell, generally protected from the sexual assaults, stabbings, and other mayhem of the general population of criminals. Now he was "fair game," and it was hard for me to sympathize with him.

Over the years, Marilyn and I each changed our attitudes about not having children. Our new preference evidenced himself at 9:00 p.m., April 19, 1990, in Fort Worth Harris Methodist Hospital, when Bryce Thomas Buffington dropped in on our lives. I had the fantastic experience of being present for his birth. I was overwhelmed with pride and cried big tears— tears of joy, this time. Being present for Bryce's birth was an experience I will never forget. Marilyn's parents and twin sister, Carolyn, drove in the next day; and my brothers and sister-in-law, Gina, visited their new nephew. It was a great family affair, overshadowed only by the absence of my parents. As had been the case on so many special occasions, my tears of joy were diluted by the fact that my son would never know my mom, and probably not my dad.

Holding Bryce in my arms, looking into his face, and thinking of the miracle of his birth also triggered some not-so-good thoughts and emotions. *When I was born, had my dad felt the pride and joy that I was now experiencing? When Oscar was born? And when Louis was born? How could he not have had similar feelings? How could he have hired two killers to murder the three of us, as the evidence suggested he had done?*

Bryce's birth meant that I now had the opportunity and the choice to become the exact opposite of the dad I had experienced. Dad was an anti-role model: someone whose footsteps you never want to follow. I didn't want to be anything like my dad. I hated much of his behavior and feared him because of some of it, but I also loved him.

I suppose that in their purest sense, love and fear cannot coexist, and they repel each other, much like water and oil. However, in life they both often do exist between two people, which was the case in my relationship with my dad. He once held me, as I held Bryce. I loved him and stood by him through thick and thin, through his drinking and philandering, his trials and incarceration. I had also feared him. If we boys did anything that he considered bad, even minor stuff, he had pulled out his big, black belt, made us bend over, and whipped us hard. We thought the lickings, the crying, and the screaming were a normal part of family life. Loving my dad despite my fear of him also seemed oddly normal.

All this has made me want to be the best father I could possibly be. I wanted Bryce to know that he is loved, and that I will always be there for him, and I will earn his respect rather than demand compliance through fear. I want him to have a different perception of what a father is, and to love me and respect me for who I am, rather than fear me.

From the beginning, part of my strategy was to be sure Bryce would never know his grandfather—which meant doing what I could to keep Dad behind bars.

Marilyn and I each wrote letters in June 1992 protesting Dad's parole. Each of them commented on the seriousness of his crime and Dad's lack of remorse. I also wrote:

> I learned from a good friend of my mother's that my father verbally, mentally, sexually, and physically abused my mother for years. My mother finally gained the courage to leave my father via divorce in June 1975. In the time after June 1975 until her death on March 20, 1976, my father verbally threatened her, stalked her, had her constantly followed by an employee of his who has been convicted of her murder, and had her fearing for her life. My mother feared going to the police because of knowing this would enrage my father even more. In the weeks prior to her murder my mother expressed to her friend that she knew my father was going to kill her. It was only a matter of time.
>
> . . . Frankly, I am scared to death of my father! Please, please do not release my father on parole!

But he was still my dad, and I still wanted to understand the "enigma wrapped in a cocoon of contradictions." I wanted to know how Dad had gone from a happily married man, a leader in church, and the father of three good boys, to a killer who seemed to have no remorse.

Perhaps it had to do with the company he kept.

CHAPTER SEVENTEEN

Letters from Jail and Prison
1988–1992

"Do not be misled: Bad company corrupts good character."
(1 Corinthians 15:33)

LETTERS FROM BEXAR COUNTY JAIL

November 3, 1988. I love you both very much. My #1 son "works" the hallway as his wife faithfully takes notes and is always good for a smile each time I turn around.

November 10, 1988. The case went to the jury 24 hours ago. Your faithful support is one of the factors helping one or more jurors to hold court.

November 1988 [*After conviction*]. My suggestion is for you to write the many questions you have to me. I will answer them all. Your mother was very special to me—I never believed the divorce would be final. Could not adjust and the drinking began. I was loved a lot by Mom but she hurt me terribly . . .

1988, Thanksgiving week. [*Letter from county jail after sentenced to return to prison in the general population.*] Dear James Jr., Marilyn, Oscar, Louis & Gina,

All my sons and daughters deserve some explanation from me; not only to help you understand the past, but to allow our family to move ahead. . . . This is not a letter of "defense," although I have taken abuse on several matters because of my silence—which now I believe additional information needs to come to your attention.

First, you must understand that I loved your mother very much and never recovered from the anger & pain caused when she told you boys Mom & I were going to separate and you guys were crying in the car on our return from Arkansas, Thanksgiving of 1974.

After her death I could not adjust to life without Mom—I went into times of deep depression and determined suicide was the only answer with you boys living with Linda Kay. That is the reason for the excessive insurance on you boys taken out after Mom's death... I was pushing Linda Kay to move up marriage date—I was determined to kill myself in a car accident... Regarding the money I received, again you must remember I was on a suicide plan with excessive insurance coverage on myself. I even practiced going 120 miles an hour on (*Highway Loop*) 1604 so when the time came I could know the Ford LTD could go fast enough to hit a concrete pillar to give me instant death & look like an accident and not a suicide...

The love Charlotte Jacobs & I shared (She loved you boys too) created guilt I could not handle following Mom's death. My whole sense of values went upside-down & reached a point I would take Charlotte to Linda Kay's house & use her bedroom.

... After the divorce, I started drinking & going out with Charles County. He was so loyal to me & you boys. I became known in the Black community & went out with Black women.

When sober, Charles would remind me of my complaints about Mom. Charles stated once in a newspaper article he did not kill Mom but that I have solicited him. I don't know, but I could have when drinking. What I do know, on the Saturday morning of Mom's death, Mom called me in Little Rock: she did want you boys for the day—but also told me Charles wanted to see her that day. I told her "TO STAY AWAY FROM CHARLES." I became alert when she told me & made her promise to not see Charles until I returned from Arkansas. My "ego" then believed that when James Buffington said something, it was God speaking.

Charles was crazy when drinking. Once in Austin we needed money—we had been drinking—I fell off asleep & next thing I know, Charles is yelling to drive off. He had robbed an ice house. But later I shared the money so I am guilty of robbery.

What did scare me is on the Monday following Mom's death, Charles brought Idell County to our house. As Charles and I were getting into the truck he gave me a slap on the hand. Was it the slap of a friend or the slap on an accomplice?—I do not know . . .

I believe Charles County knows exactly what happened. Moore & Savere I am convinced killed Mom but Charles would have been there unable to stop it . . .

When I came to jail, God was someone I would call on, but only if I could not handle things. I became a Christian in April of 1953. But Jesus was not lord of my life. Only until I was in my second year on death row, did I let Jesus become Lord in my life & I began to live a Christ centered life. I turned everything over to the Lord, and events began to change for the better . . .

I finally began what is known as "hard time" in prison. I prayed & prayed and still no peace of mind. In the quiet of my cell, I was led to hold a rosary and felt peace & began to pray to the blessed mother. I finally had "peace" and "completeness" to my faith . . .

In December of 1985 I made the decision to enter the Catholic Church.

Jim does not view many aspects of the "Letter dated '1988—Thanksgiving week'" as credible. He sees many aspects of it as evidence that his dad refused to take accountability for his actions, tried to justify them, and often blamed his behavior on Chere and others. The insurance on the boys was taken out before Chere's death, not after as his dad claims, and it was only payable if the boys died. The claim of excessive insurance on himself was a lie. He never insured his own life. Jim never heard any other reference to suicide or his dad killing himself, and believes the reference here is just another way of his dad trying to manipulate and avoid responsibility.

December 7, 1988. Good phone call with Carolyn Thurman this morning about my joining the Catholic Church.

LETTERS FROM PRISON, TEXAS DEPARTMENT OF CORRECTIONS

Christmas Night 1988. Merry Christmas. I left on my bus ride Friday morning at 10:16 a.m., and arrived @ 2:30 p.m.

I will not have a TDC number assigned to me until Tuesday.

On my bus ride I saw so many new things, some of which I could not identify.

New Year's Day 1989. It is a strange New Year's weekend without a TV or radio for football games nor a newspaper to read.

This will be an exciting year as we apply for furlough and for a parole.

January 9, 1989. I do have "faith" but feel at times I am being swallowed deeper and deeper into the TDC system.

January 18, 1989, Tuesday (1/17/89). I went before the Classification Committee here and was assigned to the Ellis I unit—but praise God it is general population and NOT death row.

February 3, 1989. I was transferred to the Ellis Unit yesterday.

February 4, 1989. I arrived Thursday 2/2/89 and was classified "minimum security"—it was pointed out to the Assistant Warden that I had not one disciplinary report in all my 11 years plus time of incarceration.

Friday, I went to work in the Dental Lab as a technician trainee.

June 6, 1989 (*Letter to Teresse, who conducted a religious service at Ellis I unit.*)—Louis never wants to have any type of communication with me except one final letter from me giving all the details of the death of his mother. That I will never see my grandchild. Oscar only wants to communicate by letter. James Jr. will continue all types of communication, but Oscar and James Jr. will cut off all communication with me unless they know everything. My dad wants to continue to communicate with me but never wants me to parole. All the boys have protested my parole including my Father.

At your next service here I hope we three can have a short time together in prayer so you can both place hands on me and pray for healing of my family.

June 11, 1989. So I will address this matter now.

1. On May 3rd I submitted new parole plan to Mr. Bush, the Ellis I unit parole officer; calling for me to live with Oscar.

4. On May 12th I received Oscar's first letter informing me that he had protested my parole and would protest furloughs and paroles as they came up.

—Oscar gets angry, Louis gets angry, James Jr gets angry—now written protests are sent to the board regarding my parole.

. . . —now to learn from James Jr. that the phone call to Mr. Pfeiffer was to protest my parole and all my family protested my parole.

NOTHING ANY OF YOU CAN SAY OR DO TO ME WILL EVER STOP THE LOVE IN MY HEART FOR YOU.

June 18, 1989. [*Letter to James's dad and Fran*] James Jr. said my parole was set off June 9th and next review will be January of 1993.

I love you Dad and never want any doubt in your mind and heart about this. James Jr. said that you were the first to protest my parole. I know you felt you were doing the right thing—it is not for me to judge what is right or wrong.

June 18, 1989. Genevieve? Life does have two sides to a coin. Did I act like a fool? YES!!! The other side of the coin is that right before I left the jail, over the phone, Genevieve said, "be silent and listen," and she then voiced her apology for using me while she worked in the jail. To me we used each other. At the time I was not aware of family financial problems and you know that. I did the right thing and introduced her to Andy and he also fell in love and they were married 5 months later. My mistakes and misjudgments with Genevieve does not make me Attila the Hun.

My world has been turned upside down for less than 5 weeks since I received Oscar's letter May the 12th

June 2, 1989. [*Letter to Msgr. Hennessy and Maria*] But let me be clear—my anger and my anger alone begin the plot against Mom . . . Mom is dead—without my anger Mom would be alive. So it is not an injustice that I have been incarcerated for such a length.

August 1989. [*Letter to Sister Frances Briseno.*] This is an emotional period of my life—I am like a man in the desert that knows only one reality—FIND WATER TO DRINK. My reality is a comparable lead in my life to continue on—SHARE THE TRUTH WITH SISTER FRANCES!!!!

There was a vague plot to kill Mom, Msgr Hennessy said because I recanted—got out of the plot with change of mind and heart, that in the eyes of God, the Church, and in man's laws that I'm innocent. Yet, after Mom's death I remained silent—took the money ($398,000.00) and in my heart, I do not feel innocent—I FEEL GUILTY!!!!!

. . . Celibacy is a daily challenge for me. Genevieve still haunts me at night—then at times I cannot deal with your attractiveness—I get up, get your picture out, and think positive thoughts of being in that picture with you . . .

March 15, 1990. [*Letter to his father*] You have "free will" and are entitled to your opinions to anyone. I didn't know we were fighting each other.

Whatever your attitude towards me may be, I still love you and able to forgive you for suggesting I would even harm my children.

June 11, 1990. I still maintain an active schedule with my job in the education department, college, Law library, church activities with the Sunday afternoon hour of prayer and Bible study I lead; plus my in-cell piddling artwork.

November 11, 1992. [*Letter to Ginny Dial, attorney and friend*] First I answered the Chapel telephone yesterday and heard: "HELLO DAD ! ! !" It was James Junior and he will be here this Saturday for a visit. . . . It has been November/December '88 since I last saw one of my sons.

CHAPTER EIGHTEEN

Meeting With a Killer

"He reveals the deep things of darkness and brings
utter darkness into the light." (Job 12:22)

I knew Charles County before Mom's murder. Before she and Dad divorced, when we were living in the Allena Baptist Church parsonage, he worked for Dad at Cliff's Fence Company, and he later worked at Jim's Fence Company as well. Charles did much of the actual fence building and drove to job sites in one of Dad's light-blue work trucks with "Jim's Fence Company" posted on the side. From time to time, I saw him at Dad's office, and he came to the house occasionally on business-related chores.

County faced trial four times for the murder of my mom. I did not attend the first trial, in 1979, as I was only sixteen years old and not allowed to attend. He was convicted of capital murder and sentenced to death. Evidence suggested he was the triggerman in the crime.

The 1979 conviction was reversed by the Texas Court of Criminal Appeals, based on evidence of prosecutorial misconduct arising when the DA reneged on his promise that if County would cooperate with the prosecution, he would not get the death penalty; and the DA's alteration of the transcript of Moore's original confession. This reversal led to a second trial where County's life was in jeopardy once again.

In May 1985, just after I graduated from college and roughly nine years after Mom was murdered, Charles County was retried, in Brownsville, Texas, on a change of venue. I drove 565 miles through lush pine forest, grassland prairies, and semi-desert scrub, across the entire eastern part of Texas, from Arkansas to Brownsville, to attend that second trial. Several friends and relatives were there testifying for the state, including my uncle, Herman, and Dad's second wife, Linda Morrey, who I had dinner with on a couple of occasions during the trial.

I stayed in the local Holiday Inn. At the end of one day early in the trial, I returned to my hotel room to find the door open, which was odd, because I was always sure to check that the door was locked when I left my room. I entered, somewhat hesitantly, and was hit in the gut by this eerie feeling that something wasn't quite right. I looked around, and things seemed slightly amiss, as though airport security had inspected my bags and done a sloppy job of putting things back in place. I couldn't explain what I was perceiving. Nothing came of the incident, but it seemed to be the first of several mysteries that surfaced during the trial.

County's retrial was largely a repeat of his first one, with most of the same characters performing. It answered some of my questions, but created almost as many new ones. Perhaps the most significant new questions came to mind when I learned that County and Moore had company when they went to Mom's apartment, looking for her on the day she was murdered.

County's father-in-law, Buck, apparently drove the truck to her place, and David Savere and a man named Buddy Savoy were along for the ride, in addition to County and Moore. I don't know what the group's intent was, or even if it had an intent. However, my mind could not rid itself of the image of five men leaving a drinking session in a pickup truck and driving from a predominantly Black community to a White section of town, looking for a White woman, and going into her apartment. Could they not have planned to harm that attractive White woman? I was convinced more than ever that we didn't know who all was involved in killing my mom.

County was convicted, for the second time, of capital murder, and was returned to death row.

Page 8-A SAN ANTONIO EXPRESS— Thur...

COUNTY GUILTY

County found guilty

Continued from Page 1A

emotion as the verdict was announced. Butts asked that the jurors be polled individually and Palmquist began calling off their names and asking them if that was their verdict. Each juror's response "Yes," came

dignity as possible — stripped down naked in the back seat of a car," Burris said.

Comparison

Burris compared Moore's emotional, and sometimes admittedly lying, testimony versus County's firm, rather

The state called 32 witnesses in the trial which recorded eight days of testimony. Late Wednesday evening, Butts issued a written statement which claimed County had been double-crossed by the district attorney's office. Butts contended County had cooperated with the district attorney in

By ALAN BAILEY
Of the Express Staff

BROWNSVILLE woman, nine-ma Charles County murder Wednes contract execut Buffington. The jury deliber minutes before retu verdict at the Came Justice as the m came to a quick clin Thursday mornin will begin hearing

County's sentence to be decided

SPECIAL TO THE NEWS
BROWNSVILLE — The jury will hear testimony

three individuals indicted for the murder of Mrs. Buffington, a 29-tear-old

backseat of her car.

Mrs. Buffington's nude body was found March 20,

parking lot of Longfellow Junior High School in Northwest San Antonio.

or given a reduced sentence in exchange for his testimony.

rtroom Wednesday ng Judge Preston Dial an Richard Hinojosa, tched a unanimous

ve," replied Hinojosa, verdict to Dial. The ad the verdict and im Palmquist, to read his court-appointed for Butts, stood up in the l.

find the defendant

DEATH FOR COUNTY

County gets death

Continued from Pag

last January, by a jury in Ta County. A third individual, Charles M accused of being an accomplice triggerman, County, is schedul stand trial for capital murder month in Bexar County. As the jury's decision was read courtroom at the Cameron Count of Justice, County stood with his appointed attorney Charles Butts. Both County, with his hands him, and Butts, with his arms stared at the floor as court cler Palmquist read the decisio as if he expected to hear the emotion was visible and County sentence in light of Wednesday's — 13 minutes — deliberatio reaching the guilty verdict. Butts had the jurors individually. And each juror resp with a firm "Yes" to the v

By ALAN BAILEY
Of the Express Staff

BROWNSVILLE — Charles County must die for the 1976 contract killing of Chere Buffington, a jury of nine men and three women decided Thursday. Jurors returned their verdict at 5:40 p.m. after deliberating less than 15 minutes in deciding whether County should die by injection or spend the rest of his life in prison. The same jurors Wednesday had found County, 30, guilty of capital murder in killing Mrs. Buffington, a 29-

asked him if he was "a killer shrink," entified so in a magazine article. Grigson said he was the subject of iat article, and he had testified in ime 50 cases involving almost 100 eople on Texas' Death Row, but he id, "I didn't put them on Death Row. hey put themselves there because iey killed one or more people."

Psychiatrist

The psychiatrist, who received his iformation about County from the San ntonio Police Department and had not ctually interviewed County, said the ict County was laughing while he fired iree shots into Mrs. Buffington's face, nd the fact he killed her while she was egging for her life, made County an xtremely dangerous sociopath. Butts did not call any witnesses to estify on County's behalf or on his good haracter. In his closing plea for the death enalty, Burris asked the jurors, "Have

San Antonio Express-News and San Antonio Light, June 1979

County's second conviction was reversed on appeal after his attorneys maintained that the trial of James Buffington produced new evidence that entitled County to yet another trial. His third trial was held in San Antonio in June 1992, sixteen years after the crime, and roughly four years after Dad confessed to his role in it. Oscar, Louis, and I all attended and usually sat on a bench with Charles' two sisters, behind the defendants' table where their brother was seated. We had become acquainted with his sisters in the second trial and felt comfortable sitting together.

However, some members of the prosecution team bombed us with looks like daggers and snarky comments laced with sarcasm. They felt that the White sons of the murder victim keeping company with the family of the alleged Black killer made an erroneous statement about our belief as to his guilt and whose side we were on, which could bias the jury in favor of acquittal. Nothing could have been further from the truth. We were being nice to them because they had been nice to us.

The State's chief witness at this trial was David Savere, then a truck driver, who told the jury, among other things, that County had tried to recruit him to help murder my mom. Savere also testified that he overheard a conversation between Dad and County where Dad told Charles he wanted his wife or one of his kids killed. Which one didn't matter, as they were all covered by insurance, but he preferred his wife be the one.

On June 16, I wrote a letter to the judge requesting "the maximum penalty of life in prison for the man who brutally murdered my mother." A few days later, the jury convicted County of murder and sentenced him to life in prison, ruling that he could not be convicted of capital murder because of prosecutorial misconduct early in the investigation. He was the last of the three defendants to be found guilty of killing Mom. After the trial, Oscar spoke for all of us when he told the *San Antonio Express-News*, "Obviously we're pleased." I told the press, "The persons involved in this murder are now serving jail time. The family has and will continue to protest the release of James Buffington Sr., Charlie Moore, and Charles County. We really want the people of San Antonio to know we will protest any effort by our father to gain parole."

⎯⎯⎯

After the last day of the trial, one of County's sisters approached me and said, "Jim, we know you have a lot of questions remaining about what happened to your mom. You've been so nice to us, so we've spoken to Charles, and he is willing to meet with you, if you would like to meet with him. He might be able to answer some of your questions."

I'm not sure why Charles and his family made that offer. The trial was over, he had been convicted of murder rather than capital murder, and he was eligible for parole, so he had little or nothing to gain—or to lose, for that matter—by talking to me. Perhaps it was a sign of remorse or a form of symbolic restitution. Or maybe just an indication that almost no one is all bad.

I wanted to know the truth about what had happened to my mom, and I had been talking to witnesses and asking questions. I assumed County would lie if it were in his best interest, but thought he might divulge some information that would fill in a few of the blank spaces in my understanding of what had happened. I quickly accepted the sister's offer to visit with her brother.

One local reporter had followed the case closely, had been good to me, and had written several very fair articles. County, his attorney, Charles Butts, and I agreed to allow him to attend our meeting with no strings attached. He could write and publish whatever he wanted.

Butts, the reporter, and I met County in the attorney visitation room in the Bexar County Jail. The three of us sat in a small visitation booth with Charles seated behind a perforated glass shield through which we could talk, but not touch. I struggled to hold myself together, to control my breathing so I could talk normally, to conceal my hands so Charles couldn't see the slight shaking, to steady myself so he couldn't see my reaction to whatever he might say.

After very brief greetings, I "lectured" County about the impact of Mom's murder, how it hurt so many people in so many ways, and that there was no doubt in my mind that he was involved. I advised him that I had been protesting Dad's and Charlie Moore's parole, and would protest his when the time came. Then I referred to my yellow legal pad and started down a long list of questions.

In response to an early question, County said, "Your dad was a good friend. He approached me about hiring someone to kill your Mom, which he had been planning since their divorce. He did not care how she was killed. At first, I said I didn't want any part of it. But your dad kept insisting. It was not about the insurance money. He was upset because he believed she had an affair with their pastor. And he was really upset that she was planning to marry another man. He said he would rather have her dead with 'Buffington' on her tombstone, than alive with someone else's name. He was very controlling and was angry at your mom."

Although I had been aware that there was probably an emotional relationship between Mom and her pastor, this was the first time I heard that Dad killed her because he believed she had an affair, or that he didn't want her to remarry. County's claim surprised me and presented more questions to ponder.

Charles said that on the day Mom was killed, she picked up him and Charlie Moore in her car. They collected some paychecks, and then she drove to a convenience store for Moore to cash his. After explaining a few more details, County continued, "I want you to know that I didn't kill your mother. The last time I saw her alive was the day she drove off with Charlie Moore in her car to cash his check. Your mom was a very nice lady, and I knew you were a nice family. I don't know who killed her."

I asked County if the plan included killing my brothers and me. He refused to answer that question but didn't deny that we were a target of the scheme.

After hearing all he had to say, I took a deep breath and responded, "Charles you had some choices. Why didn't you just go to the police and tell them my dad was trying to kill my mom?"

"Jim, I should have. But remember, I was a poor Black man. Your dad was a rich White guy. Who would the police have believed? Me or your dad? I see that I made a mistake. I wish I had done what you said."

Charles County

172

San Antonio Express-News and San Antonio Light, 1992, 1995

My meeting with County was amicable and lasted almost two hours. When it ended, I really didn't know what to believe. County had no need to lie, but neither did he need to tell the truth. I gave him the benefit of the doubt, and assumed he intended to tell the truth and had told his perception of reality. However, I didn't accept that his version of reality was always accurate, and that he was always relating events as they actually happened. I believed his claim that my dad hired him to kill my mom. However, contrary to what he said, I concluded that he was in the car when she was killed. His blue pickup truck was at the murder scene, and several witnesses said he and Moore left that bar together. I remained uncertain who actually pulled the trigger to kill Mom. That was a continuing mystery.

In the criminal justice system, to quote Yogi Berra, "it ain't over till it's over." The decision from County's third trial was reversed because of irregularities in the case, and a fourth trial was scheduled for December of 1994. I was there for the proceedings, but shortly after they began, the DA and County's lawyer negotiated a plea agreement that brought the trial to a halt. Assistant District Attorney Bill Harris seemed reluctant, defensive, but also compassionate when he told me what happened. Facing a fourth trial, the parties agreed that if County pled guilty to murder, he would be sentenced to forty years behind bars. However, he had served enough time (including good time credit) to require the judge to immediately grant him a full release, not just parole. The DA said he did not have a choice. Not appreciating the apparently subtle nuances of issues such as "required" compared to "discretion," "time" and "good time," and judge or parole board, I was not comfortable with his explanation then, and it escapes me now. But I couldn't do anything about it.

County was convicted of murdering my mother, but after approximately eighteen years behind bars, he would be walking out of prison, a free man. My brothers and I felt a mix of negative emotions: resentment,

174

anger, disappointment, and outrage, to name a few. I believed all those who were convicted—Dad, Charlie Moore, and Charles County—deserved the death penalty. That was the law, the death penalty for capital murder, and they deserved the full measure of the law. But it was the jury's decision, and not mine. In the end, I was glad I didn't have to experience an execution.

I certainly thought that at a minimum, County should have been sentenced to life without parole and required to die in prison. However, he served his legally mandated sentence and was released according to the law. I kept up with him through his attorney, Charles Butts, for many years. I understand that he married, got a job working for Sears in their tire department, and at last count was a contributing member of society, who had not been arrested since his release in 1995. Knowing this has helped me, as a victim, to heal and to recognize two sides of the death penalty debate.

CHAPTER NINETEEN

Repentance

"Though you have made me see troubles, many and bitter, you will restore my life again; from the depths of the earth you will again bring me up. You will increase my honor and comfort me once more." (Psalm 71:20-21)

Merriam-Webster defines repentance as "to turn from sin and dedicate oneself to the amendment of one's life." Repentance involves much more than a change of mind or behavior or feeling sorry for one's actions. It is more than a jailhouse conversion or temporary change until the tumult dies down. True repentance is a transformation in which a person's fundamental character and being, not just their surface behavior, become permanently different. Repentance is the process by which humans leave their sins and bad behavior behind, and radically and deliberately change their hearts and attitudes as well as their actions.

It seems that James Buffington became a different person during his return assignment to the Ellis Unit, starting in 1989. Whether his change was a jailhouse conversion or true repentance was between him and God. Jim and other family members were estranged during the first four years of this period, and had no contact with James. However, his relationships with Chaplain Richard Lopez and Ken Rawlins, a cellmate, suggest that over time he experienced a real transformation. Jim felt that he confirmed the change after they reconnected a few years later. Each of the three has described the change.

CHAPLAIN RICHARD LOPEZ

Richard Lopez was a chaplain at the Ellis prison unit during the time James was incarcerated there. Lopez later became the chaplain on death row, where he ministered to inmates in their last hours before their executions, and ulti-mately became head chaplain for the Texas prison system. After he retired from TDCJ, he worked for the Bridges To Life prison ministry.

My dad was born in Spain, immigrated to Mexico, then crossed the border to the valley town of Robstown, Texas, where he met my mother. After they married, my parents moved to Missouri City, a southern sub-urb of Houston, and became tenant farmers, growing cotton, corn, and vegetables of various sorts. Mom passed away when I was two-and-a-half years old. She was buried in Richmond, in the Brazos River bottom about twenty miles to the east.

Once a month, on Sunday after church, Dad drove us to the ceme-tery to visit her grave. We passed through Sugar Land and saw the Cen-tral prison and its men in white working in the fields seven days a week, with men carrying rifles on horses watching their every move. Dad ex-plained that they were men who had done bad things, were caught, and locked up.

When I was a young man, I began accompanying a church deacon who conducted a ministry at the Central prison. Inmates frequently shared their stories with me: so often stories of their fathers leaving them when they were very young, their mothers working two jobs to support them, and their connecting with the wrong kind of people.

These men's stories were the beginning of God calling me to prison ministry. In 1983, I started volunteering in penitentiaries on a regular basis. These experiences convinced me to minister to inmates as a con-tinuing part of my life. Prison chaplains are required to be ordained in their chosen religious tradition. Therefore I spent five years in seminary to become an ordained Catholic deacon. In June 1990, I was hired as one of three chaplains at the Ellis Unit.

The traditional role of chaplains in prisons has been to provide in-mates the opportunity to connect with God, teach them the Bible, and help them change their hearts and minds. Over time, as prisons got larg-er, the chaplain's role became more administrative, and much of the teaching and personal ministry was assumed by volunteers. The administrative part of the role continued to grow, and inmate clerks began to handle many of the administrative duties.

—

I was the Catholic chaplain, but also conducted worship services for different denominations. One day an inmate came into my office after a service and said, "Chaplain, I really enjoyed your sermon today. It was a good one with a real message. I haven't been coming to church, and would like to start attending the Catholic service if you're okay with that."

I responded, "Absolutely. The chapel is big, and there's room for men from various religions. You are absolutely welcome to come."

James Buffington began attending our Catholic services. At first, he sat on the back row, but, week by week, little by little, he began moving forward until he sat regularly on the front row. We visited briefly after most services. One day he said, "I really enjoyed the service today, but the choir wasn't very good. I was a choir director in the free world. Worked at several churches and at one time was director of the Houston Junior Symphony Orchestra. I have experience in singing and dealing with people who sing. I'd like to try to improve your choir's performance."

I answered, "We have choir practice on Wednesdays in the chapel. I'd like for you to come next Wednesday."

I explained the situation to the choir members, suggesting that we give James a shot at reorganizing and improving our choir. All agreed, and James became our new choir director.

Twenty-four vocalists were in the choir, plus a drummer and two guitarists. James melded the twenty-four voices, who sounded like a herd of bellowing cows missing their calves, into a harmonious team. He organized the men, placing them where they needed to be. He improved their posture and had them sing to the audience rather than to their songbooks. He made other changes as well, and soon they sounded stronger and better, as the real choir they were meant to be.

Bishop Fiorenza, of the Diocese of Galveston-Houston, came to the unit one Sunday and conducted Mass. The chapel was full—he was the Bishop. The choir sang several songs and responded at different parts of the Mass. After he had given his sermon and was into the Liturgy of the Eucharist, he stopped. The Bishop didn't say a word for an uncomfortable period of time, then looked at the choir and said, "I want you to know you are dynamic. I wish most church choirs were that good."

We went to my office after the Mass was completed. I invited James to join us and introduced him to the Bishop, with words to the effect of what a wonderful job he had done in preparing the choir to perform as it had that day.

The Bishop complimented James again and said, "The chaplain told me you're not Catholic."

James answered, "No, but maybe one day I will be."

James continued to direct the choir and became more involved in the chapel and the prison's religious activities. He was so effective and efficient that he became my clerk, and then clerk for all three chaplains, doing much of our administrative work. He was so well-organized that he improved many of the things we did in the office. James developed a library of Christian books and arranged for inmates to build wooden shelves to display them.

One day James came to my office and closed the door. After a few minutes just talking about nothing, he said, "Chaplain, there are some things I want to share with you."

"Okay. Whatever you share with me will stay right here. I will not speak of it to other inmates or anyone."

James then unloaded a lot of garbage that he had accumulated over a long period of time. There is a lot I don't understand about concepts such as confession, and its relationship to repentance, forgiveness, and redemption. But I suspect that he was on to something that day.

James was estranged from his father and his sons and wanted badly to reconcile with them. I encouraged him to write to them, apologize, and ask for their forgiveness. He did, but his father and sons Oscar and Louis did not respond. However, Jim began to write him an occasional letter. On a few occasions, they talked on the phone in my office, with me listening in—according to protocol—but I didn't actually meet Jim until sometime later.

I sponsored various meetings and conferences where I invited people to visit the inmates and enjoy choir performances that James was leading. They were always impressed. But James was a raving paradox. On one hand, he hired men to kill his ex-wife. He wanted to be the boss and have his way. He felt he knew everything. As they say, he "considered himself the smartest man in the room," and he came across as an arrogant know-it-all.

On the other hand, he was very gifted in so many ways. He was smart and knowledgeable. He knew what was going on in the prison, about the different gangs, about the religious and training programs, how to do things and get things done. Through our work together we developed a close, God-centered relationship, and he usually had his good side on display. This gained him a lot of respect, from inmates and prison staff. The good side of James was the side I came to know.

KEN RAWLINS, PRISON CELLMATE

Ken Rawlins grew up in Burleson, Texas. He graduated high school, got married at age twenty-six, had a daughter, divorced, and got hooked on using and selling drugs. He first went to prison on a drug charge in 1988, and passed through the revolving doors several times until he was released for the last time in June 2007. He settled down,

*got a lawful job repairing and maintaining digital equipment, and be-
came a volunteer in the Bridges To Life prison ministry. He was James
Buffington's cellmate during the summer and fall of 1992.*

The Ellis Unit was a maximum-security prison. James was there for
murder, and just about everybody else on our row was there for murder,
armed robbery, or some other violent crime. Most were facing very long
or life sentences. I was there on a seven-year sentence for possession of
a controlled substance. I served about a year of that time before I was
released.

When assigning prison cellmates ("cellies"), prison administrators
go through a process of interviews to determine your desires and needs,
and then they assign you to the first available cell. They assigned me to a
cell with James. It was a five-by-nine-foot "box" with bunk beds on one
side and a little stainless steel combination commode/sink in the corner.
That was it. I had the top bunk. There was no air conditioning and little
air circulation. It got hotter than a two-dollar pistol during the South
Texas summer.

When I arrived at my new home, I didn't know who my cellie would
be, and he was not in the cell. I thought he would probably be a Hispanic
guy because of all the Catholic stuff I had observed, such as Bible verses,
pictures of the Virgin Mary, crosses, rosaries, etc., lying around the cell.
I thought, *Oh boy, when this guy comes home from work, there's going to be a
circus in here. If he talks to me about Jesus, we're leaving the room.*

James wasn't the guy I expected. When he came home from work and
walked in the door, I let him talk first. I thought again, *If he says anything
to me about Jesus, I'm going to start throwing his stuff out the door because
I just don't want any of that.*

But he didn't. I really think the Lord put us together because I was
so opposite of him. I think James just sized me up when he walked in the
door. He said he was gone most of each day, and I should make myself at
home and feel free to use his stuff, such as headphones, radios, and things.
He also told me that if he could do anything to help me to let him know.

James worked in the chapel. He got up early in the morning, went to work, and rarely returned till 7:30 or 8:00 at night. He convinced me to go to church with him a few times, which was a monumental achievement, since I didn't want to talk to anyone about Jesus. He didn't try to push the religion stuff on to me, which I really appreciated. I didn't become a Christian until 1997.

James and I were cellmates for about six months. We each felt the other was the best cellie we ever had. We got along great. It's hard to describe, but a lot of times in prison you're with people who are not the sharpest knives in the drawer, and conversation and camaraderie are difficult. James and I could carry on a decent conversation about world events or whatever, and we became friends.

James claimed that he at one time had owned the second largest Fence Company in the state of Texas. He also said that he had belonged to some kind of men's fraternity where they met every Thursday night and wore tuxedos, but his life had surely changed for the worse.

James never told me what his crime was. I knew it was murder, because I knew he had been on death row. The only thing he told me was that he had been locked up for fifteen years and had been denied parole many times. He said he had been locked up so long that if he could get out two weeks each year to visit his kids, he would be a happy man. He talked about his kids when they were young children, and about the period of time after their mother was gone, when he and the three boys would go to other people's houses for dinner, take trips, or this or that.

He never discussed his affiliation with the church, and he never mentioned his wife. The only personal stuff he talked about was his kids, who he was not in contact with at the time. I could tell he was remorseful about what he had done, because every time he faced the subject, he would just look at the floor, shake his head, grab his forehead, and say it was too painful to talk about. He always cried. I later came to understand from Jim that this was quite surprising, as he had never seen his dad cry, aside from the one time when they went to the funeral home and viewed his ex-wife in her casket.

I sensed that James was genuinely sorry for what he did, and not just sorry that he got caught and that his life turned out so badly. If he could have taken it all back, he would have done so.

James never tried to convert me to Christianity. His convincing me to go to church a few times was a really big deal, as I was a poster boy for sin back in those days. He used a soft approach. A prisoner can spot a fake a mile away. You got to be who you're going to be. If you're not talking from your heart, they'll turn and walk away. James had a lot of time to convert those guys, many who were there with life sentences. He found what he was looking for when he found the Lord. He separated himself from this other stuff—the lies, gangs, tattoos, etc. He renewed his mind every day. He felt he was going to be locked up for life; he had been turned down for parole so many times.

This is the guy I knew. I didn't know the old one—the one who was on death row for killing his wife, Jim's mom. I knew the man he became in prison, not the one who went to prison.

JIM

I cut off all communication with Dad in late 1988 and told him he would never see me again. Most of his family and friends turned their backs on him as well. I didn't write him, send him money, or visit for approximately four years. Then in 1990, Bryce was born, and I changed my mind. As I wrapped my arms around my son, I couldn't wrap my mind around the fact that my dad had once held me that way, and then tried to have me murdered. As time passed, and as Bryce grew from an innocent baby to an adorable toddler, I continued to struggle to accept the fact that my dad had my mother murdered and wanted to have my brothers and me killed as well. I asked myself who in the world could ever kill this little boy, and how my dad had regressed from a happily married man and a leader in his church, with three good kids, to a murderer who attempted to have his kids killed.

I was also bothered by the fact that I was much like my dad. We looked alike, and had a similar personality and many of the same mannerisms. I hated resembling him and having the same name as him. I worried about the possibility of a generational curse, and that I could be on track to follow in his footsteps. I had a son now, and I needed to know how my dad became a killer, so I could be sure to avoid becoming one as well.

After reflecting on the matter for some time, I decided I needed to see Dad to figure out how he had gone from who he had been to a murderer—and how I could be sure to avoid the same journey. About four years after I cut off all contact and told him he would never see me again, I wrote him a letter, a short one, simply asking for a visit and not explaining why I wanted to see him, or stating a purpose, or expressing any emotion.

Dad responded by return mail, saying how much he loved me and how much he would like a visit. We arranged to get together a couple of weeks later. I left Arlington early on the agreed day and arrived at the Ellis Unit, where I had visited him on death row, about 10:00 a.m.

I was surprised by the visiting arrangements. I assumed they would be like those on death row, where the visitors and inmates were separated by a glass or metal screen and communicated by phone. I had never experienced a real contact visit and wasn't sure how to handle things in the big, open room that allowed touching and even hugging for those so inclined.

Dad hadn't seen me in approximately four years and wanted, or perhaps expected, some hugging. When he approached, I refused to hug him and told him that I wasn't there to reconcile. Rather, after some chitchat in an effort to become reacquainted, I told him, "I need some questions answered. I need to know how you went from a happily married man and a leader in your church, with three good kids and a great wife, to a murderer. Dad, I am just like you in so many ways, and I hate it."

I was dumbfounded by his response. He looked me directly in the eyes and said, "Jim—we can talk about that, but first let me say that I'm sorry for what I did to your mom. I'm sorry for what I did to you and your brothers."

The dad I had known would never acknowledge being wrong, and always claimed to be right about everything. I had never, ever heard my dad admit a mistake, or say he was sorry for anything, or apologize for anything. The dad I knew used such situations to manipulate. He was a charismatic manipulator, a narcissist who never said he was sorry for what he did to Mom and us boys. As I was struggling to simultaneously catch my breath and think of how to respond, he continued, "Jim, I finally hit rock bottom. Didn't hear from you, or your brothers, or my dad, or friends, or anyone really in four years. I did a lot of thinking and a lot of soul searching—and even got some good advice from people like Chaplain Lopez. I finally became a Christian. I gave my life to God—for the first time. I 'played' at church all my life. It wasn't the real thing, and I had to admit it to myself and others. I was 'religious,' but I didn't have a real relationship with Christ. All of that has changed."

Over the years, I had become convinced that my dad was a pathological liar. I also had become leery of "jailhouse religion," which someone has described as "the sudden desperate piety of an inmate who's up against it and hopes that God will somehow bail him out." Even so, this time I believed Dad was different than he had been four years earlier—at least he had changed enough that I wanted to continue the discussion and learn more about how he could have done what he did.

Dad haltingly explained that his transition from his earlier life to being a murderer was a long process. He started making bad choices, such as going to happy hours, not going home, arguments when he finally got home at 2:00 a.m., drunk, having spent all their money—while Mom worked all day and came home and fixed dinner and did homework with us boys before putting us in bed.

Dad then admitted he had an affair with Charlotte Jacobs, and Mom found out and called him on it. They went to counseling. He kept drinking and carousing. He came home one morning after a night on the town, they had an argument, and he hit her and gave her a black eye. That was the end. Mom left him and filed for divorce and full custody of my brothers and me. That brave move by my mom made Dad furious. He couldn't accept her winning—and his not being in charge. He was also financially broke. Then he was at a bar drinking and talking with some other men, and made the comment, "I wish she was dead."

That comment took on a life of its own. How much would her death cost him? He could take out life insurance on her life and the life of us three boys, and be rich, free, and still single. Soon afterward he offered two men $2,000 to murder Mom, and presumably my brothers and me. It wasn't a one-time decision of betrayal. It was a culmination of a series of bad choices.

My plan from the beginning was to just meet with Dad once, but toward the end of that session, I decided I wanted to meet again to get more questions answered. I visited him once a month after that. Over the next year, I learned more about the man he seemed to have become, put myself in his shoes, and tried to understand more about the process he had explained and how it had happened. I didn't excuse or condone what he did, but the visits helped me understand his actions better. The more I understood, the better I was able to handle my feelings.

These discussions, which convinced me that people who make bad choices really can repent, and that Dad's heart had changed from that of a narcissistic murderer to a sincere Christian, were the beginning of my process of forgiving him. I first began to deal with my anger, and slowly decided I needed to forgive him in my heart and demonstrate some compassion toward him. Over time, my negative emotions begin to fade, and I told myself that I had forgiven him. I have no clear memory of telling him that I had done so, but I know that I did. Not forgiving him would have allowed him to control me, and make me more angry, very bitter, and continually depressed. I didn't want those feelings, and I didn't want him to control me by imposing them on me. I forgave him to let myself off the hook, rather than to let him off the hook. I also told him that my forgiving him did not mean I absolved him from the consequences, and

I would continue to protest his parole and otherwise hold him accountable, as I had during the last four years. He had murdered my mother and, I believed, tried to kill me. I expected him to live with the consequences.

We also discussed him forgiving himself—that God had forgiven him, I had forgiven him, and it was okay for him to accept our forgiveness as the basis for forgiving himself. My dad was an alcoholic, a cheater, a wife beater, and a murderer. He could not excuse himself for what he had done, but he could put it behind him and move on with his life.

By the end of the year, I was hugging him during our visits, and we had established a pretty healthy father-son relationship. He never admitted to trying to have my brothers and me killed—and in fact continued to deny it, even in the face of very strong circumstantial evidence to the contrary. I didn't believe him. As is common among people who have been incarcerated for a long time, he had developed his story, and he stuck with it. I think he just couldn't bring himself to admit he hired someone to kill his own kids. I was willing to quit asking him about it and see what happened next.

CHAPTER TWENTY

Redemption

"Trust in the Lord with all your heart and lean not on your own understanding; in all your ways submit to him, and he will make your paths straight." (Proverbs 3:5-6)

CHAPLAIN RICHARD LOPEZ

One cool and blustery day in early March 1994, as I was walking into the prison, I was met by a guard and told "they" wanted me in the infirmary immediately. The prison's infirmary is a rather large facility with beds, gurneys, various medical equipment, and several nurses and doctors. Its staff typically distributes medications, patches up fight victims, addresses drug problems, and tolerates its share of hypochondriacs and malingerers.

This time was different. The first person I saw when entering the infirmary was James Buffington, strapped down on a stretcher. He saw me, blinked, contorted his face, and began to mumble, but I could not understand what he was saying.

The nurse said, "They found him outside his cell on the floor. We don't know what's wrong with him. We think he has had a stroke. There is no evidence he was taking drugs or attacked by another inmate. Not sure. We're taking him to the hospital in Huntsville."

I tried to comfort James as best I could. I grabbed his hand and told him he was being taken to the hospital, but I wasn't sure he understood. I walked beside him to the ambulance and then went immediately to the prison's record section and found contact information that he had left for his son. I called Jim to tell him what was going on.

When he answered, I got right to the point: "Jim, this is Chaplain Lopez from the Ellis prison unit. I have some disturbing news. Your dad apparently had a fall, and he is now unconscious. We're not sure what's going on. They're taking him to the hospital in Huntsville and may need to transfer him from there to John Sealy in Galveston. (*The John Sealy Hospital at the University of Texas Medical Branch at Galveston*) Just want you to know. I'm here to help if I can."

Jim replied, "Thanks, Chaplain. I'm on my way. I'll meet you at the hospital."

I drove to the Huntsville hospital and told them James's son, Jim, was on his way. They said that it was too late for Jim to come to Huntsville. The doctors had decided to fly James to John Sealy Hospital.

I asked the doctors how serious they thought it was. The answer was, "We don't know. We believe something has happened in his brain."

Several orderlies took him to an awaiting helicopter. It took off immediately, hovered briefly, then disappeared into the clear Texas sky for the 110 miles flight to Galveston.

I went to the hospital lobby to wait for Jim to arrive, sat in a small, straight-backed, uncomfortable chair, and tried to relax from a very trying day. Relaxation was elusive and hard to find, as I reflected on James's paradoxical life that included both brutal murder and selfless service, and remembered many of the stories he shared in my office. The story I remembered most vividly was the one when he had acknowledged his life sentence and said he didn't think he would ever get out of prison.

He then told me, "The one worry I have is that I do not want to die in prison."

JIM

Oscar and I arrived in Huntsville, worn out and anxious after our long, spontaneous drive from Arlington. Although we had never met Chaplain Lopez, he greeted us like long lost brothers, or perhaps as a father and sons. He explained that Dad was on his way by helicopter to Galveston, and that we needed to head in that direction immediately. We got into our cars, and Oscar and I followed the chaplain south on Highway 45.

As soon as we arrived at the Galveston hospital, a doctor told us Dad had become brain dead in the chopper somewhere over Houston, and he was still breathing, but on life support. He told us Dad had suffered a brain aneurysm that had caused a bulge or ballooning in a blood vessel that probably ruptured, causing bleeding into the brain that was taking his life. I recalled that Dad's mother, my Grandmother Glendal, had experienced the same thing twenty years earlier.

The doctors confirmed that there was no brain activity, and said they believed Dad had no chance of recovering. They said we needed to decide whether to remove him from life support and whether his organs would be donated when his breathing stopped.

We wanted to donate as many organs as feasible, but were reluctant because we thought potential recipients probably would not want them from someone they knew had been on death row. After we were told by the doctors that the donations would be anonymous, we decided to approve them. However, after they began the surgery to harvest the organs, the doctors informed us that our dad had hepatitis, and his organs could not be donated.

The more difficult decision was whether to agree to have Dad taken off life support. We called Louis and Marilyn, and the four of us discussed what to do. We made the difficult and heartrending decision to remove our dad's support and let him die.

One is never prepared to lose a parent, but in our case the real hardship was having to take his life support away. Many people might think it would be an easy call—to remove life support from the man who murdered your mother and tried to have you killed. But he was still our dad, and it was really hard to pull the plug on him. The irony was inescapable. Our dad had killed our mom and wanted us three boys killed, and now we had to decide whether to end his life. I was particularly traumatized because I had reestablished a relationship with Dad. I had been visiting him and was planning to visit him that weekend along with Marilyn, who would be seeing him for the first time in the four years since our estrangement from him. She wanted to meet this new, changed person I had been talking about.

Death often calls people to seek solace in strange ways. Perhaps I have done so. But Chaplain Lopez later told me how much Dad hated the idea of dying in prison, and I am consoled by the fact, as he probably would have been, that he didn't. He didn't die locked behind bars. Instead he left this world on a helicopter flight away from prison, and he probably would have thanked God for allowing him to die outside the prison walls.

We learned that the State provides a modest funeral service for inmates who die while incarcerated and whose bodies aren't claimed by their families. The bodies are buried in Captain Joe Byrd Cemetery in Huntsville, where an estimated 3,000 incarcerated people have been interred since it was established in 1855. Chaplain Lopez said that these funerals are incredibly sad occasions. Often no family or friends attend, and the only people present are the officiating chaplain, who makes a few comments and says a short prayer, and the inmate crew doing the burial. When family members do attend a funeral, they often have not seen or touched the individual for years, and the service becomes an awkward reconciliation that is too little, too late.

However, an inmate's family has the option to claim the body and make funeral arrangements of their choice. We elected this option. Then Louis, Oscar, and I were faced with deciding whether or not to bury Dad in the joint burial plot with the headstone he had purchased for Mom's burial. Many people, some with a legitimate interest such as Mom's family, and some in the media, felt Dad should be buried in another location away from his ex-wife. After considerable discussion, we boys decided differently. We did not want him buried on the prison grounds, nor did we prefer to have him buried next to Mom. However, as Christians, we believed it didn't really matter where he was buried. Since we already had a plot and a tombstone with his name on it, we decided to take the simplest, less-expensive option, and bury him there, and have our parents in one place. I had forgiven Dad, which made our decision seem okay to me. I'm sure he would have liked it as well.

CHAPLAIN RICHARD LOPEZ

During our downtime at the hospital, I shared some stories with Jim about his father as I had come to know him. I told Jim how his dad respected other people and had earned the respect of everyone in the Ellis unit, including inmates of all cultures, colors, and religions, or of no religion at all, and the guards, officers, and wardens. He never talked negatively about anybody and was always supportive of others. When inmates were growling at each other, he tried to talk them out of trouble. James never got in trouble himself, and never had a "case." He completed the full process to convert to Catholicism and became strong in the Church. With no formal influence, but with the influence that respect carries, he led many to God and church.

Jim thanked me for saying what I did and for revealing that side of his dad. After James's death, the family asked me to officiate at his funeral service. I drove to San Antonio to the San Jose Mission Burial Park, where a visitation was held in the chapel the evening before the interment. The visitation was well-attended by family and quite a few longtime friends of family members.

The next day the three sons and a small group of the Buffington family and close friends gathered for James's burial in a private ceremony—private, in large part, to keep the media away. I opened it with a prayer and said a few brief words. Jim made a few comments about his dad, and Irene Wilcox, a prison volunteer, sang the contemporary Christian song, "I Can Only Imagine."

I can only imagine what it will be like
When I walk, by your side
I can only imagine what my eyes will see
When your face is before me
I can only imagine
I can only imagine

I closed the ceremony with another prayer.

A day or so after his funeral, I was reflecting on James Buffington, the murderer and former death row inmate who had meant so much to me and to so many other people, and who was respected by so many for what he did and who he was. The more I thought about it, the more I wondered if we—the prison system—had given him the respect he had given us, and that I believed he deserved.

The next morning, I went to the prison's big corner office and talked to the warden, privately. I told him, "We all know the respect James Buffington had here in the prison. Among inmates, guards, everybody—the positive influence he had on so many. I'd like to do a memorial service for him. Would make it simple. Just let people gather in the chapel and pay tribute to him. I know this has never been done before, but I'm not aware of any inmate who has ever had Buffington's level of influence."

"Chaplain, what other questions do you have?" he shot back at me. "We've never had this kind of memorial service. That's all. Do you have anything else? There's no way I'm going to let you talk me into doing this. Goodbye."

I was not surprised, but I was badly disappointed. I trudged out of the office in silence.

A few days later the warden called me to his office. I went, with significant reluctance. When I opened the door to enter, my heart was beating a little too fast. It began to beat even faster when I saw the assistant wardens, some other senior staff, and several guards sitting silently around the room, seeming to glare at me. The warden looked at me from a face devoid of emotion, and said, sternly, "Chaplain, please sit down. I have something to discuss with you."

I sat down immediately on the one available chair, located in the center of the room. The warden began, "I've talked to my staff about your request from the other day—you know, a memorial service for James Buffington. We've talked about it. These guys have convinced me it's not a bad idea. We agree you can do a memorial service—a simple one. But remember, it's a one-time event. Don't ask me to do it again."

I couldn't hold back my tears. The memorial would allow all the inmates and staff that James influenced so positively to honor him and his transformed life. Hopefully it would foster a continuation of his teaching and influence by demonstrating that repentance and redemption are possible, even for a man condemned to be executed for having the mother of his children killed.

I called Jim and told him about the warden's decision, and that he and his two brothers were authorized to attend if they wished. He said he would love to attend and would talk to his brothers. Jim and his wife Marilyn, Oscar, and Louis and his wife Gina, attended. Before the memorial service, the warden gave them a tour of the prison, including death row, the general population area, and other places of interest. This was the first time they had been in a prison except for the obviously safe visits in the visitation area with James. They admitted they were "scared to death." I could sense their fear, read it on their faces, and hear it in their voices.

The chapel was large, located on the right side of a long hall that separated it from death row on the left. It was packed with extra chairs in the aisles and rear of the room. Inmates and several staff filled all the seats, and some were standing. A line of inmates formed outside, trying to get in. The three sons and two spouses sat on the front row, with more than 300 men in white prison garb sitting at their backs.

I kicked the session off with an opening prayer and then shared some comments about James and our relationship. The choir that James had led sang several songs, culminating with a rousing rendition of "Amazing Grace."

> *Amazing grace, how sweet the sound*
> *That saved a wretch like me.*
> *I once was lost, but now I am found,*
> *Was blind, but now I see.*

Inmates from different religions each gave an "open mic" talk of about two minutes, mostly sharing how James had supported everyone, regardless of race, religion, creed, or offense, and how God had touched them, and they had become Christians because of James. The warden and another ranking officer spoke about the impact that James had in the penitentiary. Many of them cried profusely and unapologetically, as they remembered the life of James Buffington.

At my request, Jim shared his experiences with his dad. He walked quickly to the podium, turned around, looked into the faces of 300 men, took a deep breath, and talked of how he had learned about God from his dad, as so many inmates had. He then said, "Please don't judge me; I'm not judging you. There's no real difference between us. You made a bad choice that got you into prison, and I haven't made such a decision. Please don't let one bad choice for which you went to prison define you. Your past does not have to define you. You need to forgive yourself and let yourself off the hook. I learned from my dad that who you really are is not what you do and say when everyone is looking, but who you really are is what you do and say when no one is looking. My dad met people in this prison, when nobody was looking, and told his story of how he ended up behind bars, asked God for forgiveness, took responsibility and accountability for his bad choices, and moved in a new direction. Go back to your living quarters, and tell others your story and the story of Jesus. Thanks for being here today and for your wonderful tributes to my dad."

At the end of Jim's comments, roughly three hours after I had kicked off the memorial, I closed it with a prayer. Then the three sons and two spouses formed a receiving line. Almost every inmate in the audience came through the line, hugged each of the sons, and shook hands with Marilyn and Gina.

To this day, in 2023, this is the only such memorial that's ever been held in a Texas prison, even though several others have been requested by families. I later learned what a turning point this was for Jim and his two brothers. Whether or not this allowed them to fully forgive their father, only they can answer, but each of them agreed that they let go of several bags that they had been carrying in their lives—bags full of fear, hurt, betrayal, and anger.

James Buffington and I became close friends, and I learned some important things from him. One of the most important was his approach to forgiveness. He acknowledged all the hurt and harm he had caused in his lifetime, especially his abuse of his wife and sons and the murder of his ex-wife. He wanted their forgiveness, and also yearned for the assurance that God had forgiven him. He put his life in God's hands and believed his acceptance of God's forgiveness allowed him to experience the love of God and the forgiveness of others. I think this is a pretty good lesson for us all.

I've been asked if I can explain the enigma of the two James Buffingtons: the cold-blooded murderer, and the man the inmates and staff at the Ellis prison came to know; the narcissistic manipulator and the selfless servant leader. I'm not sure I can explain. However when I think about it, I think of the two men who were crucified on either side of Christ. According to the Gospel of Luke, while both men were suffering the same gruesome execution in the presence of Christ, their reactions were quite different. The one on the left reviled Christ and asked to come down from his cross. The one on the right did not ask to be taken down, but instead asked to be taken up with Christ, saying, "Jesus, remember me when You come into Your kingdom."

And Jesus replied saying, "Amen, I say to you, today you will be with Me in Paradise." I believe the right side of James realized, acknowledged, and affirmed his guilt; transformed his life, accepted the cross; and placed his hope, not in this world, but in the promise of the next.

In doing so, he left a legacy of love and service that continues today.

CHAPTER TWENTY-ONE

Meeting With Another Killer

"If your brother or sister sins, go and point out their fault, just between the two of you. If they listen to you, you have won them over. But if they will not listen, take one or two others along, so that every matter may be established by the testimony of two or three witnesses."
(Matthew 18: 15–16)

One might assume that Dad's death and burial, and the memorial in his honor, should have brought closure to those of us affected by his actions, like the epilogue of a book concludes the story and wraps up any loose ends. But that was not the case for me. The memorial ended one chapter, but opened other ambiguities and questions, and I felt a need for clearer, firmer explanations of what happened to my mom and dad. The passing of years did not answer my questions or satisfy that need.

The Victim Offender Mediation Dialogue (VOMD) process of the Texas Department of Criminal Justice (TDCJ) provided an opportunity for me to meet with another killer, ask more questions, and hopefully get some answers. This unique program permits victims to have a structured, face-to-face meeting with "their" offender, if the offender agrees and admits guilt. The idea is that through VOMD, victims may receive answers to unanswered questions, which help in their healing and recovery process. It also permits offenders, in the truest sense, to acknowledge that they are responsible and accountable for their behavior.

Early in 2005, I contacted Victim Services and told them that if Charlie Moore was willing, I would like to participate in a mediation with him. The agency contacted Moore, who said "No." The matter was referred to Gene Stewart, a TDCJ employee who was the potential mediator. Gene was a tall, thin, stereotypical Texan, around sixty years old, who wore a big hat and cowboy boots, and spoke in a soft, comforting voice.

He suggested I write Moore a personal letter explaining why I wanted to meet and asking him to participate.

I wrote that I wanted to meet with him to get some questions answered, and not to try to beat him up. I gave the letter to the mediator, and he delivered it to Moore, who responded with a long letter in return that contained some self-justification, some lecturing, but mostly expressions of regret and a request for forgiveness. His letter said, among other things:

Most of all, I sincerely want you to know that I will not make any false attempts to try to make you or your brothers think that I am not as guilty as your Dad and Charles County for your Mom's death. However, being in the Spirit Realm of God, it is my desire that you and your brothers will forgive me for my involvement because it is no doubt I am grieving and have been grieving for the last twenty (20) years of my incarceration. Knowing that if I had an opportunity, I would gladly answer any questions you or your brothers wish to ask me concerning Mrs. Buffington's death.

. . . When Victim Service contacted me first time, "I allowed self thoughts to overtake the Will of God, and I refused to see you . . . but I am more than sure that you are well aware of Spiritual renewing of the Mind . . . Really what I'm asking is that "Since I'm a new brother in Christ" God through Jesus Christ open my old selfish thoughts and gave me a change of heart and desire to visit with you, and answer any questions you wish to ask, . . .

. . . Jim mostly why I fear and hurt so deep is because I knew your mom real well. She was a good mother and wife for your Dad and she did not deserve the type of death that came upon her behind your father's, County, and my evilness. Please open your heart and mind and "Forgive us," because I am deeply sorry . . . Even though I know my being sorry will not take away the hurt and pain you and your brothers has suffered . . . But please allow God's attitude to control your heart, mind, and thoughts, then no matter what happens in life we will know that God is big enough to handle the situation and make it work out for the good . . .

Jim lastly I will say this, "Not as a coverup, but as a man of God . . . Forgiveness Frees you to live again, receiving forgiveness for past mistakes and sins, and forgiving others for their mistakes and sins, are two of the most important factors in emotional healing . . .

Moore did not clearly admit he had committed the murder, as required by the mediation process. After several discussions, mediator Stewart got him to admit that he was in the car when Mom was killed, but Moore still maintained that County was the one who pulled the trigger, and not him. The mediator and I agreed that this was an admission of guilt, so we proceeded with the process.

I participated in a long preparation procedure that lasted almost a year and included a written application, extensive paperwork answering many questions in great detail, and meetings with the mediator, who was also directing Moore through a similar preparation. The mediator finally told us, "Each of you is ready to meet."

The mediation was held on July 26, 2005, at the Stiles Maximum Security Unit, about four miles southeast of Beaumont, where Moore was incarcerated. I arrived at 8:00 a.m. and entered the unit through a metal detector. A guard searched my folder of paperwork, which included my notes and family photos. The mediator and I went to the warden's office, where the warden assured me of my safety and described where we would be meeting. He asked if I had any questions, and I had none. We met in a large, open visitation room around a small table with chairs on opposite sides for the two of us, and one at the end of the table for the mediator. A guard stood to the side.

Moore was a mean-looking dude, with a big scar across his right cheek and a perpetual scowl on his face. He had a hunched-over posture and short gray hair, but all considered, carried his fifty-nine years better than one might expect of someone who had lived the way he had. When we first faced one another, he seemed a little apprehensive, as though he expected me to be really angry. He offered to shake my hand. I refused. I hadn't realized I had so much anger and disgust toward someone I had never met.

Charlie Moore

The mediator started the meeting by stating that he understood I wanted to explain what happened to me and others because of the murder of my mom and hopefully get some questions answered. Charlie said he was willing to answer the questions as best he could. Stewart asked me to go first.

I told my story in nitty-gritty, gory detail, and showed Moore individual pictures of family members affected by his crime: grandparents, parents, siblings, children, in-laws. I wanted Moore to know the ripple effect of his crime, and that it wasn't just my mom who was a victim. I explained in some detail how each of us was affected. I told him how my grandmother collapsed when she heard the news, how my grandad had to go to the morgue and identify his murdered daughter, how Mom's brother found out about her murder from the morning news of a naked dead lady being found in her car, what it was like attending the funeral and seeing Mom's face destroyed by his gunshots, what it was like attending several murder trials, how my grandad had died of a broken heart, and other difficult particulars. I wanted him to feel really bad about what he had done.

When Moore told his story, it was all about him, filled with excuses attempting to justify what he had done. His parents got divorced. His dad was an alcoholic. His dad hung around with the wrong people. His dad was in prison.

I pointed out that in many ways we had similar lives, as our fathers seemed to have behaved in much the same way. How did he end up in prison, and I didn't ?

Moore continued, saying he took up drinking and drugs, including heroin; and started hanging around with the wrong people, including my dad. He said my dad told County and him that he wanted his ex-wife killed, and "For a couple of grand, all I had to do was kill a White lady, and I could use the money to support my drug habit."

It hurt to hear this mean-looking, convicted killer say that my dad was "the wrong people." Hearing that my mom had been murdered for a "couple of grand" felt like a whole ton of bricks had been dumped on me. The crime was senseless. It all hit me so hard.

We finally got to the main reason I requested the mediation. I asked Moore to tell me what happened. He explained his involvement in the murder of my mother and also told me of his and County's attempt to get her to disclose where my brothers and I were located so they could murder us too. He said the reason it took so long to kill my mother was that they were driving around trying to find my brothers and me. My mom wouldn't tell them where we were. She kept lying, saying we were with our father, as they continued to press her, "We know you are lying. They are not with their dad. Where are your boys?"

Mom refused to disclose the information and saved our lives.

Moore explained, "Your mother came in her car to the house where County was staying to pick us up. I pulled a gun and told her to get in the back seat. She crawled over the seat into the back. Charles got in the front, I got in the back with your mom, and we drove off. We continued asking where her boys were because you were supposed to be in the car."

He continued, describing how they drove to the end of a street just past County's dad's house outside of town, where County shot her, and then they backtracked to his dad's house and took off her clothes after she was dead. County picked up a blue truck and he, Moore, drove Mom in her car to Longfellow Junior High School and left her car and body in the parking lot. After that, they went to Woodlawn Lake, met some lady friends who took mom's jewelry and some of her other belongings and threw her purse into the water. Moore drew a rough map to illustrate the route they had taken.

Before the mediation, I considered the possibility of killing Moore at some time during the process. I even considered taking a knife in a folder just in case I needed it to do the job. I did not however, as I had learned that trying to smuggle a knife into a prison wasn't a good idea. My second plan was, "I can choke the old man and, by the time these guys get me off him, he's gonna be dead. I've been to a lot of capital murder trials, and a jury will not convict me when they hear what this man did to my mom in the back seat of her car."

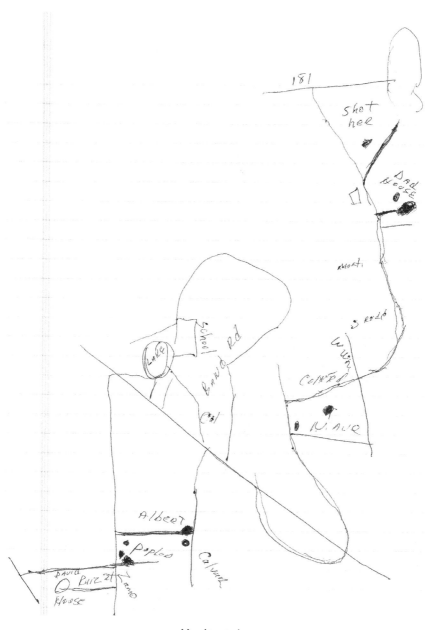

Murder route

After listening to Moore talk about what he did to my mom, my anger for him was boiling hot. The details he shared had incinerated any cooling effect that might have occurred over the almost thirty years since Mom's death, and propelled me into a rage of fury. At that exact time, it seemed logical, rational, and the right thing to do to kill him; but in the back of my mind, I was facing a real difficult choice.

I shoved back my chair, stood as tall as I could, glared angrily into Moore's eyes, and walked out of the room. I went to the bathroom, where I slammed the toilet seat, kicked a trash can, and banged my fist into the wall to discharge my anger in private, so that Moore wouldn't see how he had affected me.

I met the mediator in the hall as I was returning to the meeting room. He asked, "Are you okay?"

"I am so, so angry, but I'm not going to let him see it."

Gene said, "It's okay to show your anger in front of him."

I returned to the meeting room, sat back down in front of the man who had so violently taken my mother's life, and got more direct. I confessed that I wanted to kill him. I told him that I had made a choice to get up and leave the room instead. I explained that he made several choices before he killed my mom, "You made a choice to meet my mom at her car. You made a choice to pull out a gun. You made a choice to point the gun at my mom. You made a choice to get in her car and make her get in the back seat. You made a choice to take off her clothes." I paused and asked him, "Why didn't you make a choice to stop what you were doing before you shot her?"

Moore didn't answer my question.

I told him that I'd just learned that it takes more of a man to stop and walk away than it does to stay and make a bad choice, like he did with my mom.

As I reflected on my choice to walk away from killing Moore, I realized the role of my Christian faith in this decision. The impact of hearing in church, and reading the Bible about what Jesus would do, saved me from my anger. I also wondered if Dad could have felt a similar anger toward Mom for leaving him, when he arranged to have her killed. Yet Dad's feelings and actions trumped the lessons of Jesus that Dad had so loudly proclaimed in church.

I managed to get through the remainder of the day. I felt I had learned some things, though in the back of my mind, I didn't believe a word Moore said. He claimed County was the one who had raped and killed the White lady. He denied his fingerprints were on Mom's car, and claimed that if they were, the police planted them. He tried to make the murder less gruesome than it was, maintaining my mom quietly put her head down before County shot her and claiming he took her clothes off after he shot her. Moore then said that when a possible witness drove into the school parking lot, he told County they needed to kill him, suggesting to me that he had taken charge.

Although I thought Moore was a liar, I was glad he met with me. All considered, I was convinced that he was in the car, was the leader and the one holding the gun, and that we boys were supposed to be there and be killed.

Moore showed few signs of remorse. He blamed my dad, Charles County, and DA Charles Conaway for his situation. However, he asked for my forgiveness and wanted to know how he could pay us back. I refused to tell him that I forgave him.

The mediator wrote the following agreement, which Moore and I signed:

> Jim Buffington and Charlie Moore the undersigned, having participated in this process, do hereby affirm the following terms of agreement:
>
> 1. Charlie will remember Mom each year on her birthday, August 16, and on the anniversary of her murder, March 20. On these days, he will pray for Mom's family.
> 2. Charlie will continue the spiritual disciplines of prayer, Bible study, and church attendance.
> 3. Charlie will practice a lifestyle of truth and honesty.

The mediation lasted eight hours, with a lunch break and occasional short breaks. I closed our session with a prayer during which I prayed for Charlie. If you can pray for someone who hurt you, you probably have forgiven them. In any case, a couple of weeks later, I wrote a letter telling him that I forgave him. I realized I needed to forgive him to get rid of my anger and hatred. I still planned to protest his parole because of what he did to my mom and what he told me, which was, "I'm afraid if I got out of jail now, I might harm someone else."

I shared feedback from the mediation with Louis, Oscar, and Bryce. My decision not to try to kill Moore generated the most discussion. The initial reaction of each of them was that I should have killed him when I had a chance, as a jury would not convict, and I could have gotten away with it. Each of them held a great deal of anger. Bryce, who strongly empathized with what our family went through before he was born, was particularly angry. I have been surprised at the number of people who shared similar opinions.

Generational curses are recurring problems. Handed down from generation to generation, they kill and destroy families. The term has been defined in different ways, often with heavy religious overtones. Simply stated, when a generational curse exists, a parent influences the child in a negative way, the child continues the parent's bad behaviors, and the cycle perpetuates itself generation after generation. Generational curses can be found in any negative cycle that family members trap themselves in, including alcoholism, drug addiction, gambling addiction, poverty mindsets, extramarital affairs, spousal abuse, child abuse, and many more.

My father was a murderer. I considered trying to kill the man who murdered my mom. If I had killed Charlie, I would have continued a generational curse, and Bryce could more easily have done what his grandfather and father did. But a person can change a generational curse by his actions. I may have prevented one by my choice of not killing Charlie.

Perhaps I prevented a line of bad choices by making the right choice.

I learned several things from the mediation. I came to understand how angry I was toward Charlie Moore, who I had not met before. I got a lot of answers, even though some didn't square with the trial evidence, and I didn't think he was always telling the truth. I learned more about what happened to my mom, and I got answers as to how she met the guys who killed her; what happened, where they took her, and why; and things that happened in the school parking lot. I also got confirmation that my dad really had wanted to kill my brothers and me, which he always denied. The meeting helped me understand how things fit together. I, of course, knew Dad, and had previously met Charles County. Now I had finally come face-to-face with the third person in the plot, the one who the police and I believed actually killed my mother.

Moore said he had become a Christian in prison. I was leery as to whether his was a "jailhouse" conversion, but I listened to him, and he answered my questions. My act of forgiving him seemed to be the Christian thing to do, and it helped me greatly.

I couldn't help but think about my mom, how she was only twenty-nine when she was murdered; she'd had a couple death threats, and thought something was going to happen, but didn't know what. Her will, in which she requested that "I'll Tell the World That I'm a Christian," be sung at her funeral, is an example for us about forgiveness. When you read the words of that song, you know that she had already forgiven. If she could forgive, facing death, and leave a message for my brothers and me, then I can tell the story that Jesus changed my life, and I can forgive. If she could do it, I can do it.

It's been valuable and affirming for my brothers and me to explain to our kids how, even though a horrible tragedy happened, God continues to forgive all of us and has turned this tragedy into His good. There are still consequences, but my dad became a Christian, and Charlie Moore became a Christian. And God used them to connect me with a prison ministry that involves telling my story to prison inmates to help them turn their lives around.

CHAPTER TWENTY-TWO

Perspectives

"Get rid of all bitterness, rage and anger, brawling and slander, along with every form of malice. Be kind and compassionate to one another, forgiving each other, just as in Christ God forgave you."
(Ephesians 4: 31-32)

James's action led to the murder of one woman, but it created many victims. Chere's murder started family and friends on a trail of tears fueled by fear, sadness, uncertainty—and anger focused on Charles County and Charlie Moore as the perpetrators. Then James admitted his involvement, and the matter became more personal for Jim, his brothers, and their spouses, creating a flood of personal animosity, rage, shame, and resentment toward their dad and father-in-law. Each of them was affected differently and had to deal with it in their own way, but ultimately each had to consider whether to forgive James.

Forgiveness is a process, or journey, of granting a person free pardon and giving up anger and resentment for a hurt they caused. It involves looking back at what happened, not for the purpose of analyzing, blaming, or condemning, but for the purpose of leaving an offense behind and moving on to a better future. It does not change the past or the bad things a person did, but it does change the present and can change the future.

Forgiveness is not so much a word spoken, an action performed, or an emotion felt, as it is a way of life that fosters a deeper relationship with another. Often associated with faith, religion, and belief in God, forgiveness pertains to Christian believers, adherents of other religious traditions, and nonbelievers alike. Forgiveness embodies specific practices through which people seek to remember the past truthfully, repair hurt and brokenness, heal divisions, and reconcile relationships.

The practice of forgiveness can be a tricky proposition. Sometimes accountability, firm punishment, and justice are needed, particularly in cases of abuse and extreme violence. Sometimes a means of dealing with cycles of hatred, vengeance, and bitterness is what is needed. Forgiveness provides space for both. It serves not to absolve guilt or avoid consequences, but as a reminder of the peace that communion with God or another can provide. It breaks apart the logic of vengeance, violence, repression, and hatred, and offers love, compassion, justice, consequences, remembrance, and community.

Forgiveness requires difficult personal decisions, and people go forward with it in their own way and time. Forgiveness often is harder when it involves people in an intimate and continuous relationship than when the relationship is distant and temporary. Jim, Marilyn, Louis, Gina, and Oscar (still single at the time), all either knew James intimately or had a close connection with him. The question of forgiving him involved a history, an ongoing relationship, and presumably the possibility of reconciliation with a loved one. Each was hurt by him in a similar way. However, each of them felt different about his behavior, and each responded differently and demonstrated their own approach to forgiveness.

JIM

Forgiving Dad didn't become an issue with me until Marilyn and I visited him the night after the verdict was rendered in his second trial—the night he looked me in the eyes and said, "I did it, and she deserved it." Marilyn had not shared with me that she thought he was guilty, and until then, I believed without reservation that he was innocent of any involvement in Mom's murder. I knew he had been harsh with my brothers and me, but I thought the intimidation and whippings were normal and just what dads did to their sons. In my mind, he had never hurt me inappropriately, and there was nothing to forgive.

His confession upended my life. The shock and sadness of losing my mom took on an entirely new dimension, and Dad's confession caused me to double down on the grief of her death. I felt I had betrayed her when I focused my life on Dad and testified for him, and felt guilty that I hadn't grieved more for her. I concluded he had seduced me into supporting him. I believed in him, while he had my mom killed, didn't take any accountability for what he had done, and maintained that he was the victim. He blamed her for his bad choices, said she left him, and omitted the part that he had cheated on her, hit her, and tried to totally control her.

When Dad confessed, I saw that he had taken my mom from me, and that he had taken my father as well when he set himself on the road to prison. My pain was compounded when I came to believe he wanted to kill my brothers and me for money, rather than love us, take care of us, and provide for us. His confession led to the type of hurt and pain that seemed unforgivable, but that only forgiveness can cure.

Marilyn was not surprised that Dad killed Mom, but she was amazed that he admitted it. I was traumatized by both. My reaction to Dad's confession triggered a series of emotions that were in many ways similar to the stages of grief. The first was shock, which played out for me as numbed disbelief. Marilyn and I had attended Dad's second trial and heard the mountain of evidence against him; and at some level I had questioned his innocence, but I nevertheless was stunned at what he had done and how cavalierly he told us about it. Hearing that he had arranged Mom's murder was shocking. His blaming her and showing no remorse was an even bigger jolt.

I was overwhelmed by anger, bitterness, frustration, resentment, and desire for revenge—all directed at Dad. I was livid that he had killed Mom, but perhaps even more irate that he blamed her and betrayed me when he sat in the courtroom and listened passively as I testified to what he knew was false. I managed to control my temper and other outward expressions of fury, but inside my blood was boiling. I was so angry that, for four years, I didn't see him, visit him, write him, or have anything to do with him.

Depression is usually considered part of the grieving process. I never felt depressed in the usual sense of that word. However, for a time, and certainly when Marilyn and I visited Mom's grave immediately after his confession, I experienced overwhelming feelings of isolation, confusion, emptiness, and intense sadness and sorrow. Fortunately, my faith, Marilyn's love and support, Bryce's birth, and the backing of family and friends pulled me through the long haul. I became consumed with trying to understand how Dad got from who he was to what he did, a form of testing that I believe helped me deal with my shock and anger.

They say acceptance is part of the grieving process, but how does one accept the unacceptable? Marilyn and I came to the realization that Dad, without a doubt, hired someone to kill Mom. However, this did not mean that we felt what he did was in any way acceptable, or that we bought into any explanation he might make. Rather, it meant that I was willing to live with a new reality. I was the son of the man who had my mom murdered. I needed to accept the emotional pain of my "new" status and rebuild my life.

Accepting my new status and rebuilding my life required me to get beyond the cycle of grief about what happened and deal with the anger, betrayal, and disgust I felt toward my dad for hurting me and so many others. I tried to put myself in his shoes, and experience a feeling of empathy that would help me forgive him and move on. Without forgiveness, I no doubt would have held on to the pain Dad caused, and become bitter and vengeful, which would have allowed him to control my life. It was like anger, bitterness, betrayal, and shame filled a suitcase that I had been carrying around, and forgiving would empty it and get rid of my burden. I wouldn't forget what Dad did or pretend what he did never happened, but I wouldn't have to carry the weight around anymore.

The act of forgiving can often be complex. In my case, I was shocked almost beyond belief during our first meeting after four years of estrangement when Dad apologized and told me he was sorry for what he had done to Mom, Oscar, Louis, and me. I had never seen him do such a thing unless he was trying to manipulate someone. When he said he was sorry for what he did and told me that he had asked God into his life, I didn't necessarily believe him. But it was enough to keep me coming back. My continued periodic visits led to a true communion between us. We established a somewhat different but true father-son relationship, with forgiveness providing healing from both sides. To me it was healing to forgive my dad, and I also know it was healing to him to be forgiven.

Dad changing his life, humbling himself, and saying he was sorry was the key to my forgiving him. I could tell he meant it. I'm not sure whether I would have forgiven him had he not apologized, as it is so much easier to forgive someone if they tell you they are sorry. My plan was to continue our visits, and have Marilyn join us, as she finally believed he had changed. This did not happen because of Dad's untimely death, which raises another issue in the complex subject of forgiveness. I do not believe that forgiveness must be communicated to the forgiven person in order to be real. However, communication usually enhances the value of forgiving another. I believe my telling Dad I forgave him was a balm for his soul, and I'm happy I didn't defer telling him until it was too late.

MARILYN

Jim told me early in our relationship, around the time of our engagement, that his dad had been convicted of arranging the murder of his Mom. I was surprised, but at the time the revelation really didn't affect me personally or change anything between us. It seemed to be a matter between Jim, his brothers, his family, and his dad.

I first met James in June 1985, at the Bexar County Jail, where he had been incarcerated pending his second trial. I was nervous. I had never

Jim, Marilyn, Caitlyn, and Bryce Buffington

met an inmate or a convicted felon, nor been introduced to a future father-in-law. Fortunately, I didn't have to talk much, as Jim and his dad
were both big talkers who kept the conversation going. I accompanied
Jim to visit his dad several times before his trial. The visits were a little
awkward, as Jim thought his dad was innocent, and I strongly suspected
he was guilty.

In addition, his dad's personality was not one I was fond of. He
seemed condescending and arrogant, a self-absorbed, materialistic,
know-it-all who looked down on women. He had felt that if Chere wasn't

going to be with him, she couldn't be with anyone. He asked a lot of Jim and me, such as financial help when we didn't have money to spare, and he expected us to do what he wanted done for him. I visited him only because he was Jim's dad.

Sitting through James's second trial confirmed in my mind that he had arranged to have his ex-wife killed. When he confessed the evening after the trial, I was not surprised to learn that he was guilty, but I was shocked by his confession, shocked by the fact that he was telling us what he did and blaming it on Jim's mom.

I never saw James again after the confession.

Attending the memorial service in the prison was even scarier than my first visit with James. The warden took us on a tour of the entire penitentiary, including death row. Walking among the inmates, speculating on why they were there, observing the coffin-like cells, walking through the heavy steel doors, and hearing them bang shut behind us, was pretty scary for someone who grew up in a sheltered life, as I had.

Hearing so many testimonies that James apparently had changed and was remorseful opened several new perspectives. To me, forgiveness means acknowledging what was done between two parties, and letting go. I needed to forgive my father-in-law for what he had done to his sons—the harsh punishment he meted out and forcing them to endure the pain of their mom's brutal assassination and grow up without a mother, and with their father in prison. He had hurt me as well. I didn't have a mother-in-law, and Bryce didn't have a paternal grandmother. I was also hurt by the condescending way he treated me, how he piled his needs on us as newlyweds and was so interfering, self-absorbed, and demanding.

I have learned that forgiveness is a journey, and often a complex one. It's hard for me to pinpoint exactly when I forgave my father-in-law, as it covered the major act of his murdering Jim's mom and also those smaller hurts to me. I think that when Jim forgave his dad for the murder and for what he had done to him, I was able to do so as well. In January or February 1994, I told Jim that I would go with him to visit his dad. I thought it would be a chance for us to clear the air, and perhaps move toward a better relationship between us. But I was still hanging onto the smaller things—how James treated me; things he took from Jim, Bryce, and me; things that would have been so different if he hadn't been so selfish.

But James had the brain aneurysm and died. I think at that point I just let go without giving much thought to what it meant, or why I was letting go. He was gone. We would live our future lives without him. That was the end of it for me.

At his funeral service, I didn't really mourn him as a father-in-law, nor did I hold any hard feelings. My forgiveness of him was subtle. I didn't tell him I forgave him, take any forgiving action, or change our relationship. It seems that God spared me from having to confront the issue of whether, or when, to tell him I forgave him. I was able to just forgive him in my heart, for the big things and the little ones, and move on with my life.

The decision to let go of the little hurts—like when I thought about his asking us to buy someone a gift, put money on his account, visit him in jail on a holiday, or other such situations—was huge for me. Letting go of all the little things and not having to think about them or dwell on them brought peace to my life.

OSCAR

I don't have many early childhood memories about my dad. I was ten years old when he and Mom divorced, and eleven when Mom was killed. I do remember Mom and Dad together at church and at Grandma Mignon's house on Friday nights for dinner and card games. Their arguments and bad times seem largely blocked from my memory.

I recall some good times with Dad and my brothers, such as the three of us boys sitting on Dad's lap, singing in church, going on a drive with

Oscar, Janice, and Judson Buffington

him, being on the football team with him as the coach, eating Mexican food every Sunday. I also remember some bad times: the pain of the whippings with the belt, the trauma of my parent's divorce, the anguish of Mom's murder, the stress of all the moves and uncertainty, the feelings of being abandoned several times, the overwhelming sadness of it all. Perhaps that is my excuse for the school days I missed, the fights I fought, and the bad grades I received.

I loved going to church with the youth group and being around those folks. I graduated from high school in Malvern, earned an engineering degree from DeVry University in Dallas, and got a job with the technology company, Accenture. I met Janice on an early expat assignment in the Philippines. We fell in love and married in 2004.

I told Janice our family story six or seven months after we started dating—twenty-seven years after Mom's death, and nine years after Dad died. The passing of people and time took away some of the immediacy, and Janice's memories of life as an only child, raised in several homes by a single mother and aunts and uncles, made my story somewhat less impactful for her. She pretty much took it in stride.

Our son, Judson, was born in 2006. I lied to him about his grandparents for years, telling him my mom and dad died in an auto accident. When Louis posted some information on Facebook about our story, and the word started getting out with friends from church, I began to gradually tell Judson what happened, a little at a time. I explained that I lied to him because he was so young, and I was afraid he would be angry and believe I might be like my dad. He had a couple of questions, but not much reaction, and dropped the matter rather quickly.

For many years, I thought Dad was innocent. I was sad he was in prison, living with a bunch of really bad people, residing in a tiny, austere cell, eating that terrible prison food. I worried about what might happen to him, and tried to support him any way I could.

I was outraged when he confessed to being involved in Mom's murder. He had been so selfish and destroyed our world, changed our lives, and put everyone through the trauma resulting from what he did to Mom. My rage intensified when I learned that he probably tried to have my brothers and me killed as well. At this point, I didn't really care. He became irrelevant to me. His difficulties did not bother me at all, and at times I even felt glad he was going through his own trauma. I stopped writing him, visiting him, talking to him, or otherwise supporting him.

I'm not sure exactly what forgiveness is. I may have experienced it in the hospital when we pulled him off life support, and I could see that my long journey with him was ending. I'm not sure if I forgave him, or if I was just glad it was over. I call it forgiveness, because that's when I stopped being so angry and resentful. I was glad I didn't have to deal with him anymore—except sometimes I'm angry, or maybe just disappointed, as when my mom and dad are not present on special occasions, such as when Judson made the basketball team.

I remember agreeing that Dad should be buried next to Mom and feeling bad that I couldn't help pay for the funeral, and going to the service and trying to balance the inevitable sadness of losing a parent with the relief of him being out of my life. When we went to the prison memorial event and heard how he had changed, I was furious that he forgave himself and fixed his life, but didn't care enough about us to do it earlier.

All of this really hits home when I think of Judson. I am similar to Dad in a lot of ways, and even resemble him physically. I never let go of this fact, and sometimes worry that it will lead to my behaving as he did. So I do things differently with Judson. I try to put him first rather than myself, have a different approach to discipline, control my drinking, and such. I worry that I may act like the dad I knew, which is one of the reasons I don't share everything with other people.

I'm usually glad Dad changed, but sometimes I just don't care. I suppose that is how I let it go, got beyond it, and am done with it. I'm not sure if that is good or bad, but that's the way I deal with what Dad did, as well as many of the other hurts that occur in day-to-day life. I am usually able to just walk away, but I am sometimes concerned about the effect on my son, nieces, and nephews.

LOUIS

I was born roughly two-and-one-half years after Jim, but our memories seem further apart than that. I don't have a lot of childhood memories about Dad. I remember growing up in San Antonio and attending church services where he was worship leader, and Mom played piano. I also recall a few camping trips with Dad and playing in the first snow I saw in San Antonio. Most of my good memories are of Mom and family. I remember her reading books to me (I still have one of the books.), her singing and playing the piano, dinners on Friday nights in our grandparents' home, Mexican food lunches, and such.

Most of my memories of Dad are not positive. I had a great fear of him and the things he did to us. It often seemed as though he was trying to make us appear to be the perfect family—to always sit up straight, be quiet, pay attention; and never doze in church, use a bad word, or receive an unacceptable grade, etc. His behavior was better in the church environment or when other people were around, such as Papa Lee and Grandpa Herman and Grandma Mignon; he tried to appear to be the perfect father and project the perfect family. We loved going to church, because it was with the "good James." With just us at home, things were very different.

Almost anything that seemed contrary to the image he wanted to create was subject to harsh discipline. If I got out of line even a little, he made me pull my pants and underwear down, and he spanked me, hard, with a big leather belt, usually leaving bruises and welts. I remember how humiliating and painful it was—hurting so much that sitting down, even the next day, felt like being whipped again. Mom tried to protect us from our father and comfort us, often with little success. It was extreme. What he did to us then is now clearly understood as child abuse.

I never saw my Dad physically abuse Mom, nor do I remember any normal loving acts, such as holding hands, sitting together, or just being close. Life was always about him, and what things looked like around him.

When Mom and Dad were getting divorced, I wanted to live with Mom. I remember an incident when the decision was still in the air. I was eight or nine years old, in my room, crying my eyes out about the future I seemed to be facing. Mom came into the room, held me close, and tried her best to comfort me. I told her I wanted to live with her and not Dad. She didn't agree to that, but said, "Everything will be okay. Don't worry about it." Was she wrong!

I was ten years old when Mom was murdered. I remember crying uncontrollably, and the three of us kids being so afraid that we slept on the floor in Dad's bedroom the night we were told of her death. I was terrified about facing life without Mom and wondering what was next for my brothers and me. Years later, I wondered about what Dad was really thinking that night, and whether he felt any empathy at all, or was he just mad that we were still alive and not dead according to his plan.

From the beginning, it never occurred to me that Dad was involved in Mom's death. I assumed, without giving it much thought, that he didn't know more than I did. Even after he was arrested and locked in the county jail, I believed he was innocent. I once sent him a letter with a monopoly "Get Out of Jail Free" card enclosed. I wrote him periodically and visited him most Saturdays. I was, however, mainly indifferent about what was going on with him. I was trying to survive and start a new life without Dad; I had mentally left things up to Jim to worry about. Over time, as Jim did more investigation and we learned more and more, it began to sink in that he might be guilty.

When Dad confessed, it became obvious that his actions effectively made me an orphan at age ten and dramatically changed my life. He took away my mom, deserted me, destroyed my family, and started a chain of events that involved getting and losing a stepmother, living for a time with a family I barely knew and was not comfortable with, facing the possibility of being turned out and sent to an orphans' home unless some other family member stepped up to the plate to raise us, and living with grandparents I really didn't know, in a small town, in another state I didn't know anything about.

I married Gina when I was twenty years old and didn't have any parents at my wedding, graduated college with no parents at the ceremony, and had three kids without my parents *oohing* and *ahhing* over their grandchildren. It all made me so angry, and my anger just would not go away.

Attending the memorial service in the Ellis Unit and hearing the inmates and staff tell of all the good things Dad had done brought a new dimension to my thinking. A few months after his funeral and the memorial service, as I was surviving, but holding on to my anger toward him, I kept thinking, *I don't want anything to do with the man I knew. But I don't know the man all those inmate speakers described. Who was he, and how do I feel about him?*

This internal struggle started me thinking more about the issue of forgiveness.

⸻

Forgiveness for me was not quick. It took until I was a twenty-seven-year-old man to get rid of my anger and hatred. It was really hard to let go, but would have been much more difficult if I had not believed Dad changed. Him telling Jim that he was sorry for what he did, and hearing all the inmates' stories, convinced me that he had genuinely turned his life around.

Through the years, I had never given much thought to forgiveness, or who to forgive, for what, or how. It was a word I'd heard all my life in sermon after sermon in church, but it seemed to be for other people and for small hurts. I could forgive people for little things, but I was facing a big hurt, up close and personal. What Dad did to me was so big that I held onto my anger for all those years. His death pushed me in a different direction. He was gone. Things were final. Why should I hold onto my internal strife and anger when Dad was out of my life?

While I was struggling with this conundrum, a visiting pastor at church talked about forgiveness, citing Ephesians 4:31–32: "Get rid of all bitterness, rage and anger, brawling and slander, along with every form of malice. Be kind and compassionate to one another, forgiving each other, just as in Christ God forgave you."

As I sat silently in the pew, listening to the pastor that Sunday morning just a few months after my father died, all the sermons I'd heard, all the scripture I'd read, and all the anger I'd felt suddenly came together, like an overinflated balloon, and begged for release. The pastor presented an opportunity for a public release at the end of his sermon. I gathered my courage, stood up, and slowly but confidently walked down the aisle to the altar. Gina followed me, demonstrating her support without having any advanced knowledge of what I planned to do. I don't remember the words I used or much else that happened, but I do remember being on the floor, crying, with Gina and close friends surrounding me, as I forgave my father for what he had done to my family and me. It was a huge relief for me after all those years of holding on to the anger and hate. Acting on the words in that Bible verse, "Get rid of . . . ," finally got rid of it all.

I had rarely talked about what had happened in my life, so most people in our church were surprised at our story. The following week, I spoke to the entire congregation, telling them what happened to my mom and dad, and what I'd gone through. Most of them knew my dad had died just a few months earlier, but did not know the details of his life. They listened with empathy and continued to take us in as a true, loving family. That's how I survived without continuing down the road of anger, hate, and cynicism, possibly to alcohol and drug abuses.

GINA

My family moved around a great deal when I was growing up. I lived in twelve different homes before college. The last several were in Malvern, so I was able to stay in the same schools and have a good junior high and high school experience. Louis and I met in the eighth grade, became good friends and started dating in high school.

Louis told me how his mom died—about eight years after her murder and after we had dated about six months. Before that I had concluded that something unusual happened, but he never talked about it, and I was left to wonder. I didn't insist that he tell me the story, but did tell him it would be okay if he shared it with me and that I would treat it totally confidentially if he did. Shortly thereafter, one evening in a long and heart-rending conversation, Louis bared his soul for the first time.

225

He didn't want me to talk about it with other people, so I didn't. I was already in love with him, so his story made me want to take care of him, provide a family for him, and support him through his healing process.

Louis and I each attended the University of Arkansas, where we worked forty hours a week in addition to attending classes. About the time we started college, Louis's grandparents retired and moved to Oregon, leaving him without a home or a place to go during holidays. So he lived with my family during college breaks. He was able to compartmentalize his life and keep his trauma separate from our family, and we all enjoyed having him with us. We married during the summer between our sophomore and junior years of college, roughly ten years after his mom's death and eight years before his dad's. Louis living with my family and us marrying so young was a real blessing for us. God put us together because we both needed stability, loyalty, and unconditional love.

I became a teacher and taught kindergarten mostly until I retired in 2020. We have three children—son, Aaron; twin daughters, Emily and Erica; and two grandchildren.

I met Louis's father shortly after high school graduation, when I went with Louis and his grandfather to Texas to visit him on death row. This was the first time I'd been in a prison. My fear and reluctance were

Abby, Aaron, BethAnne, Erica, Emily, Gina, Louis, Emma Buffington

more or less offset by my interest in the strange world that was around me. Our visit was as nice as a visit to a man I didn't know on death row could be. Although I will admit to being uncomfortable, Louis's dad was very pleasant and cordial, and included me as part of the conversation.

People have said James always acted great in front of his dad, who really believed in him, thought he was innocent, and supported him financially every month until he confessed. Perhaps that was the case with his response to me, and he put on a fake mask for me as he had for his dad. I never saw him again, so I don't know how it would have been after James confessed to the murder and his dad protested his parole, cut him off, and never saw him again. In any case, after our visit, James called Louis pretty often. I spoke to him on several occasions and felt we developed a pretty good relationship.

Louis had always believed his dad was innocent, and I did as well. I didn't give it much thought until I attended his second trial in late 1988. When I heard all the evidence against him, I began to question his innocence. When he was convicted of murder rather than capital murder and would be up for parole, I was fearful that it would be granted, and he would end up living with us. Given the evidence presented during the trial, he was not someone I really wanted as a houseguest.

Louis didn't talk about the trauma much at all, but it did crop up from time to time. On one occasion when we had an argument, which was very rare for us, I got in the car and went for a short drive to calm down. When I returned, he said he thought I was leaving him as so many others had done, and had been afraid for the entire time I was gone. I decided then that I would never leave an argument with him again.

In another incident, I disciplined one of the kids, and Louis changed it and allowed the child to do what I had prohibited. I objected and maintained that his intervention was not fair to me, as it made him the "good" parent and me the "bad" one. He took a drive, and when he returned, I could see that he had been crying. He explained that his father had been abusive when he disciplined him, and he didn't want his children to see him that way.

I didn't feel betrayed by James or have any personal antagonism toward him. The murder happened long before I knew Louis and didn't directly affect me, and I had no complaints about the way James treated me. So from one perspective, I didn't feel that forgiveness was needed or appropriate. However, he hurt me vicariously, because of the way he hurt Louis. His hurting a person I loved brought the issue of forgiveness front and center.

I believe forgiveness is a choice—often a difficult one, as some hurt seems almost unforgivable. The only way I can make that choice is to realize that forgiveness is from God, who helps me forgive others. Sometimes feelings of hurt and anger reoccur after I choose to forgive, and I think about forgiveness again and again. I have to remind myself that it was God's choice too, and I don't want to renege on my commitment. Being unforgiving is not what God wants me to do.

I was impressed by the sheer number of inmates at the prison memorial service who talked about how James ministered to them and affected their lives. At home afterward, I quietly thought and prayed about how God had used that situation, and how some things that are so bad also work for good. It was obvious that my father-in-law changed and become a servant of God. It wasn't my place to judge him. Hearing how he had changed, and helped so many, helped me give up my feelings of being hurt, as well as my anger toward him. He positively affected many more lives than I have. It isn't for me to hold anything against him, given what he did for God.

In the early days, I did not encourage Louis to forgive his father because of my fear that he would be released and want to come live with us. After the memorial service, I got out of the way and allowed God to work in Louis's life until he was ready to forgive.

CHAPTER TWENTY-THREE

The Ripple Effect

"Honor your father and your mother, as the Lord your God has
commanded you, so that you may live long and that it may
go well with you in the land the Lord your God is giving you."
(Deuteronomy 5:16)

The effects of crime play out in many different places, on many different people, for long periods of time. It's like throwing a stone into a still, silent pond. The stone hits the water in one place, but its effects radiate out in a circle and affect the water in many places and for a significant time, often called the "ripple effect." Similarly, crime against one person ripples out to affect others, including the family and society—often over several generations.

James Buffington's crime touched many people, including his grandchildren whom he never met: Bryce, Jim's son, who has a son of his own; Oscar's son Judson, who is in high school; and Louis's children Aaron, who has two children; and Aaron's sisters, twins Emily and Erica. All are God-fearing, productive contributors to society, yet all were affected by the acts of their grandfather. In the following, Jim sets the stage for a discussion of the ripple effect on them, and Erica and Bryce each explains the impact on them personally—effects shared by the other grandchildren.

JIM

My two brothers and I told our children about their absent grandparents at different times and in age-appropriate ways, and from time to time each of the grandchildren heard me tell my story in church or another venue. However, although the five cousins are great friends, they had never discussed the situation with one another, and we had never discussed it as a family, until the spring of 2022.

In early 2022, Shalom World, a Catholic TV channel that offers a wide range of spiritual programming, produced a documentary, *Forgiving Their Mother's Murderer: Seventy Times Seven*, telling our family story.[1] Their film crew spent a full day in Marilyn's and my home, asking Oscar, Louis, and me a long series of questions that probed into the circumstances of Mom's murder, how it affected us, and how we dealt with the issue of forgiveness; and filming our responses. We anxiously awaited the film's production, curiously wondering whether they had accurately reflected our story and our feelings about it—as well as how each of us were presented, whether we should be prepared for a Hollywood contract, and other such irrelevant issues.

The documentary's debut was scheduled around Easter time. The entire family gathered in anticipation on a Friday night at Oscar and Janice's house to watch the final product. Janice served us a wonderful dinner, and afterward we adjourned to their big living room with the giant TV. Siblings, in-laws, and cousins found comfortable spots on the sofas, in big overstuffed chairs, and on the floor; and the show began.

Our evening was a real anomaly. We saw a serious documentary about our mom and grandmother being murdered by our dad and grandfather, who was convicted and sent to death row—a movie that laid out the heartbreaking details and didn't pull any punches. Not a word was spoken during the entire showing. However, when the show was over, we had a hilarious discussion. My brothers and I made fun of one another about how we looked in the show, who was fattest, whether Jim got too much face time, who was the best speaker, and other such trivia. James's grandkids were also surprisingly hilarious, seeming to get beyond the gravity of the topic and thoroughly enjoy the evening, laughing and carrying on about, and competing with, their fathers. I saw it as a

---

1. See https://www.shalomworld.org/episode/forgiving-their-mothers-murderer.

great demonstration of the closeness of our family and how we have handled the cards we were dealt.

Importantly, I believe that evening opened the door to a healthy sharing of our family history and, with the door open, we have learned more about the ripple effect of Dad's actions on his grandchildren whom he never met. It's fair to say that the impact on the five grandchildren has not involved a tide of counterproductive emotions or bad behavior, but has played out instead as a trickle of natural hurt, managed with a deluge of love. None of them ever met their grandfather, and they don't feel a connection with him. All were shocked when they learned what he had done and saddened by not knowing their grandmother, especially on occasions dear to them. Each has struggled with describing how they feel about the grandfather they never met, but all have some level of anger, hard feelings, and sadness.

Emily described her reaction as follows: "It kind of feels like I'm on the outside watching a true crime story about a cruel stranger. It's hard to believe that this happened to my family, and it doesn't feel real sometimes. I don't hate him. I don't love him. I don't really feel anything for him. But when I think about what he did, I do feel angry."

Buffington Brothers, kids, and grandkids: Bryce, Palmer James, Jim, Oscar, Judson, Louis, Emily, Abby, Emma, Aaron, Erica Buffington, June 2022

Judson and Aaron both feel ambivalence toward their grandfather and Aaron shared, "I am glad he turned things around at the end, happy for him even. But I am also glad I didn't have to meet him and try to have any feelings for him personally."

All of Dad's grandchildren have dealt effectively with their anger, and they have forgiven him or are working toward doing so. Erica's and Bryce's stories seem to capture the essence of all of their experiences.

ERICA

When my twin sister, Emily, and I were about thirteen, my dad sat us down and told us the truth about his dad arranging the murder of his mom. I think he omitted some of the more brutal details, but over the years we learned more of the story, mainly by listening to Uncle Jim give speeches and guest sermons. I believe I now have a pretty thorough understanding of what happened.

I don't think I was old enough to truly understand the impact when I first learned about the murder. I remember thinking, *Wow! I can't believe that happened. I can't imagine how hard that must've been.* But my understanding of the effects didn't get much deeper than that.

Then I grew up, graduated high school, watched my brother Aaron get married and have kids, and graduated college. I began to reflect more deeply on what had happened, mainly on how the trauma of losing his mom had affected my dad; how he had to watch all of the wonderful moments in his life and not get to share them with his mom; how he didn't get to see the pride and love in her face when she held her grandkids or great-grandkids; how he didn't get to sit next to his mom as she cheered on her grandkids as they walked across the stage at graduations; how he doesn't get to call her on her birthday or on Mother's Day. These and other such moments were stolen from him by his father. He snuffed out the life of a woman so young—actually almost exactly the age I am now. He broke the hearts of three little boys who loved their mom and dad very much. He destroyed their innocence and sense of safety and comfort. He did all of that for no reason. His selfishness and hatred stole the most important person in my father's life.

I come closest to feeling hatred toward my grandfather when I think about what my dad had to go through. Hearing Dad talk about how scared he was as a kid, and not knowing it was his father who caused that fear, makes me terribly angry. Dad spent years defending his father, who claimed his innocence for so long. I can't imagine the pain Dad felt when he finally learned the truth after all of those years. He didn't deserve to be put through that trauma and feel that kind of betrayal.

Notwithstanding all this, my dad is thoughtful, kind, funny, very loving, and a great husband, father, and grandfather. He has built a great life, and his mom would be so proud of him. To think that he had to go through something so horrific is very heartbreaking. To know that it was caused by his father, my grandfather, makes me incredibly sad. I wish so badly Dad could have had the opportunity to share his life with his mom.

I have forgiven my grandfather for what he did. I think I was able to forgive him because my dad and uncles forgave him. Seeing them do that made it easier for me to do it. However, I think my forgiveness is different than theirs. My dad and uncles had an intimate relationship with their dad. They had to forgive their father for the way he treated them, and for murdering their mom and putting them through tremendous pain, loss, and trauma. They had to forgive him for his actions, directed at them and their mom.

I wasn't alive when the crime happened, and I never met my grandma or my grandad. So while I did have to forgive my grandfather for what he did to my grandma, my forgiveness was mostly aimed toward the impact on the lives of my dad and uncles. I had to forgive him for hurting my dad and his brothers; for causing wounds that still affect them all these years later; for taking away memories that were never made; for the sadness of all the special events that my family didn't get to share with Chere.

My middle name is Chere. I am very honored that my parents named me after my grandmother. I am certain she was an incredible person and mother, and I am glad that I get to carry her name. But it also makes me kind of sad. I am named after a woman I never met. I don't have memories of spending time with her. She is not alive to see me have a daughter of my own. I won't get to say, "Hey, Grandma, meet your new great-granddaughter! I named her after you!"

If I have a daughter, I want to pass the name of Chere to her. But one day I will have to explain to that daughter why she was named Chere. I will have to explain to her what happened to her great-grandmother, and why it is so important that she was named after her. That is a little heartbreaking. But I know that seeing a little part of his mother get passed on to a new generation, and knowing that, as time passes, his mom is still a part of our family and we still think about her, will make my dad happy.

BRYCE

I am Jim and Marilyn's son, thirty-three years old, married to Caitlyn Buffington, and have a one-year-old son named Palmer James. When my grandmother, Chere, was twenty-nine years old, her ex-husband (my grandfather James) paid two men to murder her. If she were alive today, I would have a seventy-seven-year-old grandmother, and Palmer would have a great-grandmother. That explains the ripple effect on me and why forgiving my grandfather has been so difficult.

I was born at Harris Methodist Hospital in Fort Worth. Dad says he was overwhelmed with emotion, crying tears of joy, feeling so much love as Mom was bringing his son into the world. But he had a feeling of sadness too when Mom's family showed up to celebrate, and he knew that his parents would never be there.

My parents insisted that I was never to meet my grandfather, because he had prevented me from meeting my grandmother, and they didn't want me associating with an anti-role model. I never did. I heard about him and what he had done bit by bit as I was growing up. Mom and Dad were close to her parents, and we spent a lot of time with them.

At some point, probably during late elementary school, I became aware that I had never seen Dad's parents, and I started asking why. The answers were guarded for a time, like my grandmother "had passed away." But on a twelve-hour car ride home from vacation at Fort Walton Beach, Florida, when I was in junior high school, my parents came through with most of the story. I don't remember having any particular reaction, which is perhaps not surprising given my age and the passing of more than twenty-five years since the event.

Dad began telling the story on victim impact panels in prisons in 2003, and I frequently joined him to offer support, mainly as a silent partner. During Christmas break of my freshman year at the University of Arkansas, I accompanied him to a juvenile detention center where he was speaking. At the end of his story, one of the young men in the audience raised his hand, looked directly at me, and asked if I had forgiven my grandfather. His question was a real bombshell. I had never discussed much of our history with anyone outside of my family, and when I had heard the word "grandfather" I always thought of my mom's father: an amazing man who raised five girls and was a loving grandfather to many grandchildren before passing at the age of seventy-nine, when I was eleven. I referred to my "other grandfather (James)" as "Dad's dad."

My answer was "no." I told the group that I had not forgiven my dad's dad. In fact, I hated the man, and held anger toward him for what he did to my grandmother, my parents, and our extended family. The more I learned about him and put the pieces together, the angrier I got. He took away half of my grandparents. He took away nights, weekends, and years of our families' lives while they were in high school, college, and starting their own families, because of their time spent going to visit him, writing him, and attending his trials. And they supported him in other ways, such as putting money on his books, when doing so created a financial strain for them. They supported him when he was bold-face lying to them.

On the car ride home from the juvenile detention center, I told my dad how I felt about his father, and that he had affected me more than I realized. We talked about what had happened, and for the first time also discussed my dad's journey of forgiveness, as well as that of some of our other family members. I empathized with them and began to understand the ripple effects of one bad decision affecting so many, and how we all make mistakes. Some just realize where they are headed before others.

From the beginning, I didn't think I needed to forgive Dad's dad. Why should I forgive someone I had never met, who was dead and gone? How could I forgive in that situation? However, as I considered it more and thought about how he hurt family members, took my grandmother, and affected me, I became angrier. Then I began to see reasons for forgiving him.

Volunteering as a facilitator for small groups of offenders with the Bridges To Life prison ministry helped soften my heart to people who go down the wrong path in life. A prime example of one of life's many "coincidences" occurred when I volunteered in a small group and became friends with Ken Rawlins, my grandfather's prison cellmate during a time shortly before he died. Ken, who had been released from prison and began volunteering with Bridges To Life, told me in first person about the James Buffington he knew.

After hearing more about the memorial service inside the prison and how my dad's dad had changed, and having more discussions with my family, I began to forgive him for his choices and mistakes. We've all made mistakes and needed forgiveness, and the Bible talks about how no sin is worse than another. That's been a struggle for me to process. However, I am confident we all receive more grace from God than we deserve, and I've concluded I owe my "other grandfather" a generous helping of grace, even acknowledging his awful decisions.

Jim and Ken Rawlins, with picture of James at Bryce's wedding, February 15, 2020

Although I have forgiven Dad's dad, there has been no clearly identifiable act of forgiveness. I told myself I forgave him. I don't feel the same anger. While there will always be a little bit of anger, I don't wish anything bad on him anymore. I don't think I would have continued to volunteer in prisons, trying to help people who have done what he did, if I hadn't forgiven him. Caitlyn and I named our son Palmer James. While the name was to honor my father, I believe the use of the name "James" carries a symbolic element of forgiveness and redemption of his great-grandfather.

Perhaps mountain climbing is a good metaphor for my experience. Climbing a mountain requires a journey in two directions. A mountain climber slowly traverses difficult terrain and makes their way up the mountain. Then they change directions and take the difficult journey down. Forgiveness worked that way for me. My anger and hatred were a journey, starting at a low level and reaching a higher level as I learned more. When I had all I could handle, I changed directions and began my journey of forgiveness, with great difficulty, to the peace I felt in the beginning. My journey represented a full circle of crime and forgiveness: forgiveness that I owed to God, my family, and myself.

Now that I have my own son, I am starting to realize how much every action I take affects Palmer James, and other people as well. It's easy to ask God why certain things happen to "me," but what I should ask is why things happen to me, how can I learn and grow from them and use them for God's good. I believe this path to forgiveness has helped me to learn and grow, and will serve God by being a model for Palmer James and others. While it may seem like the end of a journey, I suspect it's only part of a bigger legacy.

JIM

During the writing of this book, Mom's brother, Herman Stieferman, passed away. We were able to visit with Herman, Dana, and their son,

Scott Stieferman, and with all of Chere Buffington's kids, grandkids, and great-grandkids shortly before his death. A group picture demonstrates how the ripple effect impacts so many people now and in the future.

Stieferman and Buffington extended family

CHAPTER TWENTY-FOUR

Legacy

"And the things you have heard me say in the presence
of many witnesses entrust to reliable people who will also
be qualified to teach others." (2 Timothy 2:2)

Shortly after Dad's memorial service in 1994, Pastor Gary Smith at my church in Arlington, Fielder Road Baptist Church (now Fielder Church), asked if he could share our story with the congregation. I was a little reluctant at first, as this would be quite a reversal of my lifetime of trying to keep the story under wraps. I could see little value in discussing my life, which I considered "normal." However, after thinking about it, I decided that what seemed so normal to our family was not normal at all to most other people. They could learn some things from hearing about what Dad did, how he changed, and how he touched so many lives—for bad and for good. Perhaps our sharing the narrative of our family would bring a measure of good from all the bad. So I agreed.

The pastor started his Sunday morning sermon as usual with several predictable platitudes, amidst the muted rumblings of a congregation with attitudes ranging from sincere reverence to pious indifference. Then his words became more direct, his tone more animated. People began to realize they were hearing about one of their own, about a friend's father paying someone to murder his mother, about crime and redemption touching their congregation.

You could hear a pin drop. People were astounded at what they were hearing, at what we went through, at the story of crime, forgiveness, and redemption among their own. When the service ended, Marilyn and I were inundated with expressions of sympathy, love, and support from friends and strangers alike. We began to see that our tragic experience conveyed a story of transformation that could be affirming and hopeful.

In our Christmas card that year, Marilyn and I shared our story more broadly. I soon began receiving requests to speak from various churches. Encouraged by the words of the Christian hymn, "Let The Redeemed Of The Lord Say So," I began accepting invitations.

What does it mean to be His
To be formed in His likeness
Know that we have a purpose
To be salt and light in the world, in the world
To be salt and light in the world
Let the redeemed of the Lord say so

The next time I spoke was at Third Baptist Church in Malvern. Although we had worshipped there, very few of the congregants knew about my parents, which they were hearing about for the first time. When I revealed my story of hurt, change, and forgiveness, I realized how much telling it was helping me heal. Just talking about it helped me form a mental picture that I could examine, critique, and expose to new thinking in ways that helped me grow.

I also came to believe that by talking about Mom and Dad, I was honoring them—my mom, and how she loved me and led me to faith; and my dad, who did some horrible things, but eventually asked for forgiveness, became a Christian, and changed his life and the life of many others. I soon realized that many people struggle with problems in their lives and need to be forgiven and/or forgive bad parents, inconsiderate siblings, cheating spouses, or other hurtful people. Several of them thanked me for telling my story and told me that it provided them a lesson in life, opening their eyes to how to forgive and ask for forgiveness.

After I told my story in approximately twenty churches and protested several parole applications of Charles County and Charlie Moore, I came to the attention of the Texas Department of Criminal Justice. A representative of their Victim Services Division contacted me and asked me to speak on a victim impact panel in a prison.

Victim impact panels are generally comprised of one to four victims of crime speaking to, and answering questions from, groups of inmates, ranging from a half-dozen to a hundred or so offenders. Those impacted by crime speak about the offenses against them and relate first-person accounts of how crime impacted their lives, and continues to do so. The purpose is to help perpetrators of crime recognize and internalize the lasting, long-term effects of what they have done to others. These stories, told without blaming or judgment, seek to create empathy in the perpetrators and leave a permanent impression that leads to changes in thinking and behavior, and prevents future offenses.

My first thought was *Absolutely not*. I was comfortable speaking in churches, but had never been in a prison except to visit Dad in the safety of a visiting area and to attend his memorial. Why should I speak to a group of criminals that in all probability included men who had killed someone else's mom? And to be candid, why should I go behind locked steel doors into the bowels of a prison where I understood there were signs posted to the effect of, "We will not negotiate for return of hostages."

However, I couldn't rid myself of that nagging feeling that I might be missing an opportunity, or perhaps even a calling. I thought about the request, prayed about it, and had additional discussions with staff of victim services. They explained that the main objective of the panels was to encourage offenders to empathize with victims, and help prevent future crimes. I finally decided that if I could possibly help prevent a crime, and help another family avoid what ours had endured, then I should bare my soul.

The first panel I participated in was in 2003 at the federal prison in Seagoville, Texas, a low-security federal correctional institution located less than an hour from my home in Arlington. Approximately ninety inmates gathered in a big gymnasium to hear a panel of four of us talk about our lives and answer their questions.

Connie Hilton spoke first. She shared her story of stepping out of her bathroom in the early morning hours of a fall day several years before and seeing a man standing in the hallway with a shotgun. She screamed, and her husband came running. The man shot and killed him. Two other men quickly joined the attacker, and the three of them beat her until she could no longer scream or move. One of the men raped her, while the other two helped themselves to their possessions. They blindfolded her, tied her up, and left her for dead. Connie's life became a living hell.

Two of the men who assaulted Connie had never been apprehended for that crime, and for all she knew, could have been in the group she was addressing. She told her awful story—similar in so many ways to what happened to my mom, except that Connie had lived to talk about it—with fearlessness, dignity, and grace. Hearing it created a real connection for me and gave me the confidence to tell my story. It seemed like Mom would have approved of me sharing her story as well.

I recounted my experience in all its gory details, including Dad's horrendous actions and his repentance. I aimed to give myself a small measure of healing and make the listeners feel as guilty as possible. I was really surprised at how the inmates connected with me, mainly because I had been an inmate's son. I got most of the questions. They asked what happened to Charles County and Charlie Moore, and I told them County had been released, but Moore was still in prison. They asked a lot of questions pertaining to forgiveness, one of which was, "If you have forgiven them, why do you protest their parole?"

"They killed my mom, and I'm going to stand up for her," I replied. "They should be in prison because that's what the jury gave them. That is the parole board's decision and not mine."

Another man asked, "What's it like to visit your dad in prison?"

I gave them some advice when I replied, "You may almost force your kids to come see you—but that's probably the worst thing you can do for them. They reconnect with you, but often it's not a good situation, involving lots of waiting time, a visit, and then they have to leave. They relive losing their dad to prison every time they leave a visit. It's like a cut on the arm that has healed with a scab, and then they visit, and the scab is knocked off and the wound is open again. The pain of losing their family member to prison comes back. I'm not saying don't do it, but from the kids' perspective, it's awful."

Sharing my story was difficult and heartbreaking, as it forced me to relive in detail that horrible time of Mom's violent death and its aftermath. But it also gave me a powerful sense of release, as if by talking about my ordeal I was able to take another step toward getting beyond it. It also helped confirm what I said at Dad's memorial—that I had much in common with the inmates I was addressing. We had a common humanity. All of us were God's creatures, engulfed by his love, but who made different choices in our lives. But for the grace of God, I could have been in their shoes.

As Connie and I were chatting after our presentations, she asked me if I'd ever heard of Bridges To Life (BTL). I said no. She explained that she was the program director for BTL, a faith-based restorative justice ministry that aims to connect communities to prisons in an effort to reduce the recidivism of released inmates, minimize the number of crime victims, and enhance public safety. Bridges To Life was founded in 1998 by Houstonian John Sage after the brutal murder of his sister in 1993. John realized the terrible toll this tragic event had taken, not only on his family's life, but also on those of his sister's friends, coworkers, and the community at large.

Connie continued, "It uses an intensive, fourteen-week process during which victim volunteers and offenders are brought together with volunteer facilitators. Victims tell their stories in small groups, which provides an opportunity for the offenders to openly discuss their crimes and understand the impact on their victims, their families, and society."

Connie said that at the end of each program a graduation ceremony is held where inmates describe what they learned from the program and how it affected their lives. She invited me to attend one of the graduations. I accepted and was impressed with what I heard. I was particularly moved by hearing offenders who had completed the program tell of how they began to feel a sense of empathy when they listened to victims tell of what happened to them and how crime affected their lives.

As I reflected on my story, I began to see that sharing it could have an equal or greater effect on inmates. Hearing of Mom's love for her three sons, that had such a huge impact on my life, could affect other lives as well. My Dad's really bad choices that led to so much pain for so many, followed by his faith decision and experience of redemption, could become a model for the incarcerated offenders. Our story could demonstrate how God can take something meant for bad and turn it to His good, and telling it would honor both my parents and their legacy.

I became a BTL volunteer a few months later. This work has strengthened my faith and provided a vehicle for me to share with others how they can overcome adversity and heal themselves. As difficult as it may be to imagine, I believe the worst of Dad's life left a legacy of good. But for him and what he did, I would not have become involved in the Bridges To Life prison ministry.

The organization began operating in 1999 when a group of sixteen volunteers, many victims of crime, conducted two-hour sessions each week for eleven consecutive weeks at one prison in Richmond, Texas. Forty-one inmates completed that project. By 2014, the organization had grown to include a paid staff of thirteen and over 500 active volunteers. That year it conducted almost 100 projects in fifty-four facilities, touching almost 4,000 offenders, mostly within the State of Texas.

Each of the projects, later expanded to fourteen weeks, addresses topics that include understanding the effects of crime and the relationship between offenders and victims; the importance of faith and stories in the healing process; responsibility and accountability for offenses; and the importance of confession, repentance, forgiveness, reconciliation, and restitution.

I began volunteering with the program after Connie's invitation in 2004, serving as a speaker, telling my story, and as a small group facilitator. On January 1, 2016, I retired from my business career at the Merrill Corporation and joined BTL as the chief operating officer. Since then,

I have had the opportunity to help the organization grow and increase its influence and impact for good. As of mid-2023, over 75,000 offenders have graduated from the BTL program since its inception, with the help of more than 3,500 volunteers. Bridges To Life projects have been conducted in more than 220 facilities, and its curriculum has been used in seventeen states and seven foreign countries. Studies confirm that BTL participation has reduced recidivism—the rate at which released offenders returned to prison—by 30 percent, and by 62 percent among those who committed a violent crime. More than 86 percent of BTL graduates do not return to prison within three years after release.

BTL is based on the principles of restorative justice, which aims to heal the harm caused by crime. There is a saying in prison that "hurt people hurt people," but through BTL I have learned that "healed people can heal people." I believe I have contributed to this success, and to improving the lives of many offenders and their families, as well as victims of crime and their families. But for Dad, I never would have done so. Seems to me that Dad left a legacy that has gone well beyond what he did at the Ellis Unit.

CHAPTER TWENTY-FIVE

Reflections

"Because of the Lord's great love we are not consumed,
for his compassions never fail. They are new every morning;
great is your faithfulness." (Lamentations 3:22–23)

Killing someone is usually considered murder. Conspiracy to commit murder is generally found to be present when one or more persons agree to kill someone, even when "agreement" is not specifically articulated, but is inferred from the conduct of the parties. The Texas Penal Code provides that a person is criminally responsible for the actions of another if they are engaged in a criminal conspiracy to commit a murder, or if they should have anticipated a murder committed by a coconspirator. A conspiracy, which involves a secret plan or agreement between people for a harmful purpose, usually leaves the victim or victims with unanswered questions and compelling riddles. That was the case here. This chapter summarizes some of Jim's reflections on the mysteries concerning what happened and why.

I guess I've told my story more than one hundred times over the years—to individuals, small groups, and large groups, in churches and in penitentiaries, to victims and to criminals. I am convinced that each telling has benefited my listeners and me. Hearing about my life helps listeners connect with others and better understand their lives, who they are, their perspectives, their interpretation of things, and their knowledge and understanding of the world, while triggering feelings and emotions such as empathy, sadness, and joy. Sharing my story has helped me reflect on my life and see new perspectives.

This book is another telling, albeit in much more detail than previous ones. I have learned from it. I've extracted more memories, discovered

249

more facts, connected more dots, seen clearer themes, and also surfaced some unanswered questions.

In addition to my dad, four individuals—and perhaps seven—arguably were part of the conspiracy to murder Mom, my brothers, and me. Charles County and Charlie Moore were for sure involved in the plot. David Savere and Charlotte Jacobs may, or may not, have been involved in the conspiracy and had a role in arranging the murder. County's dad and a couple of their drinking buddies were certainly at the wrong place at the wrong time, and could have been involved. But exactly who did what among them remains a mystery.

David Savere, the local college student, and Dad's former employee, admitted to a connection and testified twice that he heard Dad say he wanted Mom killed. There was no direct evidence that Savere was involved in the killing. He claimed he had nothing to do with it, and didn't go to the police because he thought the conversation was "not important." However, could Savere have been that close and not be complicit in the plot? Quite a few people thought he was deeply involved. Whether he was is a mystery.

Charlotte Jacobs's situation was like Savere's, as she was never charged with a crime, and exactly what part she played, if any, remains a mystery. However, according to police detectives, there was convincing circumstantial evidence from which her participation in the conspiracy could be inferred. This seemed clearly confirmed forty years later by the contents of a suitcase found in my Uncle Norris's attic.

After my uncle, Norris Buffington, passed away, his wife Carole found a small brown suitcase in the attic of their home. She passed it on to me in July, 2017, roughly forty years after Dad left it for safekeeping. I don't know whether he gave it to his brother right after the murder in 1976, or just before his arrest in 1977, or sometime between; but it's clear his purpose was to hide some things he didn't want others to know about and use against him.

When I examined the contents of the suitcase, I found that most of the things in it were not proof of a crime: truck titles, work papers, child custody papers, bank records, payroll ledgers, and such. They did, however, confirm what I already knew: that my dad was financially broke from late 1975 to Mom's murder in 1976, and he spent most of the money he did have on life insurance on Mom and us three boys, on maintaining the three of us, and on a salary for his secretary Charlotte Jacobs.

Suitcase found in the attic

Picture in suitcase

Papers and calendar in suitcase

Three items stood out. One was a picture of Jacobs in her underwear, and a second was a brown wallet that was completely empty except for a packaged condom. The third was two pages that had been torn out of Dad's office calendar. One page was for Friday, March 19, 1976 (the day before the murder) with some sort of code written on it. The other page, for Saturday March 20, 1976, was blank. Although I have never been able to break the code on the calendar page, these items removed any lingering uncertainty in my mind that my dad and Jacobs really did have an affair, and that they did plan my mom's murder for hire to get insurance money. It "closed the case," as far as I was concerned.

What Dad was thinking when he left the suitcase with his brother is a mystery. However, the contents suggest to me that he anticipated a fight for his freedom and expected to win it and return to a life more or less as it had been. Who knows what he told his brother, and who knows what turmoil it caused my uncle to "hide" the suitcase for so many years and never tell me, anyone in the family, or even his own wife, about it. I guess Norris, Jr. just put it in the attic and tried to forget about it.

The evidence presented at the second trial that County's father-in-law, Buck, apparently was driving their truck, and David Savere and a man named Buddy Savoy were along for the ride when they went to Mom's apartment, looking for her on the day she was murdered, makes me wonder whether they were involved more than just "coincidentally." Perhaps they were also participants in the conspiracy.

Three individuals were convicted and sent to prison for their roles in Mom's murder. Whether others should have been included remains an open question. The cases against them, if there ever were any, were closed years ago and remain closed today.

There also is the question of who actually shot our mom. As previously discussed, Charles County was convicted of murder, sent to death row, retried several times, served his term in prison, and was released. Moore was sentenced in a plea bargain to a seventeen-year sentence, released on parole, and subsequently sentenced to life in prison as a habitual criminal. Evidence as to who pulled the trigger is conflicting. These were the only witnesses, and each blames the other. We just do not know for sure who pulled the trigger and killed my mom.

The mysteries of who was involved in the conspiracy and who pulled the trigger are thought-provoking, but the apparent enigma that was James Buffington; and whether his "change" was real and honest is perhaps more intriguing. I am not a psychologist or sociologist, and I claim no expertise in the subject beyond that of a reasonably well-informed lay-person and a son who knew his father pretty well. I also believe some things I learned during this writing, some new perspectives I developed, and some observations I made, shed light on this question.

A person who is an enigma is a mystery, and has a confusing mixture of qualities that seem to be in opposition to one another. One never knows what that person is really thinking, or what their motives for doing something are. This seems to have been the case with James Buffington. Borrowing a phrase, he was an "enigma wrapped in a cocoon of contradictions." As previously discussed, he seemed deeply religious, an apparently faithful Christian, church leader, and loving husband and father; yet was controlling, manipulative, and abusive, locked on death row, charged with the murder of his ex-wife. He helped others, but also expected help. He conveyed equal portions of narcissism and love. He was part scripture-quoting pastor and part jailhouse lawyer. He was big (over 300 pounds) and little (less than 200 pounds). He seemed to have been so smart, and yet so dumb.

Before this writing, I had mainly characterized Dad in my mind as a "conventional" murderer, whose act of killing was motivated mostly by financial greed and his intent to collect on life insurance policies. In my mind, the enigma arose from the conflicting characteristics of an apparent Christian who hired two men to assassinate his ex-wife to enrich himself.

As I reflected on the situation however, I became convinced there was a more likely explanation, and that he was a domestic abuser intent on exercising control. Most domestic abusers are enigmas. They frequently appear to be good guys, while using emotional and physical abuse to maintain power over a partner or other family member, to control the behavior of that person, or to directly or indirectly cause her to do what they want her to do.

Most domestic abusers exhibit several common characteristics in their everyday life. They appear to be generous, but their generosity is a calculated act to control their victims and excuse their violence. They mask their insecurities with their efforts to be in control. They try to explain their jealousy and possessiveness under the guise of "love." Some claim a faith in God, and purposefully misinterpret scripture to justify their controlling actions. They are charming and portray themselves as warm, kind, and caring, but in reality are manipulative, and know exactly what to say and how to act to get what they want. They anger easily, and refuse to take responsibility for their actions. They often abuse alcohol and blame substance use for their domestic abuse. They act like a macho male and show little or no emotion. They have little regard for the law. They place blame on others and never on themselves. They have a dual personality, like Jekyll and Hyde.

Dad no doubt was after the insurance money he received when Mom was murdered, and I make no pretense of reading his mind at the time. However, I believe the weight of the evidence supports the view that he had most of the characteristics of a domestic abuser, and his driving motivation was to control his ex-wife and his sons. He had a history of abuse, and demonstrated a relationship dominated by coercive control.

Mom's boyfriend at the time of her death, Ken, said she told him about how Dad treated her when they were married: that he frequently humiliated, hassled, and belittled her, and held us three boys over her head to get things from her or to make her do things. Ken said that Mom had little money and often had almost no food in her apartment. Sometimes she did not eat for days. She was taking some heart pills, and on one occasion she decided to take all the pills at once and just end all her problems. She didn't follow through, and never considered such a dire action again.

The divorce was a trigger that threatened Dad's control and escalated his control tactics. A comment made in a bar apparently planted the idea of homicide. He planned the murder by hiring a killer. The result was the assassination. He tried to use the escalating series of bad choices— going to happy hours and returning home drunk at two in the morning, spending all their money, while Mom worked all day and came home and fixed dinner and did homework with us boys, his affair with Charlotte Jacobs, hitting Mom—to explain his ultimate act of abuse. When he couldn't control her, he had her killed, apparently intended to have us boys killed as well, and lost whatever control of his life he had. He continued his controlling efforts even after Mom's death, when he made the arrangements for her burial with little or no involvement of her family. All considered, his actions as an abuser who committed a murder seem entirely consistent, and not an enigma at all.

It seems to me that Dad probably continued his abuser's attitude and behavior for more or less fifteen years after he was arrested in 1976, until sometime after he confessed the murder in 1989 and was assigned to the Ellis Unit. During this period, he exhibited characteristics of a "jailhouse Christian" with two different personas: maintaining his innocence in the face of his own knowledge and compelling evidence to the contrary, doing "good works" for the purpose of manipulating and maintaining control, talking the talk without walking the walk. Seems to me he probably didn't change who he really was until he confessed to Marilyn and me, because he saw no reason to change.

Then when he confessed to us that he had Mom killed and lied about it all those years, and our family cut off all connection and protested his parole, he had a reason to change. He told me he "hit rock bottom." Just adopting his good-guy persona, and changing his behavior to gain favor or feeling sorry for what he had done, was not enough. He needed to transform his fundamental character, leave his sins and bad behavior behind, and radically and deliberately change his heart as well as his behavior.

Whether he actually did this, and whether he deserves credit for what he did when it seemed to be so much to his advantage after he had hit bottom, is between Dad and his Creator. But I am convinced that, even as manipulative as he was, he did not con me, Richard Lopez, Ken Rawlins, and all those inmates who believed in him. I believe he rejected his bad side and became the good guy who he previously only pretended to be. He wasn't two people at the same time. He was a violent abuser until he wasn't. He changed. After that he was the committed Christian he claimed to be. That seems to resolve the enigma.

I also became intrigued by how Oscar, Louis, and I seem to have avoided a predictable generational curse and, it seems to me, demonstrated so many of our father's positive attributes and so few of his negative ones. One example is that I may have avoided the possibility of a generational curse when I made the choice to walk away and didn't try to kill Charlie Moore during our mediation. A second example involves domestic violence and avoiding it's perpetuation. Boys who experience domestic violence grow up to have a great risk of becoming abusers themselves, and the burden of domestic violence is passed from one generation to the next. In one of many studies on this issue, researchers found that four out of five children living with violent partners eventually committed violence against their own partners as adults. Most men who grew up in violent homes do not want that for their own families. Unfortunately, they do not have a model for the right way to be a spouse and parent, and it's hard for them to figure it out on their own.

As far as I can tell, Oscar, Louis, and I are examples of sons who somehow figured it out. The trauma in our lives destroyed any feeling of security or stability, and made us feel like orphans, but at the same time strengthened our bonds as brothers. We fought each other big time, but we were always together, had a lot of fun with each other, and were each other's best friends. The divorce tightened our bonds, and after Mom was murdered, it was us against the world. Over the years, we continued to support one another—I believe with honesty, kindness, humor, and grace. We now spend time with one another and are best friends, probably closer than most siblings. We are men of faith who are committed to walking the talk, being good dads, and leading loving families.

How did Oscar, Louis, and I manage to avoid so many of our dad's bad characteristics? I suspect the answer starts with our mother. While the evidence seems to be somewhat vague as to at what age children are most influenced by their parents, it's clear that parents have a significant impact at an early age. Even with her early death, each of us remembers a mother who loved him, cared for him, and supported him, and this seems to have provided a model for our future lives. Our mom raised us to be good kids, and even in our struggles today we often ask ourselves what Mom would think. Her early good influence seems to have won out over the bad influence of our dad.

Our faith must also have been a factor. During our formative years, Dad seemed to be a role model for a life of faith, and we didn't see through his hypocrisy. Both before and after his incarceration, he insisted that we attend church and make faith part of our lives. The fact that we attended church regularly, learned what was right and what was wrong, and looked to prayer and God for guidance gave us purpose and attracted good into our lives. The many like-minded friends among church youth groups and the adult couples who "took us in" provided mentors who helped us navigate the tough times, and models of how a good family functions.

Each of us married empathetic, compassionate, supportive, helpful, caring, loving women who have our backs. We all want a stable home and do not want our wives or children to experience the trauma we experienced. Our marriages have become a source of stability and security, a confirmation of our faith, and a barrier against a generational curse.

And finally, we believe we had an awful dad, and very much want to turn our experience around and be the best dads we can be. We don't want our families to experience what we experienced, so we have become intentional about the kind of husbands and dads we want to be and the choices we make.

My life has taken a slightly different direction than Oscar's and Louis's. As the oldest sibling, I was more involved in dealing with the the aftermath of Mom's murder and the issues Dad caused. This involvement seems to have played forward in a couple of seemingly paradoxical ways.

An email I received on November 1, 2022, from the Texas Department of Criminal Justice introduces a paradox that seems to pit forgiveness against consequences:

> The Victim Services Division (VSD) sends our sincere regrets for the criminal victimization you have experienced. It is our goal to assist you in participating in the criminal justice process. This is to notify you that the TDCJ is processing (Charlie Moore's) case for review by the Texas Board of Pardons and Paroles (BPP) as of 11/01/2022. The purpose of this review is for the BPP to decide whether to release the offender to supervision. Supervision means the offender would serve the remainder of their sentence in the community under the supervision of a parole officer.
>
> ... This notification is to confirm your request to speak with the BPP during the review of this offender's case. The case will be forwarded to the BPP within the next two to six months.

... You are welcome to provide a written statement to help the BPP understand how the offense has affected you.

I am on record to protest Charlie Moore's parole anytime it is considered. I have done so every year, or every few years, since the 1980s, each time he became eligible for parole. In 2017, Moore was released on parole even though our whole family protested, and I objected in person. I told the Parole Board I was very concerned that he would harm another person again if released.

About six months later, while on TDCJ's super intensive supervision program, Moore was arrested again for trying to strangle a lady to death. Fortunately, she survived, and Moore was re-arrested, convicted, and sentenced in 2018 to two years in prison. Because he violated his parole by committing a new crime, he reverted back to his previous crime, which resulted in a life sentence. However he is still eligible for parole review.

In March 2023, as this book was being written, Marilyn and I traveled to Amarillo to make our case to keep him behind bars as he faced another parole hearing. The main discussion point at the hearing was our concern as to how to protect others from additional harm based on his past multiple crime history. Although I have forgiven him for what he did, I continue to believe that, if he were released, he might well commit another similar crime. Therefore, he must live with the consequences imposed by the State when his sentence was assessed.

The Parole Board denied Moore's parole for another two years. I plan to do this again in March of 2025, when he will be seventy-nine years old. We will continue to do what we can to be sure Moore cannot hurt anyone else.

The second seeming paradox is that I, a crime victim, work full-time to help men and women who are incarcerated for doing things like Dad, County, and Moore did to Mom. My interest in prison ministry and work with Bridges To Life is a classic example of bad leading to good, as Dad's bad behavior motivated me to become involved.

The purpose of this book is to share the power of our family story, become part of the Buffington family legacy, and foster a more-detailed and broader telling within the prison ministry community—to help both offenders and crime victims. *Betrayed By Choices* has answered several core questions about the crime itself, but has not answered some key unknowns. What is perhaps unknowable to us, and of continuing interest, is the question of how so much good could come from something so bad. How could James's life leave such a legacy of good? How could three boys faced with what we endured become what we became? Would I be leading the Bridges To Life prison ministry in its transformative processes if Dad hadn't killed Mom? Didn't Dad's legacy of redemption go well beyond what he did at the Ellis Unit?

What is very clear is that my mom left me a legacy of a mother's love, a faith that redeems, and an opportunity to "tell the world" of my story and my faith. These gifts have allowed me to avoid the prison of hate and anger, to forgive and accept forgiveness, and to share this story of love and redemption. We hope that this writing will perpetuate the legacies of Mom and Dad.

In memory of my mom, Chere Jean Stieferman Buffington

In memory of my dad, James Glen Buffington Sr.

Appendix

BUFFINGTON FAMILY

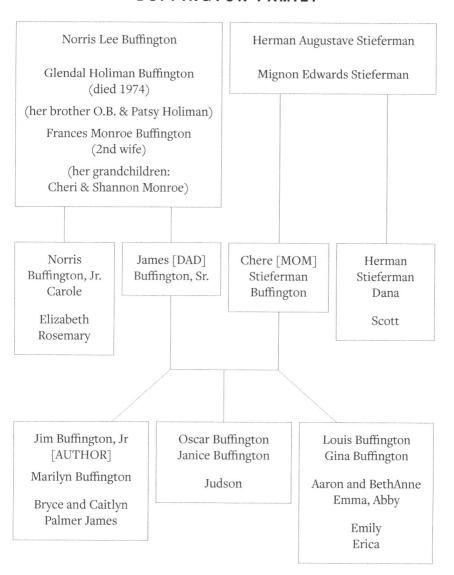

Norris Lee Buffington

Glendal Holiman Buffington
(died 1974)

(her brother O.B. & Patsy Holiman)

Frances Monroe Buffington
(2nd wife)

(her grandchildren:
Cheri & Shannon Monroe)

Herman Augustave Stieferman

Mignon Edwards Stieferman

Norris
Buffington, Jr.
Carole

Elizabeth
Rosemary

James [DAD]
Buffington, Sr.

Chere [MOM]
Stieferman
Buffington

Herman
Stieferman
Dana

Scott

Jim Buffington, Jr
[AUTHOR]

Marilyn Buffington

Bryce and Caitlyn
Palmer James

Oscar Buffington
Janice Buffington

Judson

Louis Buffington
Gina Buffington

Aaron and BethAnne
Emma, Abby

Emily
Erica

SIGNIFICANT OTHERS

Attorneys

Andy Logan: investigator for James's court-appointed attorney

Cecil Bain: James's attorney

Charles Butts: Charles County's attorney

John Hrncir: James's court-appointed attorney

Linda Sorber: James's attorney and family friend

Mark Stevens: James's court-appointed attorney

Marvin Zimmerman: James's court-appointed attorney

Tom Thurmond: James's attorney

Convicted Killers

Charles County: accused trigger man in the murder

Charlie Moore: accused trigger man in the murder

Detectives

Abel Juarez

Richard Stengle

Robert Fleming

Friends and Others

Alva Wheeler: Linda Kay Morrey's mother

Bailey Smith: evangelist

Blake Henson: Jim's friend from college and best man

Carol Gibson: Chere's friend

Carolyn McGinnis: Marilyn's twin sister

Chris Hansen: Jim's friend from high school in Austin

Connie Hilton: Bridges To Life program director

David Burnett: Jim's friend from high school in Austin

Dub Ashton: Jim's college marketing professor

Genevieve Logan: Catholic chaplain who counseled James in prison

Irene Wilcox: prison volunteer, sang at James's funeral

Janet and Ted Daniel: neighbors at the Big House

John Sage: Bridges To Life founder and CEO

Jorgen and Sandy Hoberg: family friends from church

Judy Hansen: Jim's youth choir pastor in Austin

Ken Rawlins: James's prison cellmate

Kevin and Scott Briscoe: Jim's friends from high school in Austin

Maria: James's spiritual adviser in prison

Mike Barr: Jim's friend from high school in Arkansas and college roommate

Phil and Sarah Brumley: family friends from church in Arkansas

Richard Lopez: prison chaplain

Tammy: Linda Kay Morrey's daughter

Judges and Mediators

Gene Stewart: TDCJ mediator

J.P. Gutierrez: Justice of the Peace

John G Benavides: District Court judge

Peter Michael Curry: trial judge

Pastors

Dr. Gary Smith, Fielder Church

Dr. Jimmy Draper, officiant at James and Chere's wedding

Rev. Bill Fortson, officiant at Chere's funeral

Rev. James McKee, officiant at Chere's funeral

Prosecutors

Bill Harris: assistant prosecutor in James's second trial

Charles Conaway: chief prosecutor in James's first trial

Julian Lopez: chief prosecutor in James's second trial

Trial Witnesses

Bobby Jacobs: Life insurance manager

Buddy Savoy: Charles County friend

C. W. Williamson: security guard at Longfellow Junior High School
Charlotte Jacobs: fictitious name for James's secretary
David Chasen: Life Insurance Agent
David Savere: college student and Charles County friend
Dr. Betty Schroeder: psychiatrist
Dr. James Duff: medical examiner
Dr. James Grigson: psychiatrist
Dr. Nevil Murray: psychiatrist
Dr. Richard Cameron: psychiatrist
Ed Currie: James's friend from high school
Gary White: Life Insurance Agent
Gordon Caton: Chere's former employer
Idell County: Charles County's wife
Ken McDaniel: Chere's boyfriend after the divorce
Linda Kay Morrey: James's second wife
Mary Rodgers: a friend of Charles County
Mayola Taylor: Charles County's girlfriend
Verdo County: Charles County's father
Willie Arthur "Buck" Wilburn: Charles County's father-in-law

Acknowledgments

Jim Buffington, Jr., and Kirk Blackard collaborated on the writing of *BETRAYED BY CHOICES: A Family Story of Murder, Forgiveness, and Redemption* as a forging of like minds and different experiences, with each bringing his own unique perspective to the project. Jim lived the story, a history of a major portion of his life. Over the years, he spent many hours figuring out what happened, thinking about its implications for him and others, and talking about his conclusions with people in churches and prisons. As a consequence of his experiences, he volunteered with the Bridges To Life prison ministry and became its chief operating officer. Jim and Kirk became acquainted at Bridges To Life.

Kirk is a retired lawyer and business executive, and a long-time volunteer and member of Bridges To Life's Board of Directors. He is the author of *Restoring Peace: Using Lessons from Prison to Mend Broken Relationships*, which is the centerpiece of the ministry's curriculum, along with four other books dealing with matters of crime, conflict, repentance, and forgiveness. He makes no claim to a special expertise or to having many answers in these areas. However, he believes his experiences provided a true appreciation of the questions to be asked.

BETRAYED BY CHOICES is a long and complex family story involving many people. It is based on Jim's memory, the memories of several others who were part of the story, letters written by James Buffington when he was incarcerated, correspondence among others who were involved, official records, and media reports.

The authors recognize that memory is fluid and inevitably changes over time. People remember through their own eyes or experiences, and sometimes they forget. And the consequences of events comprising this story have rippled through quite a few families and many individuals. All have been affected, each in their own way. Each has some different memories of what happened, and each might tell a slightly different version of the story. We also recognize that media reports and other documents are not always accurate, and sometimes need to be taken with a grain of salt.

In this context, we have done our best to tell a truthful story. There are no composite or fictional characters in the book. All the names used are correct names for real people, with one exception: "Charlotte Jacobs" is a fictitious name for a real person. All the events described actually happened. Many are verifiable in the records, and to the best of our understanding and recollection, all happened in substance as they are depicted. In cases where individuals could not remember specific time or sequence, we took our best guess. We also have taken the liberty of filling in some details based on the way we know things to have been, rather than a recollection of specific details.

We have included some contemporaneous dialogue in quotations. This represents the kind of conversations that occurred, in the context of known facts such as the location, the people, and the events, rather than a reference to a written record or specific memory of precise words that were spoken.

Quotation of contemporary written material, including excerpts from James's writings, is verbatim. We relied largely on James himself to unwrap the apparent enigma of his life. He was a prolific writer when he was incarcerated, and Jim retained nearly all of the letters written to him, as well as many written to others. Much of James's writing concerned mundane, day-to-day activities. Other reflected his views about life and what had happened to him. We attempted to omit most of the mundane, while including enough to give the reader a picture of what James did and who he was, painted with his own brush. We also included excerpts from several letters written by other individuals. All are quoted verbatim, with few corrections to basic errors of punctuation, style, spelling, typos, and such. A few issues that seemed important for the reader's background understanding were explained in italics.

We have also included within quotation marks current memories or feelings of several individuals. These are verbatim quotes of what individuals said or wrote in connection with interviews for this book.

Drafts of the manuscript were reviewed with Jim's younger brothers, Oscar and Louis, who lived basically the same experiences as Jim; and with Jim's wife Marilyn, who joined the family about ten years into the story and became an active participant. All agree with our telling of the story.

In summary, we have been scrupulous about the people and events we have presented as facts, and conscientious about telling the essential truth of the story, while taking some liberty with details as long as they have fostered a truthful account.

Our thanks go to many people for help in making this book what it is. First and foremost, we express our appreciation to Oscar and Louis. The book is their story as well as Jim's, although they experienced parts of it differently, and remember it through the lens of their eyes rather than Jim's. We thank them for being vulnerable enough to allow it to be written, for their total cooperation with the effort, for providing any assistance requested, and for reading early drafts to help assure the accuracy of what we were writing.

Thanks also to Marilyn, Gina, and Janice; and to James and Chere Buffington's grandkids—Aaron, Emily, Erica, Judson, and Bryce—for their participation and support.

Several individuals read the manuscript and provided invaluable feedback that significantly improved the product. Special thanks go to Alec Schrader, Tim Anderson, David Kurtz, Michele Duskin, Roy Lee Jackson, and Val Padley for all their time and efforts that made the book better than it otherwise would have been.

JIM

Thank you to Kirk Blackard for encouraging me and helping me to write this book that tells the whole story. He spent much time researching case files, trial transcripts, Dad's letters, and newspaper articles, asking questions and writing drafts. I am forever grateful for his time, guidance, and friendship through this process. We were able to capture all the details and also honor both my mom and my dad with their legacies. I am especially thankful for my incredible wife Marilyn, who has stood by my side for thirty-eight years, and for God's great faithfulness to us.

KIRK

My thanks go out to all my family and friends who have supported me over the years and to my five wonderful grandchildren. May the lessons from Jim's family help bring peace to your lives. Thanks to Jim for allowing me to help tell his story.

Made in the USA
Monee, IL
10 September 2023